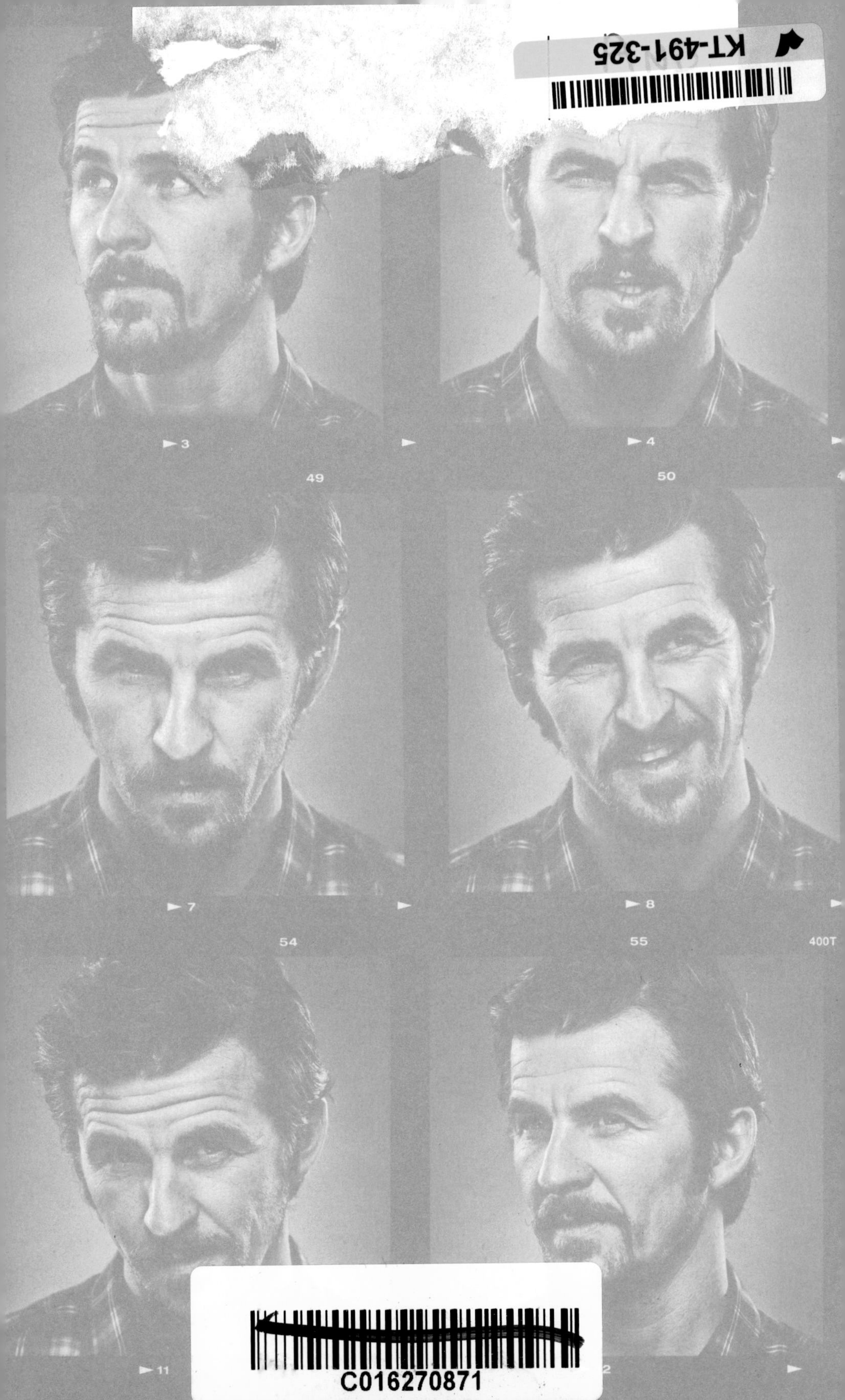

►3
►
►4
49
50
►7
►
►8
54
55
400T
►11
►

NO NONSENSE

NO NONSENSE

The Autobiography

JOEY BARTON

with Michael Calvin

SIMON &
SCHUSTER

London · New York · Sydney · Toronto · New Delhi

A CBS COMPANY

First published in Great Britain by Simon & Schuster UK Ltd, 2016
A CBS COMPANY

1 3 5 7 9 10 8 6 4 2

Simon & Schuster UK Ltd
1st Floor
222 Gray's Inn Road
London WC1X 8HB

www.simonandschuster.co.uk

Simon & Schuster Australia, Sydney
Simon & Schuster India, New Delhi

A CIP catalogue record for this book
is available from the British Library

Hardback ISBN: 978-1-4711-4758-6
Trade Paperback ISBN: 978-1-4711-4759-3
Ebook ISBN: 978-1-4711-4768-5

Typeset in the UK by M Rules
Printed and bound by CPI Group (UK) Ltd, Croydon, CR0 4YY

Simon & Schuster UK Ltd are committed to sourcing paper that is made from wood grown in sustainable forests and support the Forest Stewardship Council, the leading international forest certification organisation. Our books displaying the FSC logo are printed on FSC certified paper.

CONTENTS

CHAPTER ONE

THE VISIT

The smackhead in the corner is silently enduring the agonies of withdrawal. Hollow-eyed, sallow-skinned and sweating profusely, he constantly mops his face with rough paper towels taken from the waiting-room toilet. His plight is hypnotic and faintly heroic because, like me, he is here to visit a friend.

A young woman sits six feet away, clutching a pack of baby wipes. She has the pallor of permanent tiredness and carries the weight of too many cheap takeaways. Her toddler, absent-mindedly playing with a plastic toy, has been dressed for the occasion in a polo shirt, offset by a gold neck chain, cargo pants and pristine Nike trainers.

I'm back in a familiar place, prison, for a reality check on who I was, who I have become, and who I want to be. The victims are not necessarily those on the other side of the security scanners, the inmates who wear orange bibs and have the expectant eyes of children arriving at a birthday party.

The air is stale and the sights are stark. It smells of decay and enforced abandonment. The memories are personal and paper-cut painful. An unfulfilled threat from another time, another jail, filters through my brain: 'You're getting stabbed, Barton ... you're going to die, you maggot.'

This is HMP Preston, a Victorian relic designed for 750 men which is consistently overcrowded. It feels like a run-down NHS hospital and is set, incongruously, in an industrial estate. We are ushered through an entrance framed by a sign that reads: 'Challenging and changing offender attitudes to reduce crime in our communities.'

Even as visitors, we surrender a little of our humanity. No keys, symbols of possession. No wallets, with their dog-eared photographs and scraps of individualism. No books, in case the pages are invisibly laced with hallucinogenic drugs. No chewing gum or rail tickets, other everyday items viewed with suspicion.

Everything, apart from a small amount of loose change to buy the inmates sweets and soft drinks, is locked away, awaiting our return to normality. We are identified by a numbered ticket and a fluorescent wristband, which must be ripped off on departure.

There is a strange kind of energy, created by the trade-off between people who are locked up and those who are free to walk away when they choose. One group is desperately upbeat about the limitations of their life, and the other deliberately downplays the attractions of the outside world.

Everyone is putting on a front. The bravado is a little too close to bullshit to be entirely convincing. There's that frisson of uncertainty you feel when you know someone is lying to you, but you can't quite put your finger on how big the lie is.

I know what some of you are thinking. I'm in my element behind bars. I'm a thug, a Neanderthal, a stain on society. I'm back where I belong, with the dregs and the druggies. I am The Man Who Shamed Our Great Game, Football.

Nice try. I am desensitised to the slurs, because they form the soundtrack to my life. My past screams at me from half-forgotten headlines, crusty leader columns and ill-tempered Twitter rants, so that my hearing has become selective. If you want to understand me, my weaknesses are as important as my strengths.

It has been a long road, with more than a few speed humps to negotiate, but I finally accept myself for who I am. I couldn't be prouder of what I have achieved. Good people have given me the time and room to understand why, and how, I was out of control for so long, for most of my twenties. One of them happens to be here, serving a seven-and-a-half-year sentence for manslaughter.

Andy Taylor, Tagger to use his childhood nickname, is my closest friend outside my family. We grew up together in adjoining council estates, though he was deemed posh because he lived in a semi-detached house rather than the traditional terraced two up, two down. When he gained his sociology degree in the United States, he began to build a successful career as a football agent.

He must live with the fact that his role in a brawl in Liverpool city centre in the early hours of Friday, 19 December 2014 resulted in the death of a fellow human being. It was impossible to prove who delivered the fatal blow, but off-duty policeman Neil Doyle, recently married, did not return home.

It could so easily have been me in Tagger's position. He was the smartest of us all. I was more capable of violence. There was so much ferocity, so much anger, inside me. My behaviour was occasionally psychotic. I was involved in so many similar incidents that I look at him and think, 'Fuck me, I got so lucky there, so, so lucky.'

I was capable of serious, serious stuff. I've contemplated that on so many levels, and tried to deconstruct my actions. Without that dangerous energy, I probably wouldn't be here to tell my tale. I'd be working on a building site, or I might be dead. My intensity is the greatest gift I've been given, but equally it is the most destructive force imaginable.

I've done some bad things, but I've never killed anyone. I lost as many fights as I won, and, by chance, never caused anyone serious harm beyond superficial cuts and bruises. We all think we are immune to bad things, but events can spiral out of control and conspire against you. It scares me to realise how fragile life can be.

Do I feel guilty as I turn to go after a couple of hours, and Tagger rises from his plastic chair, which is embedded in concrete, for a farewell embrace? Not really. I never thought he would end up in jail, because of what he stands for. No one did. I care about him, since he is one of an extremely small circle of friends to whom I reach out for advice, but he has his own journey to make.

That phrase has been cheapened by the schmaltz that passes as Saturday night TV entertainment, but I'm talking about dealing with the reality that, however sorry we feel for him as a mate, another family has lost their loved one. Society dictates there is a price to be paid for that. Some will argue that such a debt can never be met.

Tagger doesn't fit the traditional prisoner profile; he is set on proving he can be a positive influence, a stronger individual through adversity. He has earned the trust of the authorities and works on the front desk, preparing inmates for court appearances. He processes newcomers, gives them their prison-issue clothing and talks them through the formalities of incarceration.

Prison is a terrifying place, with no shortage of people who will slash your face for £20 worth of weed, the hardest currency of all. Tagger is a 'listener', a mentor trained by the Samaritans. He has a single-bedded cell, or pad to use the old lag's slang, to enable him to privately counsel those who have been traumatised, mentally or physically.

He has prevented several suicides. The alternative to talking down unstable inmates is the dreaded 'Tornado roll', in which the potential victim is overwhelmed by force, trussed into a straitjacket and bundled into a holding cell for his own safety. Tagger is held in respect, on both sides of the divide.

Where we come from, we learn to be adaptable. We have an ability to operate in different worlds. Tagger plugs into emotion. He knows instinctively how to deal with people. He always reminds me of one of the favourite sayings of one of my other great mentors, Steve Black: 'People don't care what you know, until they know that you care.'

Prison worked for me, following my conviction for assault in 2008, because I had something to lose. You shouldn't need a degree in criminal justice and criminology to realise that's the key. If you're a kid on a council estate, with no education and no career prospects, and you have the opportunity to make a few quid by selling drugs, prison isn't going to be a deterrent.

It is a flawed, ancient system which needs reviewing. It may not be as obscene as the American model, where they put people down like animals, but there has to be a different way. Society has surely moved on from the era in which judicial revenge was taken by throwing an offender into jail and throwing away the key.

I'm a creature of habit. I can have a conversation with anybody, about anything, at any time. Given literally a captive audience, here was my opportunity to determine what makes people tick. I spoke to killers, blaggers, career criminals and petty thieves. They taught me that individuals aren't born evil, but things happen that make them behave in a certain way.

Fear, for me, was rocket fuel. It was me against the world. I had that little voice inside, telling me, 'No one likes you. No one thinks you've got a chance.' I might as well have been walking around with 'Fuck Off' stamped across my forehead. It was no wonder I alienated people.

Peter Kay, the counsellor who enabled me to make sense of my life before his death, used to talk about me as a self-saboteur. He took me through the process of understanding the importance of environment, whether that's a prison cell or a council estate on which no one is going to give you anything.

St John's estate, in Huyton, has a frontier feel, geographically and spiritually. It was earmarked as a social dustbin, following Liverpool's slum clearance programme, and has its own micro-climate. It's a daunting place for strangers, with its own set of predetermined yet unwritten rules. Survival instincts are deeply ingrained.

You cannot be seen as a soft touch in a school playground or on a football pitch. Show weakness on the streets, and they will steal the shirt from your back if you let them. The dynamics haven't really changed as I've progressed through my football career. Whenever I enter a dressing room for the first time, the deflector shields are up. I'm sensitive to threats, real or imagined.

I burned from rejection by Everton, my boyhood club, and learned that ignorance doesn't excuse failure. If you don't know something, find out about it, quickly. My self-protective mechanisms are almost automatic. I prepared for jail, once it became clear I would be going inside, by consciously cutting myself off from the outside world. I wanted to know what isolation felt like.

It gave me an overwhelming determination that I would never again allow anyone to take my liberty from me. I would never give them another chance to dehumanise me, by locking me behind a grey metal door. I would never again be known as a number.

I thought, 'This isn't how it is meant to be. This isn't what my life is going to be. I am going to dictate my future.' I knew it would be difficult, but I was going to do this on my own. I didn't want anyone to visit me, even going so far as to ban two of the people I hold most dear, my partner Georgia and my grandmother. I wanted to protect them from the experience.

I've always been thrown in at the deep end, and swum. Let's park the social obstacles, for a moment. Genetics were against me. They told me at Everton I was too small to make it as a footballer. I didn't have pace, lacked a trick, and wasn't overly big or strong. You need most of those five traits to make it as a pro, never mind a Premier League player, but they didn't feature in my skill set.

Throughout my life I've had self-appointed experts, coaches and schoolteachers, telling me that I won't amount to much, that my ambitions are ridiculous. They expected me to fuck everything up at some stage. I had a good go at that, by the way, but the thing that got me through was an insatiable hunger, an unadulterated love of the game. That can spill over into dangerous areas, but I found a way of competing, of coping.

I gave myself a puncher's chance by fighting and fighting, with a 'fuck you, world' attitude. I knew I was way behind my contemporaries, and was just trying to keep my head above water. I needed someone to believe in me. Jim Cassell, Manchester City's academy director, was that man. He was that rarity – a football man who possessed the sensitivity and imagination to get what I was all about.

He had a simple ethos: he treated each of his young players as unique. He offered support, up to the breaking point, and allowed us the freedom to fail on our own terms. He recognised I lacked that supposedly critical yard of pace, and doubted whether I would develop sufficiently to play at the highest level.

But, luckily for me, he identified passion as a principal asset in both his coaches and his kids. He detected the depth of my devotion. He sensed, correctly, that I would have played pub football if I didn't make it as a pro. He had the specialist knowledge and the moral courage to give me time to progress.

Kevin Keegan wanted me to be more respectful of my peers, to show some humility. That was never going to happen, because they were in my way. My dad once told me, 'If you want to be a first-teamer's mate, you'll never be a first-teamer.' I looked at the lads around me, playing for England at youth level, coming in from Ireland and abroad on pro contracts, and knew I was scrambling for employment.

I'm thinking, 'Dad has got a point.' I had to be ruthless, and develop an advantage they were not prepared for. That was fitness. I couldn't control the rate at which I grew, but I could out-work them, out-think them. I could turn each training session into a war, to make up the difference. I could stay on in the afternoons, to close the gap.

I'd play out of position, even as a senior player. I was thrown into right midfield at Newcastle, made the position my own by thinking on my feet, and helped Andy Carroll get his big move to Liverpool. I made the most of what I had. I was as comfortable as a Premier League footballer as I was a prisoner in Strangeways; that ability to adapt took me from the ducking stool, provided by the red-top tabloids and the cyber warriors, to the *Question Time* studio.

If someone throws a challenge at me, I get after it. So what if I fail? Far worse to cower at the chance to take a chance, and learn nothing. Far better to disregard the ridicule and fail gloriously. My logic is that even if I fall flat on my face, I'll have something to file away for future reference. I'm comfortable swimming in deep and dangerous waters.

Prison gave me space, allowed me to be alone with my thoughts. You interact with the outside world as and when you choose. I'm not advising anyone to go there, but it is the one place you are guaranteed to find solitude, whether you want it or not.

You must submit the telephone numbers of people you want to speak to, so they can be cleared. The bullshit around you melts away. You ask yourself, 'Who is really worth my time?' Suddenly, you realise you've got so little in common with so many people you thought were focal points of your life.

Human contact comes on your terms. I went to AA meetings in prison, primarily to interact with people instead of being in my cell, staring at four walls. I discovered a level of honesty and integrity I never experienced on a day-to-day basis in what passes as the real world. Paying others the respect of listening got me through. It made me realise I wasn't the only one in the room who felt vulnerable.

Many of the guys were trapped, rejected by society because they stole or dealt to put food on the family table. They were resigned to their fate, and had used alcohol as an anaesthetic as much as a stimulant, but they were not bad people. They merely made bad choices, and lacked the economic and emotional wherewithal to cope.

It's a complex issue, but their involvement in crime tended to be a self-fulfilling prophecy, since many came from abusive backgrounds. How could I judge them? One was a Manchester City fan, who had not been visited by his wife and kids for two years. She had moved abroad with a new man; his children would be strangers by the time he was paroled. His depression was dark and deeply affecting.

That made me realise I needed to like myself. I seized the chance to reconnect, to understand why I had such a deep-rooted dislike of what I had become. I read anything I could get my hands on, from books on Buddhist principles to brilliant insights into the institutionalised drug culture of the Tour de France.

The irony, black and bitter, was that I spoke to Tagger about making the time work for me, instead of me counting down the days and being its dutiful slave. His own fall from grace was simply unthinkable at the time. We concluded there was no point in me sitting there, feeling resentful or sorry for myself. It had to be a productive experience.

I realised I'd been living for years in a jail constructed in my own head. I had the trappings of freedom, and felt unrestrained, but it was an illusion, a falsehood. I'd closed down spiritually, emotionally and even physically in some ways. My cell was between my ears, because I felt I couldn't fit in.

I wanted people to like me. I wanted to be light-hearted, to laugh and joke with those around me, but everything I did had the opposite effect. I wanted to be a good team-mate, and yet I ended up fighting with them. I wanted to be successful, but everything I did conspired against that. I wanted to behave, to assimilate myself into society, and I couldn't. It didn't agree with me.

That frustrated me, because I wanted to conform. I was alienated to the point where I wondered whether I could handle it. It was like living in an endless anxiety dream: I was chasing something that, no matter how fast I ran or how hard I tried, I could never catch. In the end I admitted defeat. I just let it all go.

Weirdly, just by being true to myself, I found fulfilment edged closer, within reach. There is still a side of me conditioned to challenge convention, but I've learned there is a time and a place for defiance. There are still days when I feel I'm wasting energy, but I'm more at ease. I let things go because I can see the marker posts, stretching towards the horizon. I know where I want to go.

Peter Kay gave me the key to fast-forwarding my decisions. I never had the ability to say to myself, 'If I do X and Y, the consequences are Z.' I had no concept of consequence. Now I understand the outcome. It is a skill I have needed to practise, because, as Tagger says, I am emotionally driven, so that a relapse is always a possibility.

I can still be the young boy who sees sweets and eats as many as possible, as quickly as possible, before he is violently sick. I am in a profession that infantilises young men, showers them with material rewards and gives them an excuse never to grow up. It tells them what to do, what to think, how to act, without rationalising the process.

I make no excuses because I am still the child who gets so consumed by what he is doing that he has no concept of time and space. My timekeeping is erratic, to say the least. I get caught up in things because I am so passionate about what

I am doing. That might be analysing a coaching video, or obsessing when I'm beaten at golf or snooker.

Part of me, the more organised side, says, 'For fuck's sake, get that in order.' But the other side of me won't have it: 'This is the most important thing in the world, Joseph, because it is in the here and now. Nothing else matters.' At least, I suppose, I can now identify the difference.

This book is important to me, not merely because I want to reach out to those who feel isolated or frustrated, but because it is time to bury the caricature. I promise full disclosure, because I have finally come to terms with instincts and experiences that brought out the nastier aspects of my character.

I've learned that being so dogmatic, seeing everything in black-and-white terms, slows me down. I've tried to replace aggression with inquisitiveness. I won't waste my natural energy on anger and recrimination. I'll merely channel it in different ways.

The one thing I didn't understand when I was dealing, badly, with a whole range of issues was my place in the world. Peter Kay encouraged me to seek out the past. I would speak to my nan about my grandad, about their parents. A light went on inside my head. Instead of blaming Dad for not forewarning me about life's difficulties, I began to realise he was doing the best he possibly could.

One by one, the dominoes fell. Change was possible, because I represented a new generation, with an opportunity to write its own history. At precisely 4am on 28 December 2011, I discovered the power of unconditional love . . .

CHAPTER TWO
FAMILY

For once in my life I was lost for words. My mouth moved, but nothing intelligible emerged. I was awestruck, dumbstruck. I had no real idea of how I reached the corridor outside the birthing suite at Chelsea and Westminster Hospital, and I made no sense when I got there. My dad, who was sitting with Tony, Georgia's father, simply burst out laughing.

'Well,' he said. 'What is it?' I paused, for what seemed like an age: 'Er, um, it's a boy.' Cassius Joseph Barton, my first child, weighed 7lb 3oz, but he tilted the world off its axis. His first breath gave me perspective. His first cry gave me clarity. The everyday miracle of his birth brought my planets into alignment, and my family into focus.

I'm told I cut the cord, but I was in a daze. I need only close my eyes to recall the most powerful moment, when the midwife cleaned him up and gave him to Georgia to hold close to her chest. It is an eternal freeze-frame image, lodged in my brain. I had done nothing, but the love I felt for both was overpowering, humbling. I revelled in my insignificance, and marvelled at her strength.

I was not the first father to find it a surreal experience, and I am sure I will not be the last. I had been fascinated by the progression of pregnancy, from the gently swelling stomach to the other-worldly experience of watching a baby wriggle in the womb, but nothing prepared me for this. Robbie Fowler told me he was at the business end for the birth of his four kids, but I took my orders from my nan: 'Stand up this end of the bed. Hold Georgia's hand. And don't get in the way.'

I had played the previous evening in a 1-1 draw for Queens Park Rangers at Swansea. The club were brilliant: one of the staff on the bench had my mobile, with orders to haul me off the pitch and place a private jet at my disposal should the message get through from London that Georgia's labour pains had intensified. I did not need to take advantage of the gesture, but I have never forgotten it.

Bradley Orr, my team-mate and childhood friend, who has subsequently become my agent, drove me to the hospital at around midnight. He had two children, and a telltale smirk. 'Oh, this is going to change you,' he said. How could I be expected to understand such a simple truth? I was still the lone wolf. My ego was not only intact, but seemingly bombproof.

Brad knew . . .

Love is such a powerful emotion, subtly different for each of us but a uniquely unifying force. The energy shift, when the bond between parent and child is formed, takes the breath away. Everything changed that morning. That was the point when I said to myself, 'Get out of the way. You are no longer at the centre of the universe. You are not important.'

In a sense, it signalled my rebirth. Cogs were whirring in my head. The momentum of my life had shifted. I was still several months away from Manchester City, and the Carlos

Tevez clusterfuck, but things felt different. I understood, instinctively and instantly, why Dad swallowed me in a bear hug. Until then, again to quote my nan, I was one of those 'kids who don't realise what a parent is'.

I suddenly felt closer to him than it seemed possible. I understood how much I had hurt him when I shunned him because of the way I felt he lived his life. It took Cassius, innocent and unknowing, to superglue us back together. I realised he loved my very bones. After all, I was his first born, too.

At that moment, in that corridor, the years fell away. I was little Joe again, the baby who had a shock of blond hair when he arrived on the planet at Whiston Hospital, weighing 8lb 2oz, on 2 September 1982. My dad reminded me he had celebrated my birth by getting pissed with my grandad, and was evidently up for a nostalgic pre-breakfast livener.

I had to make my excuses, as I had a game three days later (we lost to a Robin van Persie goal at Arsenal), but I reconnected with my childhood. Dad wasn't perfect, but he didn't batter us, he didn't lock us in cupboards, as some did on the estate. He did what he could. He tried to give me what he thought I needed to survive, and thrive, in any environment.

He was a grafter and left home for work before 6am in all weathers. A roofer from the age of 15, his hands had the consistency of sandpaper. His face was wind-blasted, reddened and rough. He was an active man, who played sport four nights a week and drank the other three. Occasionally, he would come home exhausted, sit on the couch in his torn long johns, open a can of lager and simmer gently in front of the fire.

Cassius unknowingly created an extended family. Georgia's parents admitted they had thought me quite cold, clinical. I probably was, to be honest. Maybe not with my own flesh and blood, but I had a capacity to cut people dead, to isolate them in a heartbeat. I had a complicated relationship with my mum, but I wanted her to be part of her grandchildren's lives. I think that meant a lot to her.

The media mistakenly ran away with the idea that Cassius was named after Muhammad Ali, a lovely conceit since I admired him greatly, not only as a phenomenal athlete but as a principled man for his stance against the Vietnam War. His death on 3 June 2016, at the age of 74, triggered a global outpouring of grief and reflection that confirmed his status as The Greatest. He also featured, unwittingly, in one of the strangest experiences I have ever had at a sporting event. The jockey Martin Dwyer, a friend and fellow Evertonian, invited me to watch him ride in the French Derby at Chantilly one Sunday. It involved the works: private jet, paddock access and dinner with the owners of his horse. There were about 20 of them, from a quirky, indiscreet and deliciously mischievous family from Lexington, Kentucky.

The owner's son, Joseph Clay, took a shine to me. We got to talking about our children; it emerged we both had sons named Cassius. I made the inevitable reference to Cassius Marcellus Clay, and he replied, casually, that Ali's paternal great-grandfather John had been a pre-Civil War slave on one of his forebears' many plantations. John and his wife Sallie adopted the surname of their owner.

The original Cassius Marcellus Clay was an imposing figure, six feet six inches tall. He returned to Kentucky from war in Mexico to free the 40 slaves he had inherited, including John and Sallie, and became a prominent abolitionist. Stabbed during a debate with a pro-slavery campaigner for public office, he fought back with a bowie knife of his own. Abraham Lincoln sent him to St Petersburg in Russia for a year on government business, and he was married, at the age of 84, to a 15-year-old girl.

On reflection, that is some act to follow.

I was named after my dad, who was named after his grandad's brother. Cassius just felt right for my son. Georgia liked it, and I didn't want to burden him with the emotional baggage of naming him after me. Those closest to me have always called me Joe or Joseph, incidentally. Derek Fazackerley let the monster loose by referring to me as Joey on the Manchester City teamsheet before my Premier League debut, a 2-0 defeat at Bolton on 5 April 2003.

We are branded as Bartons, and I resolved immediately that I was going to change what the family name meant to other people. There must be another way, because every mistake, each indiscretion, all the aggravation, builds a reputation that impacts on your kids. Peter Kay visited us after the birth and was so happy, because he saw in me the man he knew existed, despite my doubts.

I was convinced I was too selfish to have children. I wasn't ready for them and honestly didn't know whether I'd have enough love to go around. I was adamant it wasn't fair to bring them into a world I didn't truly understand. I was the product of a broken home, and didn't want to put my kids through that pain.

When Georgia became pregnant, Pete called it as it is: 'Look. You've just got to throw yourself into this. Nobody's got every box covered. You'll learn on the job, basically.' He believed in me, long before I did. I often think of his advice during my favourite part of the day, the 10 minutes I have with Cassius before his bedtime, reading him a story or watching a Donald Duck cartoon.

I tell him I love him all the time. I never had that closeness with my dad because of the macho mindset of his generation. I knew he loved me, that he would do anything for me. I even saw him fight on my behalf. But as for intimacy, well, men didn't do that sort of thing. They demanded their dinner on time, made sure they had the biggest helpings, but quietly deferred to the strength of their women when they thought no one was looking.

My nan, dad's mum, is a traditional matriarch. Her warmth is wonderful and her wrath is best avoided. Peter, my grandad, converted to Roman Catholicism to marry her. Faith got her through pancreatic cancer; she could see the lights of Liverpool's two cathedrals from her hospital bed as she prayed before her operation. She told anyone on the ward who would listen that, 'I can't die because my family need me.'

She was right, you know. We named our daughter Pieta Giulia after my paternal grandparents, who acted as surrogate parents at a key stage in my life. Grandad, who started out as a slaughterman in the local abattoir and ended alongside his son on the roofs, didn't live to see her born. He didn't trust hospitals and died quickly when his cancer was diagnosed. I didn't appreciate it at the time, but he was a disciplinarian, who balanced Nan's instinct to see the good in me.

He was a clever man, the first from the family to win a grammar school scholarship, but had to take his turn in a queue of eight children. The ridicule, when he was forced to tell the PE teacher he couldn't afford a pair of cricket whites, left an indelible scar. He wasn't hung up on his humble background but he never forgot the embarrassment. Both he, and Nan, told us never to accept inferiority, real or assumed.

They were products of the terraced streets and tenements off Scotland Road in Liverpool, where pride was taken in scrubbing the solid stone steps until they gleamed. Wage packets were left, unopened, on the kitchen table on Friday night. The front room, dominated by a statue of the Virgin Mary inside a glass dome, was used on Sundays only.

Grandad was brought up to play his cards close to his chest, but prided himself on being the provider. He hated it when Nan bought a colour TV out of her part-time earnings, managing the payroll at a local factory. No one else in the close had one, and he knew that more than a few net curtains were rustling when the delivery men turned up: 'People will think I'm selling drugs if we're buying stuff like that,' he said, before demanding, in vain, that she send it back.

The ritual was repeated when she learned to drive without telling him, and bought a fifth-hand runaround after passing her test, first time. She pre-empted his complaints with a simple statement of fact: 'Trust me, Peter, if you were up to no good I'd have bought a better car than this.' Resistance was futile.

Pieta is a play on Grandad's name, and also refers to Michelangelo's statue, which depicts the body of Jesus on his mother's lap following the Crucifixion. I realise this is contradictory, since I don't believe in God and consider organised religion repressive and exploitative, but Nan loved it when she saw it in St Peter's Basilica. I've never been to Rome, but was struck by its softness and scale when I saw it in a book I was reading about artists from that period.

Nan cried when we told her Giulia was the Italian version of her name, Julia. She is a lot like me, stubborn to a fault and fiercely loyal to those who offer loyalty in return. I've got a long way to go before I can hope to match her compassion and common sense. She has lived in Molyneux Close, just off St John's estate, for 50 years. Grandad is still with her; his ashes, in a blue porcelain urn, are beside her favourite chair in the bay window.

Nothing much got past my nan, but she didn't notice my dad sneaking out along the back alley to visit a neighbour, Rita Rogers. She was in her late twenties when her husband left her with two daughters, my half-sisters Sharon and Joanne. Dad was 19, didn't drink and apparently loved nothing more than to sit in front of the telly with a tub of ice cream. Appearances were deceptive, and helped by the alibi provided by his debut for the pub football team.

Truth be told, it wasn't exactly a case for Poirot. It didn't take long to twig his bed hadn't been slept in, though the covers were disturbed. His van remained parked outside. Nan told a white lie at work that she had an early dentist's appointment, and lay in wait. When she discovered the deception, all hell broke loose. Dad was told he was stupid, an easy mark for a gold-digger. Nan, who had given birth to him when she was 17, wanted him to live a little, on her terms, before he settled down.

Nan's misgivings about Rita's family were well founded. Her four brothers, Eddie, Stephen, Paul and Tony, have all had drug-related issues and been in and out of prison. Her dad, Ned, was by all accounts an utter bastard. My dad came to loathe them, but not before he'd defied his family and walked out to set up home with Rita in Wingate Towers, a high-rise block of flats on the nearby Bluebell estate.

My nan refused to speak to him for two years, until she was accosted while out shopping one morning and congratulated on her new grandchild. She knew nothing about my birth, but managed to bluff her way through the small talk by insisting, 'The baby's lovely, a chubby little thing like our Joe.' Her sister advised her to be a good Christian, buy a pot plant as a present to mark my arrival, and pay her respects. She saw me, announced that I was 'gorgeous' and gave Rita, my mum, the benefit of the doubt.

A truce of sorts was established, but any resemblance to the *Little House on the Prairie* was entirely coincidental. Dad disliked Mum's brothers so intensely he refused to allow them over the threshold. They used to wait until he was out, playing football, before visiting. No wonder, really. They tended to bring their dubious business home with them.

I was alone, following football stories on Teletext in my parents' bedroom one afternoon, when I was startled by someone hammering on the front door. It was my one of my uncles, sweating and short of breath. When he knew the coast was clear, he barged past me and bounded up the stairs into my bedroom. I just managed to make it in behind him, before he locked the door.

He went to speak, but evidently decided actions were better than words. He tipped his bag upside down, so that the contents cascaded on to my Everton duvet. There were more £5, £10 and £20 notes than I could count, screwed up in dishevelled bundles. 'I've borrowed this from the post office,' he said, as I wondered briefly whether my eyeballs would ever return to their sockets.

'Hide this for me for a couple of days and you can keep the coins.'

Now he had my attention. It was worth risking Dad's backhander, which carried an infinitely greater threat than the long arm of the law. There was about £16 in loose change on the bed, enough for half a dozen Subbuteo teams. It was hardly the Great Train Robbery, so what passed as my conscience was clear. I didn't give the morality of the situation a second thought. I was well on the way to being a St John's boy.

I grew up on Boundary Road, literally the wrong side of the tracks. It was another world on the other side of the railway, where Nan ruled the roost, but even she could not be protected from tragic, terrifying reality. Her daughter Julie was six months pregnant with my cousin Josh when his father Joe was killed in the Bluebell pub, which used to dominate the estate in Huyton on which Steven Gerrard grew up.

Joe worked in London during the week and played local park football, but was originally from Manchester, never something to advertise when the beers are being thrown down in a Scouse pub on a Sunday afternoon. He got into a loud argument over a game of pool, stupidly started by a smartass comment about a sponsored head-shaving event involving the regulars. Two lads followed him into the toilet; one hit him on the back of the head with a pool cue. He died instantly.

The pair claimed self-defence and were acquitted of manslaughter, but the law of the concrete jungle applied. They knew, better than anyone, that their lives were cheap. They fled the area with their families before vengeance could be taken.

The human cost was terrible. Both Julie, who lost one of the twins she was carrying due to the shock, and my uncle Paul, who had been with Joe and was consumed by guilt at his failure to protect him, suffered from subsequent depression. I was too young to understand, and have only the vaguest memories of anguished family gatherings, but violence was a fact of everyday life.

Ice-cream men fought in the streets during one of the more bizarre turf wars. The corner shop was protected by concrete barriers, but was still regularly ram-raided. Drug dealers controlled the high-rises. The police didn't dare arrive in groups of fewer than six: their vans were bombarded by bricks and their patrol cars were torched if they were left unguarded while they chased local scallies down blind alleys. Once the bizzies were lured into the rat runs near the Labour club, they were lost. I retain affection for the place, despite its rough edges, because it is home to good people doing their best in difficult circumstances. Dad was a man's man, in the days when that phrase didn't offend the easily offended. He was a good fighter and a great drinker. He could lend his hand to anything. If you needed a shed building, a roof mending or a fence erecting, he was up for the job. He painted the house, converted the dining room into a playroom, and knocked a wall down to install a new kitchen.

He was softly spoken but could handle himself. Although he played football at the weekends, thereby avoiding involvement in most of their most notorious exploits, he was a member of the Huyton Baddies, a group of casuals who caused havoc following Liverpool and, to a lesser extent, Everton around Europe in the eighties.

Their greatest urban legend features a circus strongman, who rather rashly threw a Baddie through the window of a local pub because he attempted to chat up his companion, a trapeze artist. A council of war was called, and the following evening the big top was stormed. The strongman was beaten up, together with the ringmaster and any member of the supporting cast foolish enough not to flee. The tent was burned down and, for good measure, someone decided to release the animals from their cages.

The story goes that a lion was shot outside the King's Head pub. A tiger was cornered outside Betty's Hair Salon in Mortimer Street. An elephant rampaged across the common and was heading into town until a police SWAT team, supported by vets, imposed some sort of order on chaos.

If that episode had cartoonish elements, cold-blooded cruelty scarred the landscape. Paul Hagan, who worked as a roofer with my dad, was beaten to death with his friend Francis Perry by two bouncers wielding metal baseball bats. Their fatal mistake was to make a beeline for the wrong girls in the wrong place, a Southport nightclub. The court heard that one of the killers, Sean Jackman, urinated on the dead men.

Dad had a set of unwritten rules, shaped by circumstance. Protect your own. Back your mates up. Big sticks where necessary, but no tools, knives or guns. Rely on your fists, whenever possible. Impose your own form of justice, without fear or favour. I am reminded of the consequences of that regime, on a daily basis, by a scar across the end of my nose.

I was approaching my fourth birthday when I was playing with two plastic cars in a concrete tunnel in the playground at Sylvester school. From what little I remember, and according to what I have since been able to piece together, an Alsatian appeared at the other end of the tunnel. I tried to be friendly. It mauled me, biting my temple, nose and face. My half-sisters Sharon and Joanne, who had left me for a few seconds, were alerted by my screams.

They fought the dog off, and helped Nan get me to hospital, where I stayed for 10 days. The doctors were worried about me losing the sight in my right eye, and they decided I needed minor plastic surgery on my nose. Dad was tracked down to the local pub, where, after making sure I was in good hands, he borrowed a mate's van and headed towards the playground.

He was enraged to discover the dog was still off the leash. It had avoided capture and was roaming across the school playing fields. Dad drove through the gates, ran it down, and reversed over it to ensure it was dead. He leaped out to confront the panic-stricken owner, who lived nearby and saved himself from a beating by apologising profusely.

'Fuck off back to your house,' he was told. The man saw the fire in Dad's eyes, and knew better than to argue. He returned to collect the corpse under the cover of darkness, and never complained about the vigilante action. It was the St John's way. Everyone respected Dad for his football, and his fury. It wasn't abnormal. It was an accepted form of behaviour.

He didn't need a textbook on social conditioning to know his parental duty was to make sure no one fucked with me. All I could do was imitate and intimidate in my own small, less-than-sweet way. The lessons he administered were sharp, unsubtle, but undeniably effective. They began in earnest when I was six, soon after the birth of my twin brothers, Michael and Andrew.

He hated bullying, because he had been picked on as a kid. I overstepped the mark one November afternoon by punching the living daylights out of a lad who'd tried to stop me pinching his bike. His mum came to the door to complain, and I knew what was coming. I concentrated on Dad's slippers; when they began to move I accelerated towards the first step on the stairs and tried to slip under the slap. Some hope.

Our gang worked out pretty quickly that there was limited safety in numbers. When we were seven Paul Morson, a lad who lived with his mum at the top of our road, used to prey on us individually, and take our pocket money. Everyone knew him as Birdie. He was 10, and thought he was the business. His mistake was to underestimate our desperation; we simply attacked him as a group, and gave him a bit of a shoeing.

He got his revenge, of course, when we let our guard down and walked around on our own. We'd simply regroup, and beat him up again. He soon got bored of the indignity. He became a bit of a rogue, and disappeared in 2011. Two men were jailed for life for his murder, after being found guilty of abducting him, and torturing him with a hammer. His body has never been found; some say it was thrown in the Manchester Ship Canal, others believe it was chopped up and fed to pigs.

Everyone knew the faultlines on the estate before they knew their six times table. Get caught on Cowper Way, and your trainers and pocket money would be nicked. The back-doubles on the way home from my cousin's house on Scott Avenue were dangerous, but on this particular day I decided they were worth the risk because I figured the bigger boys would be having their tea.

Big mistake. I ran into a rival gang who gave me a kicking. A lad called Chrissie Hogg, who was about 12, ran off with my football. I arrived home, whimpering and feeling sorry for myself. 'What are you crying for?' Dad asked, reasonably enough. When I explained the ambush, he went to the cupboard under the stairs, which contained the electricity meter. As in so many houses, it had been fiddled with a filed-down coin.

He rummaged through discarded trainers and emerged with a wooden rounders bat. 'Here,' he said. 'Don't come back into this house crying, ever again. Never let someone take anything from you. If he is bigger than you, hit him with a stick. If he pulls a knife, run. Do you understand? Go and fucking sort it.'

He pushed me out of the front door, and left me to my fate. It wasn't long before I reached the point of no return. The older lads were playing with my ball. They saw me, and laughed. 'Want some more?' they sneered. I had no option. I ran at the nearest kid, screaming like a banshee and swinging the bat at anything that moved. I managed no more than a glancing blow, but they scattered and left the ball behind. Chrissie Hogg never went near me again.

So that was the way it was going to be. I could protect myself by cultivating a reputation as a lunatic. Any time I was confronted, I had to go over the top in terms of spite and aggression. I couldn't show a flicker of fear. If they didn't know what I was capable of, they were too scared to take the necessary risk to find out. Feeling lucky, punks?

I was a law unto myself, even at junior school, where I'd get sent out of class, kick the fire exit open, and run home. Mum would take me back, but the cycle was quickly repeated. I'd answer back to the teachers, refuse to stand outside the headmaster's office to await punishment, and leg it. If anyone apprehended me, I'd wriggle free and invite them to do their worst.

Ridiculously, it worked. They tried to pander to my better nature, on the assumption it existed, because they knew the process was futile. I sensed the teachers' weakness when they were confronted by someone who didn't really want to learn. My classmates were in awe and a little afraid, because I'd simply tell people to fuck off.

Yet it was a front. People were reluctant to engage with me, and preferred to leave me alone. When we played football in the street they'd be fearful of tackling me because they couldn't trust me to react normally. On one level that was great, because I felt somehow safe. But on a deeper level, it was killing me.

I was bright enough to know that the only person I was really hurting was myself. I felt lonely, isolated, lost. I needed structure, reassurance. The real problem was that there were no rules with my mum. I did pretty much as I pleased. I yearned for Sunday nights at my nan's, where I developed the love of tea and toast that still irritates my nutritionists. It was served on a brown leather ottoman, and accompanied by her parables and stories, such as the one about Spring-heeled Jack, a Victorian bogeyman who was supposed to have been spotted on the roof of St Francis Xavier Church in Everton.

Grandad took advantage of the diversion, and used to sneak into the garden shed for a cheeky smoke. He gave me my favourite toy as a toddler, a plastic hammer. I badgered him for small nails, spare pieces of wood, and made a fuss if I didn't get them. Dad, seeing my wilfulness, made sure I had a regular supply of plastic footballs to kick against the fence.

He excelled at every sport, and was paid to play football. He was non-league, but the best player on the estate. He was respected, admired. He quickly became everything I wanted to be. Football gave him an edge, a strange sheen. He was my hero, and the game was my escape route.

CHAPTER THREE
JOLLY BOYS AND THE BISTO KID

Dave Taylor is a very lucky man. There have been Kamikaze pilots with greater regard for their own safety. He somehow survived the biggest decision of his managerial career, dropping my dad for a Wembley final. It might have only been the FA Vase, but 29 years are not remotely long enough to ease the pain or dilute the anger.

Dad was left out of Warrington Town's 3-2 defeat by St Helens Town in 1987, despite scoring in a 3-0 aggregate win over Collier Row in the semi-final. All he cares to keep from that fateful day at the old Empire Stadium are a loser's medal, awarded as an unused substitute, and a few photographs of a five-year-old, who was smuggled on to the pitch by his uncle Paul to take a pre-match penalty.

I scored, of course, though Dad insists John O'Brien, the goalkeeper, deliberately dived over it. He'd like to lose the details of his disappointment in the mists of time, but they come in handy when he tries to reinvent himself as a cross between Duncan Ferguson and Duncan McKenzie. A move was inevitable, and by the time I was eight he was patrolling midfield for Knowsley United in the Northern Premier League.

My football journey had begun. It took in Whitley Bay and Colwyn Bay, Gainsborough Trinity and Goole Town, Barrow and Bishop Auckland. The coach journeys and the dressing-room rituals were private pleasures. I peered through the fog of pre-match roll-ups and glimpsed the joy of working men playing a boys' game for beer tokens. Their results might have been in the small print, but they were stars.

No one talked down to me on those special Saturdays. They even tried to kick me on Tuesdays and Thursdays if I was a little too cheeky when I joined in training with Bradley Orr, whose dad Pedro was manager. We were ejected, kicking and screaming, whenever they wanted to work on team shape. On game day we would act as mascots, and run out in spare adult kits. Our shirts were like nightgowns and our shorts were held up with string, but we showboated for England in the warm-ups.

We were sent to fetch any balls kicked over the fence during home matches, though Brad and I preferred to sit in borrowed warm-up jackets at the end of the bench. We were spellbound by what was going on around us. We'd take everything in, from the body language of the players to the manager, shouting and swearing at the referee, linesman or opposing manager. Even at that age, I was quietly working out how I would set up the team.

The ground was owned by Terry Phillips, a bodybuilder who won the Mr Universe title four times in the seventies and eighties. The boys were paid out of the proceeds from the fruit machines. Attendance figures were fictional, so the books could be cooked. Dad discovered that his cousin Tony Kelly, who played 500 league games in midfield for Wigan,

Shrewsbury and Bolton, had secretly negotiated a second wage packet; it was swiftly retrieved, and placed behind the bar each week.

The dressing room was a treasure trove of knocked-off gear, ranging from suits to CD players, perfume to pots and pans. Win or lose, they were on the booze: raiding parties used to lay waste to off-licences on the way home. The older lads provided a diversion for some of the petty thieves, who would walk out with cases of lager, which lubricated the endless card games at the back of the bus.

Dad, who loved a laugh as much as he loved a tackle, had a decent voice. His party piece was to sing Deacon Blue's 'Dignity'. Brad's old fella massacred Ringo Starr's 'You're Sixteen'. The team had their version of the rugby song, 'Alouette'. I've used variations of that throughout my career; Nobby Nolan insisted on it being the theme tune for our celebrations at Newcastle in 2010, when we were promoted back to the Premier League. It was wheeled out when Burnley repeated the feat in 2016.

I was blessed to have that upbringing, that football education. I understood the importance of camaraderie, team spirit, a collective ethos. Knowsley punched above their weight season after season because they had players who cared. I was captivated by their genuine love of the game. It has remained with me because that is the first trait I look for in any team-mate.

There was no envy, no resentment at the optimism and opportunity of youth. When they knew I was in Everton's academy, no one burst my bubble. They'd all been at clubs, and come close to making it, and could so easily have been sour and cynical. Nobody went, 'Nah, dream on, kid.' They might have taken the piss in public so that I knew my place, but they quietly told me to believe.

Those rough-arsed footballers taught me that the human chemistry has to be right, regardless of the level at which you play. It is about a blend of styles and personalities, a commitment to a common goal. A bank manager must be able to partner a potential bank robber in central midfield. A central defender must acknowledge the courage of an irritating little shit of a winger who knows he is going to be kicked, yet still tries to push the ball past an opposing fullback.

Strokes were pulled on these Jolly Boys outings, and no one stood on ceremony. Dad excelled himself at Eastwood Town, where things got a bit spicy and he was sent off for leaving his foot in once too often. The home fans had been giving him stick, so instead of walking down the tunnel, he decided to vault the fence. He laid out the noisiest of his critics, removing his two front teeth with a single punch.

He happened to be an off-duty policeman, so the inevitable call for reinforcements was made, and the Keystone Cops chase was on. Dad wasn't going to hang around for the team bus, because he knew he would be nicked, but left word he was to be picked up at the first motorway service station on the northbound carriageway. He sprinted out of the stadium, in street shoes and his kit.

His getaway driver was the Lord Mayor of Liverpool, who happened to be Brad's grandad and club chairman. The police searched the dressing room and prowled between parked cars like confused bloodhounds. The boys, of course, obeyed the law of omertà. The teamsheet might have offered Nottinghamshire's finest an unavoidable clue, but players couldn't remember Dad's name, and didn't know where he lived.

Someone smuggled his suit and boots on to the coach, which pulled up as planned at the service station. Dad leaped into the luggage compartment for a few miles before everyone was convinced the coast was clear, and he was applauded on to his seat. He couldn't play for a couple of weeks, because the East Midlands police turned up at subsequent matches, and played as a ringer for a few months before the heat died down.

He broke cover to appear on *Match of the Day* in 1993, when they played Carlisle United in the first round of the FA Cup at Goodison Park. To get there, Knowsley had to beat Stafford Rangers, who were two leagues above them in the Conference, in a second replay, following 1-1 and 2-2 draws.

I used to be able to play football in the run-off areas during the game at Alt Park, and nick on to the pitch at half-time for a kickabout. Not on this Tuesday night. The estate had emptied, and the scallies stole in through holes in the fences. No one could move. We even had stewards. It felt like a real football club.

With 10 minutes to go, and Knowsley winning 1-0, goalkeeper Lee Williams, a chunky Welsh lad, brought down a Stafford forward in a one-against-one situation outside his penalty area, and was sent off. There was no substitute keeper, so Dad volunteered to go in goal, where his style was closer to Mike Tyson than Joe Hart. He couldn't catch the ball to save his life, but he ran through a ruck at corners, trampled over the centre forward, and gave it a right-hander. The ball fled, beyond the halfway line.

It was some sight. His borrowed jersey didn't fit and he had a maniacal look in his eye. He was a lower league version of Monk, the mad Scottish keeper played by Jason Statham in the Vinnie Jones film, *Mean Machine*. People didn't know whether to laugh, cheer or gasp, so they did a mixture of all three. The crowd sounded as if they were on helium.

When, somehow, Knowsley held on, the scallies invaded the pitch and let fireworks off. Everyone was asking, 'What the fuck's going on?' The Carlisle players were similarly bemused when they arrived at Goodison to find Dad blocking the narrow corridor between the home and away dressing rooms. He was making use of the only convenient socket to plug in his razor and shave his head. The full-time pros meekly waited for him to finish before going in to change.

The culture shock would have deepened had they known other aspects of his pre-match routine. Dad had a touch of OCD, and had to hoover the house from top to bottom before he could take us to games. We had to sit obediently on the settee while he brushed the rug until it was spotless, and virtually threadbare. Mum, bless her, preferred shopping.

He had his chance to be a hero after 10 minutes, hitting the bar after going clear with only the keeper to beat. Carlisle won 4-1, but they knew they were in a game. I wouldn't have liked to play against my dad, because he was a really tough bastard and Knowsley could put it about a bit.

They provided a finishing school for young pros at Liverpool and Everton, who were routinely roughed up in Liverpool Senior Cup ties. I can still see the fear and bewilderment in Michael Branch's eyes when the boys used him for target practice. He was the Chosen One, a 17-year-old spoken of as Everton's equivalent of Michael Owen and Robbie Fowler, but he looked lost.

That was prophetic, since, at 37, Branch is serving seven years for supplying amphetamines and cocaine. When football turned sour, and the struggle became too wearing, he succumbed to the streets. I know a hundred lads with a lot less talent from an identical background who made the same alarmingly simple life choice, and went into the drug trade. Some are up to no good on a ridiculous scale.

They don't have two heads. They were once ordinary kids. Some have had the stuffing kicked out of them, others simply don't care. Dad fell out with a neighbour because he conditioned his son to the inevitability of joining the family business, dealing and distributing industrial quantities of the stuff. He knew how vulnerable I was, but football gave me just enough scope to survive.

I had no choice in my allegiances, since he ensured I was blue from birth. I had my first Everton kit before I could walk, and by the time I was six I understood the consequences of indoctrination. I just missed out on the great Everton team of the mid-eighties, when Gary Lineker, Andy Gray and Peter Reid were denied fulfilment by the European ban on English clubs, and had to settle for relative dross.

I was first taken to Goodison by a mate of Dad's. Bob was known to everyone as Striker. We stood in the Lower Bullens, close to the dugouts. It was from there that I first sensed the scale and speed of the game. I bought old programmes from St Luke's Church, between the Gwladys Street End and Goodison Road stand, and eventually queued for spares, getting into the ground for £4 as a Junior Evertonian.

I kept goal in the playground until I was seven, because they said I spoiled things by being too good as an outfield player. I was closer in spirit to David James than Big Nev Southall, as I was easily bored. I got fed up waiting for the game to happen in front of me and consciously made things as difficult as possible by under-hitting passes to my defenders, so I had to redeem myself with a save.

I still get the gloves on after training, when the lads are taking shooting practice. I'm unorthodox, but effective. It drove my gaffer at Burnley, Sean Dyche, mad. He used to spot me from a distance and yell: 'What the fucking hell are you doing? Imagine you are a manager. Imagine someone shoots and you put your shoulder out? If someone else was doing that you'd be moaning.'

Fair do's, but I learned long ago that rules are there to be broken . . .

At seven, I was officially too young to play for my Roman Catholic junior school, St Agnes. Mr Alcock, our PE teacher, quietly ignored that because he wanted to win the area's top trophy, the Hanson Cup. We did, twice, with me up front. That didn't stop me playing as a ringer for another school, whenever they needed a result. Mr McCormack, their PE teacher, was putting his career on the line because they would have been thrown out of the league if any of my mates had grassed me up.

Everyone knew me by my nickname, Danger Mouse. Just like the cartoon character, I was first in, headfirst, if anything happened. It didn't matter if that was a scrap or a dare to launch myself off the highest diving board in the leisure centre. No one bothered to hold me back. I laugh about it now, but I keep him for posterity as a tattoo on my left foot, to remind me of the wild child within.

Brad and I used to play for Pine DIY, sponsored by a chain of stores owned by Phil Thompson, the Liverpool captain. It was one of those typically hyped youth teams, a collection of pot hunters which consisted of all the best kids in the area. At heart, though, I was at home on the pavements, or the glass-strewn gravel on which we played pick-up games.

I'd leave my ball in the bushes outside St Agnes each morning, and play fantasy football on the way home. Dustbins were international defenders, to be dazzled by my close control. I dominated central midfield, playing deft one-twos off post-boxes and parked cars. The owners would bang on windows or bawl abuse, but they'd be lost in the roar of an imaginary crowd.

I fended for myself. After school I'd change into my Everton shirt, trackie bottoms and trainers, and be out. Each street would have its posse. There were up to 20 of us, of all ages, plotting and practising for games that rapidly descended into gang warfare. Losing bragging rights in school or on the estate was not an option, so tackles became progressively worse and the assaults became more spiteful.

Inevitably, it all kicked off. When I was first involved, I made myself scarce. But gradually the violence became an end in itself. I began to love fighting as much as I loved football. As so often, a scar, this time on my right hand, tells the story. That was where I punched John Beaton's buck teeth, and had to prise my fist free. The legend of the Bisto Kid was born.

We became mates in later years, but he ran home to get his dad, who pinned me down when we resumed scrapping. John, known as Bisto because he looked like the lad in the gravy adverts, saw his chance and got in a few free punches to my unprotected face and stomach. A line had been crossed. No one, least of all an adult, steps in when the fight is fair. 'Sound,' I said, as I wrenched myself free. 'No problem. If that's how it is, we'll sort it right now.'

My hand was streaming with blood from where I had chipped his teeth, so I didn't need to play the drama queen too enthusiastically when I found Dad in the pub and explained the circumstances. He calmly put his pint to one side and said, 'Come on.' It was about a two-minute walk to Bisto's house, and Dad left me sitting on the wall in a square front garden, dominated by a large conifer.

Barry, Bisto's elder brother, tried and failed to convince my dad that his old fella wasn't in. I saw the look of panic as he was told: 'If you don't get him, I'm going to come in and get him. I'll give a slap to anyone who gets in the way, and that includes you.' In that tumbleweed moment my conscience began to whisper:

'He's going to fill him in.'

'Yeah, I know. But he had hold of me. He deserves it.'

'No he doesn't. You should learn to fight your own battles.'

'Yeah, I know. But I'm too far in now. I can't say, "Listen, let's leave it."'

My reverie was interrupted by the appearance of Bisto's dad at the door. I could only see his head, but he looked sheepish, with good reason. Dad dragged him out and the conifer began to thrash around, as if tormented by a sudden wind. A disembodied voice barked out the order, 'Stay away from him', and I was suddenly on my own. Dad left without further word, to pick up his pint as if nothing had happened. He knew I'd see his bloodied victim picking himself up from a privet hedge.

It's funny how age offers perspective and cheap wisdom. If I'd known then what I know now, that Bisto's family had been fractured by his mum's death from cancer, would I have been so set on revenge? I honestly don't know, but remorse isn't the sign of weakness I once assumed. It is only when I return to the estate that I realise how small my world was.

Our mini-Wembley seemed huge but it is in fact a small triangle of council-trimmed grass. The lamppost at which I aimed for hour after hour, so that I could pass accurately with both feet, has gone, and the road is scarred by black-and-white signs that bark 'No Ball Games', that brusque summary of officialdom's contempt for childhood.

Goals were scrawled on garage doors. We would play cricket, 20 a side, in a quadrant. Fours were hit into nearby gardens, sixes on roofs. Smashed windows stopped play quicker than a cloudburst in the county matches Lancashire used to stage across Liverpool, at Aigburth. What are the kids supposed to do these days? No wonder the estate is scarred by wilful destruction. Factories and community centres, where we used to play table tennis, have been burned down. The artificial pitch on which we once played melted when older boys used it to torch stolen cars.

Opportunity can be lost in so many ways. My cousin Paul Taylor, middle son of my Auntie Theresa, was seen as a future star. Liverpool loved his left foot and his ability to make a ball talk. They couldn't tolerate his habit of thieving anything that wasn't nailed down. His direction of travel was confirmed the moment he broke into Anfield's fabled boot room, and stripped it of 30 pairs of the first team's finest.

News of a bunch of scallies strutting around in Robbie Fowler's Nike Tiempos, and the adidas Predators once worn by Paul Ince, inevitably got back. The club demanded their return, and kicked Paul out. He couldn't give a toss. He had an aversion to authority, and took it in his stride in the same way he dealt with being excluded from school. His sticky fingers were to be the least of his, and our, problems.

Close my eyes, and I can see other familiar faces. Tagger and Mash. Cambo and poor old Birdie. Entire families – the Lubys, McElhinneys and Lackens – all up for whatever life presented. Senses heightened, I can hear my grandad's faltering voice, when I rushed from a kickabout into his kitchen to ask what was happening at Hillsborough on the afternoon of 15 April 1989.

'They're dying, son. They're dying . . .'

He had a portable radio clamped to his ear, and motioned me through the connecting door towards the television. I sat with him for more than an hour, monitoring the fragments of an unfolding tragedy until it was time to buy the *Echo*, and confront the facts, as they saw them. Seventy-four dead, according to initial reports. Ninety-six victims would require justice more than two decades later.

Everton were at Wembley, having beaten Norwich City 1-0 in the other semi-final at Villa Park. It seemed obscene even to mention it. Many from St John's were caught up in the tragedy. I overheard their horror stories, of contorted bodies, botched rescue attempts and politically orchestrated malice. Details varied, in degree, but there was unanimous agreement on one issue: the *Sun*'s front-page headline, 'The Truth', was the greatest, foulest lie of its generation.

The city that rag impugned on the whim of its masters could not be beaten down. It rallied, and pride filtered from funereal grief. An honourable goalless draw in Liverpool's first match following the disaster, a derby at Goodison, suited the mood. Cup final day, 20 May, cauterised the wounds, without healing them.

Blues sat next to reds in street parties which were only interrupted for the match, when normal tribal rules applied. The kid in me loved Ian Rush. He was the sort of striker I admired from afar, clever, clinical, calm under unimaginable pressure. The fan in me hated him when he scored twice in extra time to give the other lot the trophy the nation craved.

I was nine when Harry Tyrrell, the scout who ran my Sunday morning team and the local newsagent's, engineered my successful trial for the Everton academy. My best mate Frankie Lacken was snapped up by Liverpool. He was born on the same day, in the same hospital, as me. His family moved in next door but one and our fathers, who met in the maternity ward, were friends.

Stephen, his elder brother, boxed, like his dad. Warren, his younger brother, was a good footballer. We were the best in our respective years at senior school, but Frankie was better than me.

The mini derby matches between St Thomas Becket High School and Seel Road Comprehensive drew a swarm of excited pupils around the pitch we shared behind the local chippy. When we played in a local cup final I was introduced to the pressure and power of expectation. I got as big a buzz from the abuse as I did from the shrieking, salivating encouragement.

The game was frantic, full-on, but little different in intensity to our street scuffles. Frankie and I exchanged backhanded compliments in the form of a stud down the Achilles heel and a kick boxer's knee-high lunge. The difference was that the shame of defeat was obvious and instant. We won 3-1 and the losers shrank away, belittled as warriors.

I last met the Lacken brothers four years ago, at Glastonbury. They were in the nightclub business in Puerto Banus, on the Costa del Sol. Frankie had been a decent semi-professional player, but was in the process of leaving football behind. I'll let the sociologists ponder the nature/nurture debate, but the Lackens' back garden did stage another rite of passage.

Boxing was in the genes of both our families. On my nan's side, Bob Culshaw won the ABA junior bantamweight title in 1999. Peter Culshaw, who fought as the 'The Choirboy', won the ABA light flyweight title in 1991. A Commonwealth champion, he won world titles at flyweight and super flyweight as a professional.

Frankie's dad fought for England, and had a punchbag in his shed, at which we would take a swing when the mood took us. We were little scrotes, but styled ourselves as mean and magnificent. On summer afternoons, the beer, barbecues and boxing gloves would come out, and a makeshift ring was strung up near the rose bushes.

Don't run away with the idea that this was the human equivalent of cockfighting, but when sons are sparring in front of their fathers they are damned if they are going to back down. We had no headguards or mouthpieces, just big gloves and a desperate desire to impress. A bloody nose did no one any harm. It was good preparation for the playground.

Something was obviously stirring. One day Dad broke cover. I was 12, and it was time for a man-to-man chat. 'How do you fight?' he asked me. 'There are some bigger kids than you at the senior school. Don't try and box them. They're heavier, stronger and have a longer reach. This is what you need when it comes to a fight. Stand here.'

I did as I was told.

'The first thing you do, with your left hand, is grab the other boy's neck as hard as you can. Grab his school tie or shirt, and never let go. Now, put your head straight down, towards the floor and grab my neck.'

This was getting weird, but I complied.

'Now. Just keep throwing punches with your right hand, like a piston, and aim at the top of your fist. Don't lift your head up at any stage. They'll just hit the top of your head, which is the hardest part of your body. Keep punching. Pop, pop, pop. Eventually they will raise their chin with the effort. All you need is to connect once on the button, and they're gone. Never let go of that neck until they stop. I've won so many fights with that technique, in pubs and town centres.'

How can that be a conversation between a grown man and a 12-year-old? I can't conceive of doing something similar. As I grew up, a mess of conflicting emotions, I railed against him for not teaching me something more constructive. I yearned to be shown another way. It took me years to understand the depth of his devotion, and what he was trying to achieve.

This wasn't about emotional development. His world was a dark and dangerous place, as rough as fuck. He's living the drinking, the drugging, the violence, the randomness of it all. He knows words won't help me. He's telling me how to act, giving me skills that will get me through the most dangerous time, before I reach 17 or 18. As he saw it, that's when I would be in the Premier League. That's when I would have left the gangs, and the scrapping, behind. To use a football cliché, he was setting my stall out, early doors.

If I put myself in his position, would I want my son to understand how I have done things I am not proud of? Would I take the risk of that being a hindrance, rather than a help? I am not trying to excuse myself, or rationalise my many mistakes, but maybe in 10 years' time it will be good for Cassius to truly understand the environment that produced me.

It was a hard place, with harsh, often deadly, lessons.

CHAPTER FOUR
TICKING

Tommy One-arm had obvious psychiatric problems, but seemed harmless enough. He lived in a flat overlooking the school field where we played football, and often gave chase to the boys who threw stones at his windows. He would work himself into a rage, but soon give up.

His real name was Leo Gavan. In quieter moments, we'd see him hanging around the chippy and the off-licence on the estate. He claimed he played for Real Madrid, and was the best one-armed goalkeeper in the world, but couldn't return to Spain because he was afraid of flying.

He was a timebomb. On one cold Sunday morning in February 1996, he didn't take the medication prescribed for his schizophrenia. A group of lads smashed one of his windows, and took shelter on a nearby flat roof when he went berserk.

Incensed he was physically unable to reach them, he returned to the flat, broke up his furniture and threw it into the street. He then lay in wait, watching from a back window. When his tormentors climbed down, he grabbed a carving knife and set off in pursuit.

They reached the local flower park, where we would play football on the bowling green when the old fellas weren't around, and scattered. Gavan cornered Lee Kinch, who had not been involved in the fracas, in a garden and stabbed him once, through the heart. He was 14, and died instantly.

I was in the leisure centre when a lad on a bike gabbled the news. Naturally, we headed to the crime scene to gawp and gossip. It seemed unreal. Lee was a popular lad at school, and lived close to my mate Mash. His funeral, which we all attended, was horrendous.

Gavan was sectioned under the Mental Health Act, as a political storm broke about the failings of the council's Care in the Community programme. He was deemed fit to plead guilty to manslaughter on the grounds of diminished responsibility two years later, and returned to full-time supervision.

Life went on, and continued to be summarily snatched away. Another lad, brother of a girl who was a year below me at school, hanged himself in the trees. No one saw fit to retrieve the rope for several days, so it became a macabre tourist attraction for bored teenagers.

Kids are ghouls, aren't they? A similar thing happened when Sean Catlin, another school friend, was crushed to death. He was playing a game of jumping on a moving bus, but miscalculated, lost his grip and fell forwards, underneath the back wheels. It took weeks for the bloodstains to fade from the road.

I never saw the benefits of such a game, but we kept doing stupid things, oblivious to the dangers. Our games of chicken, running across the carriageway of the nearby M62, carried on as normal. The police caught us, threw us into a cell for effect and made us walk home from Huyton Village, but they might as well have not bothered.

Even everyday activities, such as a game of golf on a municipal course in Widnes with Frankie Lacken and another friend, John Neil, had the potential for chaos. A gang of local lads demanded our clubs, attacked us, and got more than they bargained for during the subsequent brawl when Frankie hit their leader, an older man aged around 30 named Colin, across the side of the head with a 7-iron.

They fled, terrified by the instant intensity of the violence. We went into fugitive mode, reckoning it was unsafe to take public transport or a taxi because we were covered in blood. We walked to a local A&E department, only to glimpse Colin being attended to in a nearby cubicle. He was oblivious to our presence, and didn't seem the type to alert the bizzies, but we thought better of hanging around to have our faces and hands stitched. Frankie was more concerned by the irreversible damage done to the 7-iron, his favourite club. He often blamed its loss when I beat him in subsequent games of golf.

There was a strange normality to renegade behaviour. We used to incite the local smackheads by making raids on their drug dens in the boarded-up flats above the shops. They would try to chase us through the eaves and gaps in connecting walls, so we simply climbed on the roof to wait them out.

We took to whispering so they wouldn't know we were around, but quickly got bored. We knocked holes in ceilings and tossed bricks and tiles at them to wind them up. Our escape routes, rat runs through what were once attics, were pitch-black, but we knew our way around them by teenage telepathy.

Each derelict building was an adventure, and full of surprises. An old bed or a stained set of curtains with which to ring our camp were one thing. State-of-the-art surveillance equipment, discovered by chance in an adjoining attic, was entirely another. We took one look at the cameras and recording devices and decided the nous of bigger boys was needed.

They surveyed the stash, and quickly worked out we had stumbled on an undercover police operation to monitor the activities of a known drug dealer, who operated his business empire from an unprepossessing end-of-terrace house opposite the abandoned building.

Nothing was said, but a couple of days later we copped a few quid off an intermediary. The bigger boys got more money, but ours was enough for a new footie kit, a secret stash of Panini stickers and the odd ticket to watch Everton. As far as we were concerned, it was a victimless crime. The police could do one.

It was a disconcerting time. I started to suffer from bad acne, as puberty began to kick in. I was hyper-sensitive to slights, and paranoid about showing even a flicker of fear. The part of my brain hard-wired to anarchic, illogical and self-destructive behaviour was still active. People would give me a swerve, because I just wasn't worth the risk.

The fabric of my life was in danger of being torn apart. On one level, we had regular holidays in Portugal, Mum and Dad didn't fight too often within our earshot, and it was obvious we were loved. On another level, though, the strain was increasingly obvious. Dad was so much younger than Mum. He wanted to be out with the boys, and regularly went on weekend benders.

Mum would leave us with babysitters, because my half-sisters had left home, and join him in the pub, whether he liked it or not. As an adult, I can rationalise her actions. She was fearful of losing him, resentful at her lack of freedom. This was real life, not some *Daily Mail* you-can-have-it-all fantasy. As a child, though, it stimulated a sense of emptiness.

I needed a maternal influence, and found it in my nan. She was the one who cooked the Sunday roast, cleaned our clothes and made sure we were bathed and in bed at the right time. She was the one who thought nothing of imposing a 7pm curfew, and embarrassing me by dragging me away from mischief. She used to hand out my uncles' oversized Stone Roses tee-shirts for me to wear in bed, because she didn't run to pyjamas. She was a rock.

I used to hate Sunday mornings, when my parents were trying to sleep off the lock-in. I loathed the cronies, sprawled on the settee where they lapsed into unconsciousness. I got tired of rifling through Dad's kecks to sweep up enough loose change to sort out my subs, and buy sweets and a drink after football. I didn't mind running to matches, because my stamina was my secret weapon, but I wished I got the lifts home other lads took for granted.

I felt I was in the way. There was only one course of action, which presented itself when Dad returned from another session to find his clothes cut to ribbons, and a few belongings stuffed into three black bin bags, tossed into the front garden. There had been explosions before, when Mum refused to allow him over the threshold, but this was terminal. I let him in silently through the sliding glass doors at the back to retrieve what he could, and soon joined him at my nan's.

No one really wins in that situation. Andrew was really tight with Mum, so Dad instantly became the Antichrist. Mum's suspicions were confirmed when a new woman quickly turned up on the scene. I held that against him for a while, but eventually decided life was too short. As a woman, Nan understood the magnitude of the betrayal, but as a mother her love was unbreakable.

Mum was pretty feisty, but understood Nan's rules of

engagement. Never, ever, fall out with your own. Nan was willing to help out with childcare, and expected a line to be drawn under historic tensions. Her job was to stabilise things, and she understood how fundamental football was to my future.

My life had reached a crossroads. Drugs were everywhere on the estate, and I wasn't daft. Dad's generation was into frighteningly cheap cocaine. There were tales of lines being chopped in the pub, and hoovered up at house parties. I could either go down to the park on Friday nights, to get high with school friends who were quickly progressing from weed to tabs of acid, or I could limit myself to the adrenaline high of competition.

I was fortunate that I didn't like the taste of hard drink. Dad offered me my first pint when I was 15 but I didn't touch alcohol until my 17th birthday, when I was taken out by my uncle Tom to Natterjacks disco bar on Roby Road in Huyton. Swigging warm sweet cider from plastic bottles in draughty bus shelters wasn't my idea of a good time.

For a while, I was caught in the crossfire of wanting to be in the old gang, having a good time getting up to no good, and wanting to make new friends, and to make something of myself through football. The telly in Nan's lounge, beside a roaring fire, was my tutor and bodyguard.

I was a child of Italia 90, of Roger Milla's slinky street dance and Gazza's distraught tears. Milky pictures from the Welsh language channel, S4C, allowed me to study the princes of the Italian game – Ancelotti, Baggio, Baresi and Maldini. Then Gazza took his fake breasts to Lazio, and Channel 4 offered weekly masterclasses from Batistuta, Donadoni and co.

I fell in love during USA 94. They called Gheorghe Hagi the 'Maradona of the Carpathians', yet he was in a different league to the wild-eyed, drugged-up genius who was sent home in disgrace. The Romanian was small, but shielded the ball ferociously and used it stylishly. One goal, in the 3-2 second-round win over Argentina, stays with me from childhood. Hagi picks the ball up, just inside his own half wide on the left. He takes out four opponents with a single pass, and sprints into space to receive the return. It is hot, airless and frantic in the Rose Bowl in Pasadena, yet he freezes time. He jinks inside and rolls another pass, which evades three covering defenders and gives Ilie Dumitrescu a tap-in. Wow. He scores later, with his wrong foot, but nothing beats that.

I just wanted to be him. I loved his arrogance, organising the wall for his goalkeeper at free kicks, and cutting team-mates dead when they wanted to take a throw-in instead of him. I cut my socks down and put white tape around the top in his honour, and begged for six months for a pair of his Lotto Stadio boots. I felt like crying when a minor growth spurt meant they were too small, too soon.

Gazza fascinated me, because I empathised with his restlessness and poorly hidden unhappiness. My horizons were being broadened by the game, and its inherent disciplines, but I was torn between diligence and recklessness. The dark side of my character was largely dormant, but never far from the surface. It intermittently threatened everything I held dear.

I was ticking, ticking, ticking.

I would get into needless scuffles during training sessions at Everton, like a child testing the limits of a parent's love. Black moods would overtake me without reason or warning. I played well in the Milk Cup youth tournament in Northern Ireland, but got into all kinds of bother when I threw a borrowed set of golf clubs off a cliff and into the sea.

I couldn't honestly explain why I did it. I was the toddler

who stuck his fingers into the electricity socket to see the panic and concern on adults' faces, yet I was indulged. Football clubs have their own moral codes, shaped by expedience rather than ethical standards, and my promise was deemed more important than my immaturity. I'd grow out of it.

The coaches told me to lighten up, that it was sometimes better to walk away from conflict rather than to front up and try to take on the world. They probably knew they were wasting their breath, but honour was satisfied on both sides.

I was being noticed. At the end of one of my Sunday morning matches a familiar figure introduced himself. He asked how things were going at Everton, and suggested that he could find a place for me in Liverpool's academy. I couldn't believe it. I was being tapped up by Steve Heighway, the former Liverpool winger who was developing a reputation as one of football's greatest talent spotters.

It was a beautiful, old-school scenario. Steve's wife worked at Seel Road Comprehensive, and got some of my mates there to put in a good word. I knew I could have learned so much under him, but also knew there was no way the ultimate betrayal would be allowed. Steve was persistent, if nothing else, and rang our home several times before Dad took the call. He barely had a chance to explain how impressed he had been with me when he was cut short. 'No, no, no, no,' Dad exclaimed, 'We're Evertonians, mate.' With that, he put the phone down. Job done, family honour protected.

Superficially, things were progressing smoothly. Though development coaches decry a results-based approach, my group at Bellefield had built an unbeaten run across two seasons. I should have been smart enough to recognise the warning signs when Neil Dewsnip was recruited to run the academy, since he represented everything I resented.

He had a narrow teaching background and was a smooth political operator. What really upset me, though, was his fundamentalist approach to the game. He was a disciple of power and physique, size and strength. He had an obsession about young players being bundled off the ball, and concentrated on the development of big, well-balanced lads who could retain possession.

It soon became obvious that he felt I was too small – ironically the same drawback that once threatened to hold back his star pupil, Steven Gerrard, whom he had taught PE at the Cardinal Heenan Catholic High School in West Derby. All I could do was get my nut down, work hard, and expose the stupidity of his prejudice.

Decisions were being reached so haphazardly that Leighton Baines failed two different trials with us, an oversight that was to cost £6m when he was eventually signed from Wigan, but word was out that I was among nine Everton players being considered for a place in the FA's National School of Excellence at Lilleshall. This was a Big Deal.

Lilleshall, a former stately home set in a 30,000-acre estate in Shropshire, was football's Hogwarts. It was home for two years to the 16 best players in the country aged between 14 and 16. The idea was simple, too simple as it turned out. Train the best with the best. Consume them with football. Teach them to be internationals. That reckoned without the standard of coaching, which proved to be over-managed and mediocre.

We weren't to know that, when the trials process began at Stockport County. This featured the top clubs in the Northwest; Everton's contingent, which included Phil Jagielka and Bradley Orr, was pitted against the most promising lads from Manchester United, Liverpool, Blackburn and

Manchester City. This was my type of challenge, every man for himself.

Assessors split us into two groups, and I was told cursorily that I'd be playing at right back. If that was a ploy, to see if I would sulk, it didn't work. I looked around in the tunnel beforehand, and saw the telltale signs of inner turmoil – quickness of breath and darting eyes. I had them where I wanted them.

I've always had a sixth sense, which tells me when I'm going to play well. It generates confidence and coolness. The bigger the occasion, the bigger the stakes, the bigger my performance. By half-time I'd done enough to be moved into my advertised position, central midfield. I was one of three Everton lads who went through to the next stage.

I was given my third position in my second trial game. They played me up front, despite me being comfortably the smallest kid in the group. My opposing centre halves, two big lumps from the Midlands, couldn't resist a smirk, but they weren't laughing when I scored a hat-trick. Game on. I was to be Everton's only representative in the final.

Not for the first time, I was to learn that life was unfair. My versatility was a handicap, because I was now competing for a place with specialists, who were selected in positions they had played in all their lives. I was asked to play another unfamiliar role, left midfield, and although I felt I acquitted myself well, I knew I wouldn't survive the cull.

No fewer than 234 boys passed through Lilleshall in the 15 years it operated, before Howard Wilkinson opened a corporate can of worms by announcing the establishment of a club-based academy system. Some, like Michael Owen, Sol Campbell, Nick Barmby and Jermain Defoe, made it all the way to the top, but most were quickly lost to the game.

One lad, much closer to home, used it as a formative experience. Tom Culshaw, my second cousin, played for England Schoolboys and progressed as far as being Liverpool's reserve-team captain before opting to work in coaching and education. He is a big mate of Steven Gerrard and now looks after the under-13s at Liverpool's academy.

Despite the pretensions of men like Dewsnip, who was to spend 17 years at Everton before becoming an England age-group coach, youth development is an inexact science. Just as Bob Paisley used to say, the first two yards are in your head at the highest level; the most important few inches are between an emerging player's ears.

I felt no shame, then, going back to Bellefield as a narrow failure. I was established in the system on schoolboy forms, though my headmaster did threaten to refuse to give his approval when I called a teacher 'green teeth'. I was respected by my team-mates and ready to do whatever was necessary to improve.

I hated losing, even in the cross-country at school, where I would wear down the best runner, a tall, wiry lad called Neil Kearns, by simply refusing to go away. I'd be on his heels, talking to him: 'Whatever it takes, la'. I'm just biding my time.' It used to freak him out so badly he would try a desperate sprint before flaming out, and giving up.

I looked around me at Everton and saw too many Neil Kearns. They had more natural talent than me. They had more mature, better-developed bodies. But they didn't want it to hurt. They didn't have my love of unpromising odds. I fancied a 30:70 tackle in training. They would shy away from it, to save themselves for later.

Some good it did me. A couple of months later, Dad and Nan were called into a Portakabin at the training ground for the usual end-of-season review. Dewsnip, who had earlier released Phil Jagielka and was systematically scything through the squad, did not stand on ceremony. 'He's finished at Everton,' he said. 'I'm sorry but that's how it goes.'

I was playing *Championship Manager* in my bedroom when the kitchen phone was answered by Grandad. 'Joe. It's your nan for you,' he shouted. I moved across the landing into her bedroom, lay down on the floor, and picked up the extension. 'Look, lad,' she said, 'they've said they're going to release you.

'You keep your head up, because I'm the sort of lady you'll knock down once, but you won't do it twice. If people want to ignore me, or fall out with me, I won't give them the opportunity to do it twice. There's no one better than you. They may have a bigger house or more money, but there's no one better than you.'

Her words didn't register until later, because I felt as if every ounce of air had been kicked out of me. I sobbed when I put the phone down, because I was trying to make sense of my life. I was powerless to stop my mum and dad splitting up. I couldn't do anything about puberty, or my struggle to fit in at school. But, surely, when I'm rejected by football, I can control that . . .

My thoughts raced, and the fighter made himself heard.

You know what, they're wrong. All of them. The careers teachers who smiled condescendingly when you said you were going to be a footballer, and told you to be realistic. They're wrong. The coach who got rid of you because you're not built like a brick shithouse. He's wrong as well.

Fuck 'em.

You are not a victim. They will not break you. They won't make you beg. Your background might cost you in years to come, because the line between aggression and self-assertion is pretty blurred, but right now the estate is your sanctuary. What right have they got to try to kill your dream?

Their system stinks. Too many academies are full of bitter, angry coaches who think the under-12s are beneath them. They want the cars, cash and recognition that come from being with the first team. They can't get over the fact they never made it.

You can surrender, as so many do, or you can scream and scrap. You are a late developer. You are improving every day. No one, but no one, wants it more than you. You are going to feed this down their throats. No more feeling sorry for yourself. Dry your eyes, man the fuck up, and get on with it.

Grandad's cold-eyed reaction when I went downstairs – 'You're just going to have to knuckle down, aren't you?' – was just what I needed. This was just another obstacle to overcome, another setback to be taken care of. Someone will see sense soon. Won't they?

An hour passes. The phone rings again. It is Barry Poynton who left Everton just before Dewsnip arrived. He is head of recruitment at Manchester City's academy, and wants me to go there for a trial. He says all the right things, striking the right balance between subtle surprise at my release and a challenge to my competitive nature.

Dad and I get more such calls over the next day or so. Preston North End like the look of me. So, too, do Leeds United. City were in the Championship at the time but it felt right to go with Barry. He was the first to react, to sense the opportunity in my bad news. Let's face it, he also had a vested interest in proving Everton wrong.

It wasn't a fairy tale. It never is with me, is it? I really struggled for my first two and a half years at City. I hated the travelling, an hour each way on a good day, depending on traffic. Frankie Bunn, one of the coaches, was especially good to me, but life was a series of Groundhog Days. Other coaches didn't fancy me. Too small, they'd say. Too small …

If you are at a physical disadvantage in an athletic sport, where you have to be strong and fast, you'd better develop alternative options. I'm not suited to tippy-tappy academy football. My blood has to be up, and my senses need to be sharp. I'm a player of ragged edges. No one will ever describe me as neat and tidy, freshly washed and ironed. I have to get down and dirty.

Jim Cassell was the only one who saw anything in me. He began as a scout, when his playing career with Bury was ended by a knee injury, and developed a coach's eye, which looks beyond the obvious. He didn't really know what he had on his hands, though he sensed I would play for nothing rather than walk away. Something intangible, something inexplicable to those who don't understand that football is a people business, told him to give me one last chance.

'Everything in me says we have to get rid of you, Joe,' he told me. 'You don't look like you are going to be big enough. You are never going to have the speed that should be necessary at the top level. But you have something in your eyes. I can't put my finger on it. I like that. You've got six months to show me something, or you are gone.'

At least Cass was upfront. I was still convinced I would make it, but I appreciated his honesty. I respected him, because of the straightness of his character and the authenticity of his experience. Football is full of bullshitters, career cowards who are two-faced and operate double standards. He told me as it was – as it is to this day. Shape up or ship out.

I'd be lying if I said I didn't think of doing the latter. My first instinct was to go back into non-league, with a good club like Marine, Bootle or Southport, and rebuild my reputation. I spent a week labouring on the roofs during the summer break, cutting my hands to ribbons ferrying tiles up the ladders, before retreating to the van with a vow I would never return. I had 10 GCSEs, but they were about as much use as Boy Scout badges.

Dad was adamant I had to eke out any time I had left at City. He wasn't one for paternal platitudes, but he put things into perfect perspective. 'You've got to handle disappointment because you get let down a lot in life,' he told me. 'Stay there. Use the gym. Make it work for you. They'll see what you can do eventually. At least you're on a wage. You'll be getting paid to stay fit.'

I was on the princely sum of £72 a week and understood how much my football meant to my dad. He would definitely have made it as a pro, but he didn't have that 'fuck you' mentality you need. I've seen him be ultra-competitive, go way over the top, but he'd probably want to have a pint after the match with the bloke he was threatening to kill.

He feared an age-old working-class drama was starting to play out. Estates like St John's are, essentially, unlocked cells. The long walk to freedom is hazardous, and littered with mantraps. There is a temptation to accept your fate as preordained, turn in on yourself, and succumb to resentment, frustration and societal expectation.

All my mates were bevvying, birding or drugging. Many were completing their apprenticeship in criminality. If I had been weaker, mentally, I would have been lost. You don't submit a CV in these situations, but it was made very clear to me that I'd rise very quickly through the ranks in the local drug syndicate. The going rate for a successful enforcer was several thousand pounds a week, in ready cash of course.

Dad knew the alternative scenario as well as I did. He was working six-week shifts in Ireland, but on his fortnight off, he took to accompanying me on eight-mile runs on his bike. He had me doing sets of 10 shuttle runs up and down the embankment of the M62. Knees high, arms swinging, lungs burning. No pain, no gain.

It was a Scouse version of *Rocky*, with a sprint through the boarded-up badlands of St John's being Liverpool's answer to Rocky's triumphant run up the 72 steps towards the Museum of Art in Philadelphia.

Gonna fly now . . .

CHAPTER FIVE
MAKING IT

So, you want to be a professional footballer. I might not be the best example to follow, but I would have loved to meet someone like me during my struggle to make it at Manchester City. This is my take on why I pulled through, after Jim Cassell rewarded me with a one-year pro contract on £300 a week. I didn't listen too intently when I was a kid, but what do you have to lose?

We all have inner turmoil. There's nobody who doesn't have that quiet terror of being found out. Some drink to suppress it, some drug it. Some seek cheap, empty sex, and others need the release of a mad gamble. Nobody's perfect. I certainly don't profess to be perfect. Actually, I'm probably as complex as it gets.

We all walk around, insisting that everything's sound and we don't need anyone's help, but we're all vulnerable from time to time. The sooner you start talking about your fears, the better. If I had been open to that early in my career, it would have helped enormously. I bottled everything up. Football told me that being true to myself was a sign of weakness.

People condemn me for being outspoken. I merely say what I am thinking. When I'm asked a question, I try to answer as honestly as I possibly can. The consequences are what they are. Remember, this industry isn't the be-all and end-all. There's so much more going on in the world. Football just happens to be something that people are really interested in.

I now see the game as a tool to influence people in a positive way. For years I used its power in a terrible manner. I inflicted a lot of pain and hurt on those closest to me. But for every squeaky-clean idol like Michael Owen or David Beckham, there is a darker role model like me. I've been a car crash. All my glorious fuck-ups are out there, so let's not waste time on bullshit.

I know the world has changed. Kids of 17 live on their phones. They don't read the papers. It is not that they feel my principles and morals are unimportant, but they are simply unaware of them. They are the values of a different time, another era. One thing does not change, though: in football it is kill or be killed.

Kids like you are trying to take my job. That's the reality of the situation, and I ain't going to give my job away. I'm not going to let you take food out of the mouths of my children. You will have to rip that shirt off my back. For that to happen either I have to decline physically, or you are going to be mentally stronger than me. Really? How far are you willing to go?

Are you going to do that by going out with your mates on a Saturday night? Are you going to do that by sitting around and moaning about what's going on in the academy? Are you going to do that by cutting corners? I'm not cutting any corners, by the way. I will make it my business to discover your weaknesses. That's why I have played as long as I have, at the level I have.

Don't talk to me about talent. Listen to Conor McGregor, the UFC fighter. I did, and agreed with every word he said: 'There's no talent here, this is hard work. This is an obsession. Talent does not exist. We are all equal as human beings. You could be anyone if you put in the time. You will reach the top, and that is that. I am not talented, I am obsessed.'

Successful footballers are not normal. They are borderline psychotic, because they will trample over anyone who gets in their way. Normal people don't get to the highest levels in life. Normal people don't climb Everest, sail around the world, or think nothing about playing football in front of 70,000 people. Normal people sit in the café, play bingo, go to work, come home, and repeat the same routine the following week.

I'd see it as really offensive if someone told me I was normal. I'm quite happy with who I am, and I am trying to affect the world around me in whatever way I can, but I am not normal. I am pushing personal boundaries as far and as fast as possible. Life is about seeing how far you can get under your own steam.

Now, if you come to me and say, 'Joe, what is the most important lesson you could teach me?', I'd ignore the artificial nature of the question and give you a straight answer. It is, simply, love what you do. That is the secret of long-term success.

My love of the game kept me going through the darkest times. Not the money. Not the bollocks that comes with it. I ran on pure, unadulterated love. That is what gets you through the days when the bells and whistles fail, when the world seems a cold and unforgiving place.

I also asked questions, loads of questions. Even now, when I go into an environment where I feel intellectually inferior, I'm not afraid of making myself a nuisance by simply seeking knowledge. In football terms I knew I couldn't beat people physically or technically, but I could be mentally stronger than anyone who had an eye on my job.

I was drawn to strong characters, like Peter Schmeichel. He wasn't a person you could warm to, because he let no one in, but I might have just caught him at an opportune moment. He was getting a massage in the dressing room at Maine Road. His head was down and he was lying naked, lost in the rhythm of the oil being rubbed into his body by one of the physios.

I was a nobody, a kid making his way in the reserves. I pulled up a small stool next to him and asked him questions for 30 minutes. They had nothing to do with the games he had played or the saves he had made. They were about his mind. Why he put up with me I just don't know. Maybe I caught him at a time when he was feeling a bit vulnerable or disarmed, but I ended up prising gold dust out of him.

'Where are you at?' he asked, talking to the floor. I explained I'd been playing well but, typically for a young player, I'd have a run of 10 good games then throw in a couple of mares. 'I haven't had a bad game for four years,' he said, and I laughed, thinking he was joking. He was 37 or 38 at the time.

Slowly, he lifted his head and looked me in the eye: 'I'm telling you, I've not had a bad game for four years. My teammates have had a bad game in front of me, and I've made one or two mistakes, but overall I've not had a bad game for four years. Before that I went six or seven years without a bad one.' I'm thinking this is a wind-up, but he was deadly serious.

He started talking to me about his frame of mind. He taught me about willing things into existence. He explained why he was the best keeper in the world, and how he got there: 'Look, if you think you'll have a bad game, you're going to have a bad game. Even if you are playing well and you think, "I am due a bad one", you will suddenly play poorly. Everyone makes mistakes. It's normal. But champions, world-class players who have long, successful careers, get over their mistakes in a heartbeat. They follow a mistake with something good.'

He unlocked a forgotten memory from the hard times I had as a YT. I suddenly remembered Alex Gibson, the youth-team coach, saying, 'If you make a mistake in a game, if you play a bad pass, buy yourself two simple ones and then you're back in the positive.' Maybe I should have listened to him with more intensity, instead of brooding about his lack of faith.

People saw Schmeichel's mindset as arrogance. I remember them saying, 'He's a cunt, big-time, big ego.' His attributes didn't fit the mould of being a good team-mate. He was very selfish, very self-centred, very ego-driven, but he was a fucking winner. You knew, looking in his eyes, and watching the way he trained, prepared, carried himself and spoke, that he was a successful human being.

He would go out to training 10 minutes early, and move any footballs in his net to the sidelines. Their presence in his goal offended him. Any player who idly attempted to chip him in a practice match would get a volley of abuse and the ball belted at his head. Fall below his professional standards and he would tear off his gloves, and stalk back to the changing room.

I looked at him and thought, 'Yeah, I might have to step on a few people here. They might not like me, but I'm going to have longevity in this game.' That's why, when I went into the first team, I never came out of it. I saw other kids go in, go out, shake it all about, but they didn't last. I was there for keeps.

My mind, not my ability, got me through all the stuff that happened afterwards, going to jail, playing in the Premier League with idiots abusing my kids. I dealt with the madness head-on. Schmeichel's single-mindedness made a huge impact on me. I'd always try to nick a little knowledge from my team-mates, the likes of Fowler, McManaman and Anelka. Questions, questions. Don't ask, don't get.

In my experience football is still a very reactive sport. Do that run, do that gym session, stand there, move there, do this, do that. React, react, react, react. We are telling kids, 'This is the tactic I want you to play. When the ball comes here this is how I want you to turn. When this happens this is what I want you to do.' We're not teaching them to be proactive.

It becomes much of a muchness because everyone can predict what you can do and when you will do it. As a young player, you should dare to be different. Look at Dele Alli. Touch, flick it over your head, volley it in. No one taught him to do that; that's a kid playing football on the street. That's someone who is enjoying his football, who has not had coaching constraints.

He's not had someone nowhere near as talented trying to coerce him into playing a certain way, stifling his creativity. Our academy systems are flawed. We've got to let players develop independently up to the age of 13 or 14. We're not helping by taking them into academies at six and subjecting them to the whims of an academy coach who could well be substandard, and preoccupied with personal ambitions of working towards the first team.

Let's face it, we don't have a great record of producing outstanding coaches. They bend to the wind that's blowing in the Premier League. Do we want big, strong physical players or small technical players? Do we want to play like the Germans, the Spanish or the French? Too many kids are being discarded too quickly, with too little thought.

We're playing a numbers game. Jamie Vardy, Charlie Austin, Dele Alli and countless others have developed outside their business model. How many players of their potential do we lose? If the people who ran our academies ran our economy the country would be bankrupt. They're saying, 'Give me a hundred quid. I'll give you two quid back in five years.' Some investment! Ninety-eight per cent waste . . .

But you are here to learn how to beat the odds. Everyone develops their own survival strategy. Be careful. The dressing room is a harsh environment because it is full of young men with an inability to communicate at a deep, emotional level. It is not a place to admit vulnerability. Insecurity means the humour is barbed, and I have seen kids destroyed.

I was lucky at City. Senior players like Kevin Horlock caned us, but he integrated us into the group. Andy Morrison, the captain, was, let's say, a little different. I was always a bit cheeky, a little chirpy. The other first-year YT lads were timid, but I didn't give a shit. All pros try to create an 'us and them' mentality, which makes them unapproachable, but I had no fear factor because of what I'd seen with my dad, on the road with Knowsley United.

I'd answer back, which didn't go down too well. I refused to be their slave, because I already had my training-ground job, cleaning the showers. I also, even then, had my eyes on their shirts. I saw this as part of the psychological warfare that would eventually end with me in the first team. I wouldn't let them think they could get one over on me. But I did make one mistake.

A big mistake.

My group of YTs were in the indoor dome at Platt Lane one afternoon, before City moved to the Carrington complex. Morrison was in the gym, kicking the ball against the wall before a session, and we decided to have a game of dare. Jocky was a bit of a bully, a scrapper, and even the senior pros were petrified of him, but I drew the short straw and had to do something to him.

My plan was to wait until his back was turned and kick a ball in his general direction. It landed nowhere near him, and by the time he realised what was going on we had scarpered. We were pretty pleased with ourselves until, after training, he caught us in the youth-team showers and blocked the only exit. This, by the way, is the man whose autobiography was entitled *The Good, the Mad and the Ugly.*

'Who kicked the ball?' he said, in the sort of tone that told us this would not end well. 'I am going to hit every fucking one of yous if you don't tell me.' The lads were not doing a great job of disguising their anguished glances in my direction, so I decided I was going to have to take what was coming.

'It was me, Jock.'

'Right, come with me.'

He ordered me to lie face down, and pushed my head into the floor with the palm of his hand. I was determined not to whimper and show him he was hurting me, but he just kept pushing and pushing. The pain was indescribable. I didn't cry, honestly. But my eyes watered with the pain. When he let me up he simply said, 'Never fucking do that again.'

He had made his point, that I had to know my place, and never mentioned it again. I never held it against him, and kinda saw where he was coming from. I'd been caught being a cheeky bastard. Now I'm a senior pro I don't mind a lad with a bit of edge. I'd much prefer that to the kids who play nice and polite. You need people pushing boundaries.

When I was 17, I was running around like a lunatic, getting sent off in training, because I had such an overpowering hunger to play professional football. There was only one place at the dinner table, and I was determined to be the one who was going to eat. I went after the alpha males, and I could see some of them thinking, 'Fucking hell. That's the way you get my shirt.'

Never forget, I'm seeking weakness. I'm scheming, building a dossier on everyone, because every friend is a potential enemy. I literally do have a little black book. I might put the hammer on someone in training, get a little physical, and he might give up at that point. Noted. Next time there is scope for confrontation, bang, I have already worked out what is going to hurt him.

People are doing the same to me, but I am better at the black ops stuff than them. I've never physically punched someone during a training session, but my language can be threatening. I am frighteningly articulate and terribly cruel when I am angry, or angling for an advantage. I find a way to cut straight through your heart. I'm hardened to violence of the tongue, because of the life experiences I've had.

I've always been prepared to sacrifice more than anyone else. I used to hear the lads in my youth team talking about going out on Saturday night, or on a Tuesday after a ressie game. I'd have a quiet chuckle. I'm thinking, 'I'm getting closer to you. You might be ahead of me, but I'll be really ready for training tomorrow. You won't. That's me closing the gap on you.'

I had fallen into the lifetime habit of being out for at least two and a half hours every day, working on my basics, having balls fed to me for heading or shooting practice. I wanted to be Joe Calzaghe, the boxer who never dropped his intensity. Watch some of his great fights. He may lack the ring smarts of some of his best opponents, but he wore them down with his relentlessness and then imposed his will.

Be honest. Will you be the one who never quits, who tracks

back to make a tackle in the 94th minute when the game is long since won? Will you go again when your throat is burning and your stomach seems saturated by molten lead? Will you train on your own and force yourself to do one final shuttle run, knowing it will end in a shower of sick? If you can say yes, you could be a man, my son.

Forget the money. I hear of a lad on 36 grand a week at 17. He's probably never going to kick a ball for the first team. That is going to fry his brain, and that's not his fault. The majority of young players don't come from the best social or economic background. You can't blame him for taking the money, because no one is going to turn their nose up at a fortune.

The ignorance out there is frightening. I once spoke to a good young player about the importance of looking after himself, financially. He didn't have a clue what a mortgage was. He kept his money under the bed. He reasoned that if he wanted a house he would take it out and buy one, like he would a piece of fruit.

There's a moral responsibility to educate these kids, to give them a pathway, and it's been negated. There should be a salary cap for young players. Give them a maximum of £250 a week at 18, rising to £5,000 at 19, and keep the rest in trust funds which can only be accessed when they are 35, or retired. That still gives the market economy plenty of time and freedom to move.

If you have an agent at 17, and he is telling the club they can't do this or that because he has to protect your brand or your image, have a word. Don't put the gold-encrusted cart before the horse. Get out there and learn your trade, play real football. Feel what it is like to be elbowed in the face by a lower-league defender who needs the £150 win bonus to pay his mortgage.

Forget the fripperies. I was listening to some young lads recently, wondering whether they should rub ice on their faces before they go out for a game. Cristiano Ronaldo does so, because he wants his face to glow for the TV cameras. The difference is, he is one of the best two players in the world, whose life is minutely dedicated to his career. He has always put in the hours to ensure he operates optimally, whatever the showbiz bollocks. He is not preparing to run out before two men and a dog in a development fixture.

The game will change massively in your lifetime. Football is still miles off the pace, compared to the NFL and NBA. Look at the time, effort and intelligence involved in those two sports. A top-level player is a product of a 10-year sequence of single-minded application of the highest possible quality of advice and information.

Where is football going? It is a given that you can only train people physiologically for a certain amount of time each day, let's say two hours. You can't ask someone to perform on a Saturday and then blast them all week. Our science is generally good, and improving in its practicality, but the real step change is going to come in mindsets and mentality.

We've already seen Dr Steve Peters come over, to work with Liverpool and England, but he can't have the requisite impact because he is trying to do the wrong thing. The principle is right but the message is wrong. I think he is brilliant, but he is a clinical psychiatrist, whose professional instinct is to control fires, dampen them down. As a footballer your flames have to be fanned. Your blood needs to be up.

We still think of football as an endurance sport, but it is now a high-intensity interval sport. It involves lots of small, high-speed interactions. Demands on the body come in short, sharp blasts. To be honest, I don't think many clubs or coaches have got their heads around that evolution of the game. There are still far too many stupid soft tissue injuries.

We can improve physically, but the great leap forward will be in the mind. The Belgians are particularly advanced in the area of brain training, a discipline designed to improve the number and clarity of pictures in a young player's brain when he receives the ball. Their experts reckon that Lionel Messi's brain processes around 120 images of his immediate options, and their outcomes, in that split second.

As an interval sport, football is an emotional game. The collective emotion of 11 individuals can overcome those with greater talent, if they want it more and put something extra into their work. External support is vital. I know this will sound cheesy, but when you know your fans are rooting for you, when you hear the low rumble of a supportive chant at a key moment, it does lift you.

Materially, the game is in a fantastic position. But it won't always be so. Sport, like life, is cyclical. Empires rise and fall. Kings live and die. By rationalising what we are doing now, in a position of financial strength, I am also trying to prepare your generation for a new survival strategy, based on heart and hunger.

Look at the financial markets. Generally, when things are going well, people say, 'Happy days. Let's buy, let's borrow, let's lend.' Then, suddenly, Armageddon strikes. Everyone goes, 'Oh shit.' That's when the clever people emerge. You only realise who hasn't got trunks on when the tide goes out. Who in football hasn't invested in a pair of trunks? We'll find out soon enough.

Speaking of trunks, we need to address the popular misconception that it is best to avoid meeting your heroes, because most of them aren't what you've built them up to be. That misses the point. By discovering just how human they actually are, you appreciate that anything is attainable in life. They are ordinary people – not normal, ordinary – who have achieved extraordinary things.

Stuart Pearce was an icon of mine. You know, Euro 96, his mad penalty and all that. All of a sudden I am at City as a kid, and he is joining in my session, absolutely lamping balls at people. He'd smash it at you from a range of about two yards, and bollock you if you couldn't get hold of it. I didn't understand at the time, but he was obviously testing us. Some would respond; others would shrink a bit. He had his information, his insight.

He trained as he played, all out. He was an interesting mixture, being an introverted character with extrovert tendencies. He fascinated me during match days, when two youth-team players would be assigned to do the chores in the first-team dressing room, to give us a feel for things.

Most of the youth-team lads would linger in the tunnel and watch the pre-match warm-up, but Pearcey was never there. He was allowed to prepare in his own way, and I would sit in the corner of the dressing room, slyly hoping he wouldn't notice me while he did his warm-up. It was some show.

He wore nothing but his socks, shinpads and a pair of white pants. He would work himself into a frenzy, stretching, striding, jumping, grunting. He'd be sweating, staring, scary. I'm thinking, 'What the fuck is this? He's a lunatic.' Now I am older, I can understand why, psychologically, it worked for him. He was in the zone, his way.

But back then, I just thought, 'Wow. Whatever it takes. I am seeing behind the curtain here. This is not what they let you watch on TV.' Little did I know there would be plenty of time to ponder Pearcey's weaknesses. Our time together at City would prove to be eventful . . .

CHAPTER SIX
CARPE DIEM

Arthur Cox was on me before I could react. A solid, bull-necked man, powerful despite being in his early sixties, he had his hands around my throat and had pinned me against a wall in the canteen at Manchester City's training ground. His eyes were ablaze, and his weathered face was taut with contempt. His words were a murderous hail of machine-gun bullets.

'How can you not get in the first team? What the fuck are you doing? There's something wrong. You're not working hard enough. You're not dedicating your life to this. Is that it? Listen, there's nothing stopping you here. You should be playing. If you don't knuckle down, I will fucking have you. I'm going to box your ears. You're a disgrace. You've got to go harder. Go. Fucking. Harder.'

He let me loose and, for once, I knew better than to protest. This was what tough love felt like. Puzzling, pulverising, intimidating, energising. I was 19 and perversely thrilled he was on my case. Promoted from chief scout to be Kevin Keegan's assistant, Coxy was cunning, watchful and deadly.

Sixteen years managing Chesterfield, Newcastle United and Derby County had turned him into a cross between Yoda and Luca Brasi, Don Corleone's personal enforcer.

He was Keegan's sounding board, the Yin to his Yang. Kevin had the influence of office, but diluted it, within reason, because he loved football, and footballers. He was bubbly, infectious, innocent in his determination to involve himself in training. He would instigate frantic sessions of head tennis, and hang around to serve up headers and volleys for anyone willing to share his endless childhood.

Arthur's interactions with players were darker, more profound. He lurked in the background, sensing weakness, stalking the feckless and the careless. His aggression was tinged by a revealing envy, since his dreams of being a professional footballer had been shattered long before, by injury sustained in a reserve match for Coventry City.

I loved him. I was a kid, struggling with life, hustling to make my way in the game. He burrowed inside my brain. I was immediately unbalanced whenever he walked past me, shaking his head slowly and silently. What have I done? What does he know? What is he thinking? What has he heard? Why does he care? Why does he bother with me?

When he sat me down and asked, 'Where do you think you're at?', the world condensed until it felt as claustrophobic as a confessional. He had a piercing stare, designed to unnerve, but somehow, deep down, I knew he cared. He'd obviously done his homework on me, with Jim Cassell and Alex Gibson. He appreciated how close I'd come to being kicked out.

He sought out Asa Hartford, my reserve-team manager, and attended most of our home games at Hyde United's ground. He was hard on me, very hard, but occasionally I would catch a glimpse of an animated gesture when I put a reducer on a senior pro who felt the stiffs were beneath him. My restlessness and juvenile ruthlessness fitted snugly into his value system.

As someone who had a fantastic career despite being better suited, physically, to working life as one of Santa's elves, Keegan obviously identified with my determination to compensate for my lack of stature. In hindsight, he was trying to teach me to better myself, without explaining fully what he wanted, or why he wanted it. He had too much trust in my ability to pick things up; I needed clearer guidance, greater detail, rather than management by assumption.

I was too immature to grasp why he hated the hassle of a kid treating a Tuesday training exercise as a cup final, when he was trying to get his head around his team for Saturday and his most valuable players fancied a gentle workout. His old-school belief in the hierarchy of the dressing room meant he loathed my lack of respect for my peers. He demanded unity, incompatible in my eyes with personal ambition.

The four lads ahead of me in my preferred position might as well have had targets imprinted on their foreheads.

Terry Dunfield had an easier passage through the academy. He was a better technical footballer, two-footed and composed. But, like me, he was a prisoner of his upbringing. He was a nice middle-class kid from Canada, whose deference was instinctive and ruinous, since it signalled softness. I quickly realised he could not cope with my physicality, so I smashed him at every opportunity.

He made nine first-team appearances before he asked Keegan to release him, to take up a three-year contract at Bury. He had the strength of character to overcome a career-threatening injury, a broken kneecap, and he captained his country. He played effectively in the lower leagues and North America until 2015, but with me, he stood no chance.

One down, three to go . . .

Ali Benarbia was a super bloke, engaging and encouraging, up to a point. A French-Algerian whose skill on the ball made him a fan favourite, he had survived hard schools at Monaco, Bordeaux and PSG. He saw me coming. He was too quick for me, too streetwise. Yet he struggled with the pace of the Premier League. He left within three months of my first-team debut, to take up semi-retirement in Qatar.

Nice knowing you, pal . . .

Kevin Horlock, a holding midfield player capable of great delivery from set pieces, was a Northern Ireland international, lively, funny and popular. He had already entered City legend by being sent off for 'aggressive walking' towards the referee in a goalless draw at Bournemouth. He made 232 appearances over seven years, across three divisions, but was sold to West Ham a week after Ali left.

See ya, mate . . .

That left Eyal Berkovic, an Israeli international who thought his pedigree deserved special privileges. The notoriety of being kicked in the face by John Hartson, in retaliation for a petulant slap following a training-ground tackle at West Ham, merely marked him as a victim, awaiting his fate. Don't waste your compassion on him.

He was on 30 grand a week, compared to my £300, but this was about bottle rather than bank balance. He was just another body, a diva who dared to dwell on the ball. The inevitable occurred in a practice match. I went in hard and low, won possession and left a little on him. I was up, looking to release a forward pass, while he was rolling around, clutching his leg and squealing like a stuck pig.

'Sort him out,' he wailed. Keegan complied. 'Joey, get inside,' he yelled. I'd been dismissed for doing my job. I had no intention of breaking Berkovic's leg, or doing lasting damage. I wanted to look good by making him look bad. I wanted to earn respect and opportunity. It was my way of proving that someone of his temperament could not be trusted. I was right. Keegan tired of his tantrums and sold him within nine months.

Good riddance . . .

I had a love-hate relationship with Derek Fazackerley, Kevin's senior coach. He liked my spikiness, but bristled when I refused to let him bully me. I didn't mind him riding me hard, but stood my ground when he crossed the line. I'd challenge him for taking the easy option of having a pop at me, instead of dealing with more established players who tossed it off when the mood took them.

Coxy knew which buttons to press. 'No ifs. No buts. No bollocks,' he would say, whenever I felt aggrieved. 'Work harder.' He quietly worked on Keegan, and used a lifetime's political nous to get what he wanted. 'Put the kid on the bench,' he advised him. 'That'll be our way of telling the board we need money for new players.'

That's why I walked into the away dressing room at the Riverside Stadium, at 1.30pm on Saturday, 23 November 2002, to find my first-team shirt, number 41, folded neatly on the bench. I should have taken more care of it, but I lost myself in the moment. This was my destiny. I might only have been one of the substitutes, but I considered myself a man among men.

Monkey see, monkey do. I mimicked the other subs, seasoned pros who carried their shirts and shinpads to the bench before placing them under their seat. What I failed to notice, since I was concentrating so hard on the match and the manager's body language it narrowed my field of vision, was that they took them back to the dressing room at half-time.

Middlesbrough established a two-goal lead early in the second half, Ugo Ehiogu and Alen Boksic converting crosses from Geremi, who scored a third after Nico Anelka had pulled one back. That was Keegan's trigger to turn towards me, and utter the words I had longed to hear: 'Warm up, Joe – you're going on.' I was about to discover this feel-good film was a disaster movie.

I leaned down, found my pads, but scraped my fingertips on cold concrete when I reached for my shirt. I began to panic. Where the fuck is it? How can it have disappeared? How can something like this be happening on my debut? I shot a glance at the crowd beside the dugout and felt bile rise to the back of my throat as intuition kicked in. One of those bastards had reached over and stolen it at half-time. He had done me in cold blood.

I scanned blank faces, started to act my age, and begged: 'Give us me shirt back. Please. I promise you can have it at the end of the game.'

Keegan glanced sideways, a sixth sense stirred by the delay. 'Someone's robbed me shirt, gaffer,' I eventually said, through a cotton-wool mouth.

His face flushed from bewilderment to anger. 'Get him another one, quick,' he barked at Les Chapman, the kit man.

'Sorry, boss, I only printed one for him because I didn't know he was in the squad until late yesterday.'

Keegan knew the rules. I had to wear my preassigned number. A blank shirt was no good. He did a cartoon double take between Chappy and me: 'You fucking what? For fuck's sake . . .'

He seemed in imminent danger of a heart attack when his

wild eyes alighted on Ali Benarbia. 'I suppose you've got a shirt?' he said, acidly. Ali nodded.

'Right, you're on. You, Barton, fucking sit down ...'

The papers were full of it. Classic City, they crowed. The Comedy Club is open for business, yet again. Keegan couldn't resist a variation on the theme of the Scouse hubcap story. 'Unbelievable,' he confirmed to Sky Sports. 'His shirt disappeared. I was going to give him some experience. That's life, though he should know better coming from Liverpool.'

All I could hear, in my head, was Dad's voice: 'You're going to get one chance, Joe. You've got to take it with both hands.' I sat on the bus and wept. The hard man was being ridiculed as a punter's fall guy. Keegan's prejudices were justified. I was a parody pro, a wrong 'un who had it coming to him. My world was in bits.

I didn't make another squad for five months. Scunthorpe United were interested, but insisted on a trial, in advance of a proposed loan. True to form, I was knocked out contesting a header. When I came around in hospital they told me I had damaged the balance mechanism in my inner ear. I couldn't sit up without projectile vomiting. It took six weeks for the room to stop spinning.

I couldn't drink, though I was beginning to get the taste. I retreated instead into the melancholy world of Morrissey, and Johnny Marr's multi-layered, melodic riffs. I got into The Smiths quite late, because of my initial infatuation with Oasis, but they spoke to my soul. They challenged convention, addressing issues like depression, homophobia and child abuse in a literate, ironic fashion. Their music opened another window for me.

Maybe, just maybe, there was another life out there, waiting to be experienced and articulated.

Or maybe I was destined to throw it all away.

My wild streak rapidly resurfaced on a lads' night out with Frankie Lacken, which ended with a borrowed club car, a metallic blue Vectra, hurtling through a car showroom window in Chorley. For once, alcohol was not the cause. We swerved to miss an animal, hit a speed hump, and lost control because our attention had been distracted.

Hearing the alarms wailing, and having been showered in glass, we panicked and legged it, intending to argue the car had been stolen. The police picked us up trying to make our way home, after being alerted by our taxi driver, and had to take Frankie to hospital for stitches in a chest wound. I had been lucky and escaped unhurt.

The fact we had not been drinking worked in our favour with the magistrate, who dismissed a charge of leaving the scene of an accident. I decided abject apology was the only course of action when I was called in to see Keegan. I accepted the bollocking, and promised to pay off the repair bill at £150 a week.

My football education involved an unlikely tutor, and one of the game's typically unexpected friendships. My new mate was Robbie Fowler, who joined City in January 2003. My old mates regarded his arrival at Nan's house, to pick me up on the way to training, as a religious experience. There seemed more chance of a unicorn being ridden through the public bar of the Huyton Park pub than a Scouse deity communing with snotty-nosed scallies, crowding around his BMW.

I knew him as Bob, not God.

He came to my rescue when I was banned from driving for accumulating too many points. My first car, a Fiesta I bought as a finance company bodge job, was destined for the scrap-yard. Bob's lifts saved me half an hour's walk and a 60-minute journey on public transport to City's new training ground at Carrington. He eventually offered to lend me 23 grand for my first proper ride, a Mercedes 230 CE Coupe, content I would pay him back monthly, without interest.

To this day, I still do not know why he made such a deeply personal gesture. It makes me unashamedly emotional. Maybe he identified with me, because of the similarity of our backgrounds. Maybe it was an extension of the working-class solidarity that had led him to support the striking dockers. All I knew, without fear or favour, was that this wasn't another Billy Big Bollocks footballer flashing the cash.

Those lifts taught me the eternal truth that no one or nothing is forever. He acknowledged his star was dimming. He had gone from Liverpool to Leeds, who agreed to pay a percentage of his wages at City. As his passenger, I listened to him unburden himself about sudden insecurity and the quiet terror of remorseless decline. I thought, 'This can't be real. This is Robbie fucking Fowler,' but I could sense him trying to channel my youthful positivity.

His vulnerability scared me shitless. I asked myself, 'Does this happen to all of us? Is this how you behave when you see your career slipping away?' Bob was 29, and suddenly struggling in front of goal. I can only make sense of his predicament by viewing it from my current perspective, as a 34-year-old seeking to suck the marrow out of life as a professional footballer.

His body was beginning to betray him. His mind was contaminated by self-doubt. He could no longer trust his instincts. His reactions were dulled fractionally, fatefully. I represented the coming generation, the tsunami on the horizon that was destined to sweep him away. I resolved, there and then, to lock those fears, those destructive emotions, deep within my subconsciousness. The survivor in me knew I needed to keep him close.

He was sitting next to me when Keegan read out the team to play at Bolton on Grand National Day, Saturday, 5 April 2003. I knew I was close to a reprieve, because Coxy was rampaging around like Godzilla with toothache, and I'd been drafted into the squad as a precaution because Marc-Vivien Foe had picked up a bug. 'Did I hear him right?' I asked Bob. His grin was unusually eloquent.

We lost to goals by Henrik Pedersen and Ivan Campo either side of half-time, but I played well. The frenzy of a Premier League fixture felt natural; I was able mentally to compress time, so I could think quickly and creatively. I hadn't been infected by the fear spread by a run of only one win in seven games. I looked around the dressing room and knew I belonged. Drop me if you dare.

I kept my place for a goalless home draw against Middlesbrough, when I was named man of the match for an effective man-marking job on Juninho. I picked up my first booking and my first goal at White Hart Lane on Good Friday. We took the lead after three minutes with a free header by David Sommeil, and I effectively sealed the win 18 minutes later. The video of my big moment is still there, for posterity, on the City website.

I win a tackle in midfield, and the move flows down the right to Anelka. His weak shot is parried by Kasey Keller, Fowler makes himself busy, and the ball breaks to me on the edge of the area. I open my body instinctively and hit it sweetly, deliberately, with the inside of my right boot. Goran Bunjevcevic, the Spurs defender, reads the line of the shot but can only divert it past Keller.

God, how young I look. The haircut is severe but my face is

fresh and illuminated by excitement. I run towards the Shelf and do a full-length, face-down, legs-up Klinsmann dive before being swamped by my team-mates. Little did I know it, but at that precise moment, hidden in the away end at the far corner of the ground, Dad fainted. He was hauled to his feet by Dave Barton, who is not a relation but once saved me from a stampeding police horse at Goodison.

I try to put myself in my old fella's position. He's surrounded by his mates, celebrating his son's arrival as a Premier League player. He's a football man down to his jockstrap, and appreciates how fragile life can be. I'm his first born. We fought against overwhelming odds, together. We plotted my route to the top, together. No wonder his stomach turned somersaults, and he hit the deck. I owed it to him to make sure no one would ever rob my shirt again, literally or metaphorically.

I stayed in the team until the end of the season, and signed a new contract worth six grand a week. Not drug enforcement money, but close enough to tempt one local entrepreneur to ask for a 10-grand loan, to be paid back as 20 within a week. Suspecting, correctly, that it was required for a shipment from Amsterdam, I declined and put the money towards buying Nan's council house.

I was in her lounge on the afternoon of 26 June, watching Marc-Vivien Foe play for Cameroon against Colombia in the Confederations Cup semi-final at the Stade de Gerland in Lyon, when the unthinkable occurred. He collapsed, was tended on the pitch for 45 minutes, but died as a result of an undiscovered heart condition.

I was numb. How could this be? Marco was supremely fit, a dynamic box-to-box midfield player who had appeared in 35 of our 38 Premier League games that season. He scored

City's final goal at Maine Road before the move to Eastlands. He had a laid-back personality, and seemed impervious to the game's gnawing insecurities. I sat in his memorial service, at Manchester Cathedral, and made a silent pledge.

Carpe diem, Joseph. Seize the day.

Marco's shirt number, 23, was retired and, despite the depth and authenticity of everyone's grief, life went on. Keegan signed Paul Bosvelt and Claudio Reyna, serious midfield players, established internationals and natural leaders. I can see now that Kevin was buying himself insurance against his perception of my youthful inconsistency, but at the time it felt like a betrayal.

He didn't understand my psychology. I wanted to be trusted to play backs-to-the-wall football every week. I didn't care if the new recruits showed me their medals. I was ready. I would be their worst nightmare. I would make myself undroppable. I played 39 games during the 2003/04 season, which proved more enlightening than my manager might have wished.

The cracks in the facade of Keegan's authority began to appear in our final training session before we flew to a second-round UEFA Cup tie in western Poland in November. He had waited 72 hours to announce to the group he was fining Robbie Fowler and me £500 for being 10 minutes late for the bus to Newcastle the previous Friday. We were bang to rights, since we hadn't allowed enough time to negotiate the traffic from a shopping trip to the Trafford Centre, but Bob was indignant.

'I'm not paying.'

Instantly, about 25 pairs of eyes widened, and shifted to the manager.

'You are.'

It initially had the feel of one of those scenes from a spaghetti western, where bystanders weigh up the survival prospects of rival gunslingers while making a mental note of where to hide if bullets start to fly. Unforgivably, it quickly degenerated into a yah-boo, sucks-to-you spat that would have shamed *Sesame Street*.

Everyone knew it was wrong to call out the gaffer so starkly and so publicly, but Keegan's juvenile response invited disrespect. It got worse a day later, when Coxy advised me to pay up or I wouldn't play in the tie, against rank outsiders Groclin Dyskobolia. I borrowed the readies from the boys in the card school, and dutifully trotted up to the manager's room. He took the cash without a word.

Steve McManaman advised Bob to do likewise, to keep the peace. He agreed to do so with spectacularly bad grace, but when he returned to Macca's room his poker face dissolved quickly. He reached into his pocket and smugly handed me £500. Keegan had returned our fines, on the proviso we didn't tell the lads.

What was the point of the charade? It was an unnecessary drama, an unprofessional distraction. It gave us an undeserved excuse for playing poorly in the goalless draw which resulted in our elimination on the away goals rule. Most damagingly, the manager's behaviour smacked of weakness. It was the St John's equivalent of allowing your bike to be nicked.

We didn't win again for three months, and the dressing room became a place of petty intrigues, whispers and moans. I was in and out of the team during a toxic 10-match spell. It was only a matter of time before I mirrored the mood, and defied the boss. The flashpoint came in mid-April, when he left me out once too often, without explanation, for a home game against Southampton.

I waited for the match to kick off before leaving the stadium to play a round of golf at Bowring Park, a municipal course just off the M62. I was on the fifth fairway when news came through that we had lost 3-1, and were only two points off the relegation zone. I was delighted. Fuck him. That'll teach him to scapegoat me.

Keegan's heart wasn't in the subsequent bollocking. He was hurt that I should be so adamant I had nothing to apologise for. He couldn't comprehend what he regarded as my lack of loyalty. We were each, in our way, showing signs of a silent struggle. He was trying to maintain the illusion of his leadership qualities, while I was trying to subdue an insistent inner voice.

My inner child was scared, vulnerable, fearful. He taunted me that I was about to be found out as a fraud. He misrepresented what could have been a rational managerial decision, to ease the burden on a young player in order to protect him from burnout, as a full-blown challenge to my masculinity. He distorted Keegan's silence and lack of sensitivity into a career-threatening snub.

The manager didn't understand what that shirt meant to me, even though he put me back in the team immediately. It was a comfort blanket, which soothed the kid who was conditioned to mistrust and misadventure. I was on the edge. I had started drinking heavily, getting into the occasional scuffle on nights out. The more scrapes I encountered, the bigger target I became.

It was a catch-22 situation. Keegan was right to worry, because I was struggling to cope with life in the spotlight. I was starting to lose control, to set a pattern of problems. Yet I felt I couldn't share my insecurities with him, because he represented the type of authority figure I had been programmed to distrust.

The manager struggled to differentiate between the player and the person. He sat with me in his office for hours, but couldn't understand that the fiery nature which made me an effective footballer was also making me a nasty bastard. He simply didn't understand the underlying issue: that I was fighting for my existence.

We fell out again in July, during a tetchy pre-season friendly at Doncaster, the League Two champions. They were captained by John Doolan, an Evertonian who is now coaching at the Finch Farm academy, but he missed most of the mayhem because he was substituted in order to have stitches inserted in a head wound. Paul Green, his mate in central midfield, went in late on me three times in the opening 20 minutes. I wasn't about to give him a fourth opportunity to make a name for himself.

Estate rules applied. Green lingered in possession a fraction too long, which gave me the chance to scrape my studs down his shin. He shrieked and sat on the ball, so I kicked it out from underneath him without due care and attention. He deserved the kicking, and the referee did well to contain a 10-man brawl.

It doesn't take much for footballers to turn feral. Macca, Danny Mills and Richard Dunne all began to put it about a bit. Jermaine McSporran, a striker who belonged in a Spike Milligan poem rather than a team of scufflers, responded in kind. His partner Leo Fortune-West, a lower-league lump, then lunged at me. He would have broken my leg had it remained planted, but I was alert enough to leap in the air to minimise the damage. A badly cut leg was, in the circumstances, a relief.

Keegan hooked me at half-time, which turned into a screaming match. He made things worse by hanging me out to dry in the press conference: 'Joey thinks he can look after himself, but when you start doing things like that, people sort you out. I have a problem with any player who just wants to go out and be physical all the time. There is no future in that.'

Bastard. Kevin's memory was as selective as the script for his moral lecture. We were closer in spirit than he dared acknowledge. Take a look at his head's-gone brawl with Billy Bremner at the 1974 Charity Shield, where he was decked by a Johnny Giles right hook before being sent off with the Leeds captain. They tore off their shirts as TV commentator Barry Davies bemoaned the 'unacceptable face of English football', and both received an 11-match ban.

Keegan, like me, was self-made. He was defined by his work ethic, his determination to make the most of himself. We got on infinitely better at Newcastle, where I was more mature, and the impetuosity of youth had eased. He was more aware of my demons, phenomenally receptive to the self-analysis I had undergone in prison.

Maybe, at City, we were the right combination at the wrong club at the wrong time. I can honestly say he is the only person I have encountered in the game who loves football more than me. It took time for me to appreciate the magnitude of his achievement, as a scrawny kid from Scunthorpe who defied the doubters to win a European Cup with Liverpool and Hamburg.

How sad, then, that he has been worn down by football's sharp edges. When things were beginning to splinter at City, it was probably as well that he never heard the snide asides that he'd been broken by the impossibility of managing England. The feeling of rejection must have hurt him so badly. How has he been reduced to such a peripheral figure when the values he represents have never been more important?

I realise this opens me up to a charge of hypocrisy, given what I was about to put him through as 2004 drew to a close, but he should still be centrally involved in the game.

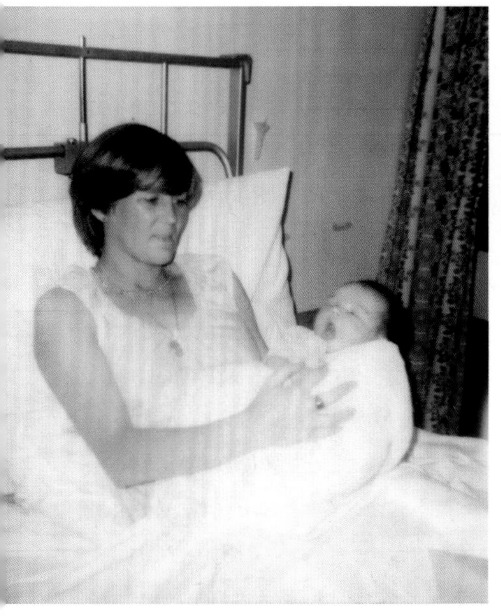

y debut. With Mum in Whiston ospital, 2 September 1982.

Picture of innocence? First day at school.

each Boy. Note the England otball shorts.

My first Communion. One of Nan's happiest days.

Barton family moments: (*top*) in the garden with my dad, my hero; (*middle*) on holiday with Mum; (*bottom*) living legacy, with my nan, Julia, and grandad, Peter.

Getting the football bug: (*from top to bottom*) with Dad at Wembley after Warrington Town got to the final of the FA Vase; showing off some early medals; Cousin Josh and I meet Gary Speed at Everton.

The stuff of dreams. Signing schoolboy forms for Everton, with Dad watching on

The Everton youth team. I'm second from the right on the front row, with my friend Bradley Orr to my left. Like me, Phil Jagielka, second from left at the back, was released.

Getty Images

No one was robbing this shirt, following my nightmare at the Riverside. My first team debut at Bolton on 5 April 2003.

ortrait of the artist as a oung man. I scored my rst senior goal in this ame, at Spurs.

PA/Empics

PA/Empics

The Guvnors. Kevin Keegan is the only man I've met who loves football mor
than me. Arthur Cox, an old-school shirt-and-tie man, didn't miss a thing.

Getty Images

Don't take liberties. A full and frank exchange of views during a pre-season friendly against Doncaster Rovers. Hooked at half time, I fell out spectacularly with my manager.

Celebrating with Robbie Fowler. Liverpool fans called him God; I knew him as Bob.

Getty Images

Playing in the Premier League Asia Trophy before the bar brawl which led to me being sent home from Thailand. The nightmare had only just begun.

amily: My brother Andrew is my best friend. Peter Kay saved me from myself n more than one occasion.

Getty Images

I went on to celebrate a last-gasp Man City equaliser at Goodison in February 2006 by baring my backside to the Everton fans who had goaded me. Cue yet another superficial controversy.

PA

Arriving for my court hearing, following the training-ground incident with Ousmane Dabo. I was on crutches after fracturing a metatarsal.

CHAPTER SEVEN

NO SMOKE WITHOUT FIRE

As a connoisseur of nightclub brawls, this was one of the most violent I have seen. It kicked off when Nico Anelka and a bunch of his mates decided to recreate the Alamo in the VIP area of a bar in central Manchester. They took on allcomers with anything that came to hand and, for once, I heeded heartfelt advice.

'Come on, Joe, stay out of the way,' said Robbie Fowler, who was sitting with me and Steve McManaman on the edge of hostilities. They knew there'd be hell to pay in the morning, since collateral damage from footballers' Christmas parties is as inevitable as death and taxes. Right on cue, Kevin Stuhr Ellegaard, our reserve goalkeeper, was knocked out by a crude right-hander.

I've seen variations on the theme down the years. Football clubs are volatile places, in which resentment is usually expressed in the relatively controlled environment of a training ground, where everyone is sober. Put the same people in an artificial situation each December, add silly quantities of drink to the mix, and the consequences are predictable.

Someone, typically the quiet one, says something he can't really take back. Someone else, similarly emboldened by alcohol, invites a teammate outside for a straightener. Sometimes this needs to happen, especially when the team is struggling. Harsh words and handbags tend to flush the toxins out of the system. The trick is to avoid the involvement of civilians, contain the fallout, and avert preying eyes or camera phones.

Anelka, a sumptuous plyer but a solitary, conflicted character, got away with it that evening. He'd taken his lumps in the fracas, but, just as when he confronted Kevin Keegan in a public row which involved the manager comically screeching, 'Speak English', the consequences were minimised. There wasn't a murmur about his party piece in the media, apart from three lines at the end of a piece hanging me out to dry.

They're artless toilers in the red-top tabloids. They prefer simplistic slurs, half-truths and innuendo to nuance and facts which inconveniently undermine preset agendas. They made sure all anyone wanted to talk about was me and a youth-team player who had been kicked out of the bar an hour before the French contingent went to war.

Jamie Tandy. A nonentity, but you might have heard of him.

Here's the myth: innocent kid has cigar stubbed out in his eye by thuggish Premier League star. He suffers 'major psychiatric deterioration' and his promising football career disintegrates. His life is ruined, since he drinks heavily and has difficulty sustaining personal relationships.

Here's the reality: gobshite invites retaliation by setting fire to the shirt of a player who was a year above him in the academy and comes from a similar background. He lacks the character to eke out a career in professional sport and is consumed by self-pity. He is convicted of assaulting two female partners.

Was I in the wrong on that night out? Absolutely. Do I regret what I did to Tandy? Every single day. Would I change the outcome? In a heartbeat. Do I have sympathy for him? Not in a million years.

I have grown tired of being the excuse for his sad self-justification. More than a decade on, he is still blaming me for his intermittent jail time and periodic appearances before the judiciary. My concern is reserved for those he has hurt along the way, the girlfriends he has left bloodied and bruised.

For the record, I never intended to stub that cigar out in his eye. Have you ever considered how difficult that is? The victim's instinct is to turn away. There are so many distortions in the story – from the fantasy that I was dressed as Jimmy Savile to the downright lie I held Tandy down before inflicting damage – that it needs to be told from the start.

We were on the lash, in fancy dress, from 11 that morning. I went as one of the Beatles from their mop-top era in the mid-sixties, John Lennon if memory serves. It started to get silly in mid-afternoon, when Robbie Fowler set light to the tassels on Paul Bosvelt's pirate uniform. He retaliated by setting fire to Bob's commando outfit, and everyone wanted in on the act.

It was childish, but bloody funny. Nicky Weaver's Ali G wig got the treatment and I spotted my chance with Tandy, whom I knew from the reserve team. He was wearing a white sailor's uniform with a silly peaked cap, and I saw he was distracted by the mayhem. All it took was a quick strike on a plastic lighter, and his jacket began to smoulder.

He was livid, and started whingeing about losing his £100 deposit on the gear. I was vaguely aware he came from Wythenshawe, a tough, sprawling estate on the south side of Manchester, so it was no surprise that he made a point of retaliating quickly. It was no big deal. We were all bevvied, and the bouncers circulated quickly, confiscating lighters.

A couple of hours later, it was forfeit time. The younger players were forced to sing for the senior pros. I did a karaoke Beatles number, but Tandy's song abused Scousers. I was too pissed to draw the obvious inference, but he was shouted down by the boys. By just after eight o'clock we had all changed into street clothes, eaten, and got back on it in a private area at the bar.

It was a time for tall tales and taller drinks. I sat in a square with Danny Mills, Shaun Wright-Phillips and his brother Bradley. We were swapping stories about managers when I felt a strange dampness on my back, followed by instant, searing pain. The bottom six inches of my white shirt were on fire. I ripped it off, sending the buttons flying, and stamped out the flames.

I'm bare-chested, demeaned, dangerous. I've been bred to bite back, to take revenge. No one makes me look small, or stupid. Tandy, standing five yards away, tried to be too clever by half. He was studiously looking in the opposite direction, making out he was the only person in the room oblivious to my distress.

I think clearly when I'm angry, even though my actions are irrational. Tandy had made me look a fool. I can still remember the thought process as my eyes settled quickly on the glass ashtray in the centre of our table: 'You cheeky little cunt. No one gets away with that. You are getting hit with this.' The ashtray was bolted to the table, so I grabbed Danny's cigar, which was smouldering on the rim.

My logic was warped, shaped by instinct and circumstance. I intended to inflict pain by stubbing the cigar out on the back of his head. But, as I advanced, he must have sensed my presence. He turned into my path. I was committed to my lunge, and the cigar hit him on the lower eyelid. He fell backwards, clutching his face.

The scene takes on a surreal, slow-motion quality. I feel several sets of arms entwine around my body, pulling me backwards. I struggle and scream that I want to finish the job, by battering him. I see Sylvain Distin, our club captain, leading him to the toilets to assess the damage. I sense his shock when he returns. 'Christ,' he says 'you've got him in the eye.'

I compute the consequences in a millisecond. I'm suddenly cold, scared. This is out of control. I could have blinded him. I might have meant to burn his hair, even scald his skull, but no one will dwell on detail. This is serious. I need to see him for myself.

'Where is he? . . . You're fucking dead, Barton . . .'

My thoughts are interrupted by the sight of Tandy's elder brother running at me. I stand my ground, brace my body, adopt the pose. It is an automatic process, honed on the streets and in the Lackens' garden in St John's. I slip the first punch, manoeuvre myself into position, and hit him on the chin with two quick jabs. He stumbles backwards and I hit him twice more. He bounces off the wall, and crumples on to the floor.

He is not getting up in a hurry, but I have no time to contemplate the next move. Jamie Tandy is running at me with a banshee wail. He's an easier target, because he is seized by rage, panic and fear. His first punch, a roundhouse right hook, misses by six inches. He's wide open. I give him several digs to the stomach, which wind him, and hit him in the face, exacerbating the original injury. The lads and the bouncers pull us apart, and the brothers are launched out of the club.

I'm bundled to a table, out of harm's way. Steve McManaman, Trevor Sinclair and Robbie Fowler form a tight, protective semicircle around me. Bob gives me his jacket and orders me to calm down. I'm not listening. The adrenaline is surging. I'm breathing deeply, rapidly. The madness of the last few minutes unfolds in my mind like a grotesque *Gangs of New York* parody.

I'm suddenly aware of Bob's voice in my ear. 'Get a grip,' he says. 'This is a massive problem.' I'm still drunk, but the defiance starts to dilute. Before the madness mutates, and Nico's crew bring a chaotic night to a close, I begin to form a game plan. I need to get to Tandy first thing in the morning, before we are called in to see Keegan. He needs to understand how football works.

I am not condoning what I did. It was malicious, reckless, indefensible. But I know what is coming. There'll be a lot of talk about the club's image, and our responsibilities as role models, but ultimately, as players, we are commodities. I've just signed a new contract. I'm a first-team regular, an emerging cult hero. Tandy is a borderline reserve, who will probably never play at the highest level. I'm valuable. He's expendable.

I'm aware the following exchange may sound callous. It is easy to misinterpret my actions as those of a bully. But when I found Tandy at the training ground I had to gauge the emotional and physical fallout. Could he handle the bitter reality of our situation? Did he have any interest in a pragmatic solution? His eye was a mess; his eyelid and lower lashes were singed.

'Look,' I said. 'We're both going to get in the shit for this. I'll take my end of it, but, to be honest, we're better playing this down. It was tit for tat. You don't burn my shirt, I don't come at you with the cigar. It is going to be easier for them to fuck you over, because you are not playing in the first team week in, week out.'

He smiled, sourly. 'No way,' he said. 'You're fucking out of order.'

I shrugged. 'Sound. Play it out however you want to play it out.'

We were both fined and I took the biggest hit, losing four weeks' money, around £60,000. He was eventually sent on loan to Koge, a provincial club in Denmark. Instead of using it as an invaluable development opportunity, as other young players had done before him, he became bitter, twisted and self-destructive. He played semi-professionally in Australia, cleaned windows and trawled around non-league in the North of England. I often wonder whether his revenge, selling the story to the *Sun*, was worth it from his point of view.

I'm still living with the consequences of the double-page spread, complete with close-up photographs and judgemental, moralistic 'reporting'. Every halfwit on social media thinks he is the first to throw a cigar-themed insult at me, but the damage is deeper than such dribbling, since initial coverage of the incident crystallised the view of me as an unfeeling, unprincipled thug.

People began running with half-truths, leaping to the conclusion that I intended to blind him. At the risk of becoming boring through repetition, I do not condone my actions. But the headlines were hollow. There was no semblance of balance, no reference to provocation. Stupidly, I had thrown the burned shirt into the bin at the club. I had no tangible evidence with which to defend my name. Trebles all round, chaps.

It was open season on me. I was an easy target for the paparazzi, a demon to be exorcised in print. It was an editorial duty to think the worst of me, whatever the circumstances. The rules of the game became clear the following May, when I accidentally ran over a Liverpool fan who had been celebrating the team's defeat of Chelsea in the Champions League semi-final.

It was 2am, and the city centre was bedlam. People were singing, intermittently blocking the road outside O'Neill's pub. I'd watched the game with some mates, but hadn't been drinking. I tried to swerve to miss the fan, who stumbled into my path, heard that dreaded, resonant thud and stopped immediately.

I had been doing no more than 10mph, and was breathalysed on the scene. Police confirmed I was stone-cold sober, unlike the Reds fans who abused me as I waited with the victim before the ambulance arrived. I went to see the guy in hospital a couple of days later. His leg was broken, but he was apologetic.

He offered to call the papers, to put his side of a typically one-sided story, but there was no point. Truth is an early victim of perpetual circulation wars. The story was spun to fit the stereotype of a rich, reckless footballer causing havoc when he should have been tucked up in bed with a malted milk and a copy of the Gideon Bible.

If only they knew . . .

I did have a problem. When things were going well I had an instinct to intervene, to my detriment. I was struggling with myself. The compensation of playing well wasn't enough. I needed regular transfusions of anger. I began scanning the papers for negative stories about me, so I had something at which to rage. I looked on fans' forums, listened to local radio. The amount of time I wasted on such self-flagellation was ridiculous.

Come to me with a bunch of roses, and I am looking for

the thorns. I want to pierce the skin with them, feel the tang of pain and watch the rivulet of blood run down my finger. I want you to dislike me, because that gives me the fury I use as fuel. Write me off. Belittle my family and my character. You know you want to.

Who am I kidding? I was grossly unhappy. I was drinking to try to escape my misery. It provided a brief, cherished release. The weirdest thing was that I was playing really well, and becoming increasingly insecure. The drink dulled the pressure of expectation. It muffled my tormentor, the voice inside my head.

The mantra was unyielding, unchanging, unrelenting: 'They're all going to realise you're a chancer. They'll see you're shit. You're weak, Mr Strongman. You want to be the people's friend. You're sensitive. You're skin deep. They're going to see right through you. They'll discover everything about you, and use it against you.'

Imagine that rattling around your brain. Someone would say something smarmy, or give me an unguarded glance. The voice would be off again . . .

'This cunt thinks he's better than you. Who's he? He needs to be told. Tell him how much you're earning. Tell him exactly what you think of him. Tell him if he does anything about it physically, you'll go head-to-head with him. Put him on his toes, challenge his manhood. Promise to destroy him.'

Surprise, surprise, I became a target. A Premier League ponce to be taken down a peg or two. I might throw myself into a tackle in front of millions, but compared to really hard men I'm nothing. The fights you've never read about are the ones I've lost, when I've been smashed by a random juicehead or been given a good kicking by bouncers in a darkened alleyway. I'd get away with cuts, bruises, a sore jaw.

I'm hardly going to go to the police and say, 'Excuse me, officer, I've just been filled in.' I was seized by illogical, convoluted bravado. I took pride in the fact I'd never been knocked out, apart from in the clash of heads during that painfully irrelevant trial match at Scunthorpe. I took confidence from the granite chip on my shoulder.

How perverse was that? My values were inverted. Achievement was something to be mistrusted, even resented. Rejection was something to be relished, a reconnection with the streets on which my sense of justice and self-worth was formed. I wouldn't back down from anything. My moral compass was going haywire.

It took me years to understand the turmoil, to ask myself the most pertinent question: Who actually wins in a fight? You can win and go to jail. You can lose and go to hospital, or a morgue. At that stage in my life, fighting was all I knew. My values were forged in a brutal environment, where it is considered better to front up and die than curl up and surrender.

Unsurprisingly, Stuart Pearce wasn't aware of what he had on his hands when he became caretaker manager, following Keegan's departure that March. We judged one another on assumptions and superficialities. He saw me as a diligent, urgent and consistent presence in his midfield. I liked what he stood for. I'd always communicated well with him, and obviously had the utmost respect for him as a player.

I had seen him flitting around the edges as a coach, quietly measuring the strength and direction of the political winds. He wasn't being disloyal to Keegan, but he was subtly distancing himself from him. That's fine. Ambition manifests itself in many ways. Just as coaches work out how to avoid being casualties during periods of regime change, players make snap judgements about managers, based on self-interest.

A small group of us, including Richard Dunne, concluded that it wouldn't be the worst thing in the world for Pearcey to get the job full time. There was no bullshit with him. He was fair. He was inclusive and recognised our influence, as core members of the group. We liaised on strategies, tactics, formations. We wanted to play for him. We helped to get him on the directors' radar by going on a nice little run until the end of the season.

It couldn't last. It never does. When he got the job that summer, he changed. He felt he had to impose himself. He no longer courted opinion; he imposed his principles and personality on us. Approachability was recast as weakness. That was his prerogative, but on the pre-season tour of Thailand the delicacy of his position and the troublesome nature of his inheritance became clear.

We were playing in the second edition of the Premier League Asia Trophy, one of those absurdly overhyped four-team tournaments designed to sell shirts and provide televised methadone for football fans suffering mid-summer withdrawal symptoms. We were up against Bolton, Everton and the Thailand Under-23 team.

I scored in our so-called semi-final against Bolton, which we lost 5-4 on penalties following a 1-1 draw in normal time. That was enough for me to be 'rested', along with Richard Dunne, from the third-place playoff, in which we beat Everton 4-2 on penalties. Pearce was quite happy to allow us a couple of beers with the team meal. It was a rookie's mistake, since his concession was a little too liberating.

I take after my grandad, in that I am an angry, articulate drunk. He was the nicest man you could wish to meet, but spiteful, verbally, after he'd had a few. He would use alcohol to project his deepest frustrations on to those he loved most.

I'm more indiscriminate. When Dunney had the bright idea of ordering a couple of bottles of wine, and then a couple more, the tenor of the night was set.

By 2am we had taken root in Blackie's, the ground-floor sports bar. We were steaming. There was a bit of boys-on-tour banter between Chappy, the kit man, Tim Flowers, our goalkeeping coach, and a group of journos, including James Cooper of Sky Sports News, but nothing insulting or out of order. It had been a thought-provoking day, which Danny Mills and Steve Jordan had spent coaching children displaced by the tsunami.

I started chatting football with an Everton fan, who knew of my allegiances and asked for my opinion on my boyhood club. The mood changed when he was joined by his son and a friend. Suddenly, there was an edge to the atmosphere. I don't know if he felt the need to show off, but he began to denigrate Robbie Fowler as a cokehead and a coward, because he wasn't on the trip.

Bob was injured, and I wasn't going to put up with lazy, vindictive lies about him. This was beyond football; it involved the integrity of a close friend. I could feel the mist start to descend: 'Look, mate. Firstly, you don't know the fella. Secondly, you're a tit. Fuck off. Just do one. I don't need you, or your shit, in my space. Go away.'

'Are you going to make me go away?'

'Yeah, if you want.'

Before the confrontation could develop his son blindsided me, and kicked me in the shin. My pain sensors were numbed, because of the drink, but I went through the mental checklist that signalled impending chaos. The kid looked young, 15 as it turned out. From where I come, it doesn't matter how old you are if you kick a grown man at 3am, in a bar where everyone is pissed. You are old enough to get a slap. You are getting yours, son.

I hit him with an open palm, rather than a fist, and meant it to sting. This might appear to be appalling, an affront to cosy suburban ethics, but I prefer to think of it as a life lesson that would have been infinitely harsher had it been imposed at the Huyton Park pub. According to an eyewitness, I growled at the kid: 'I'm going to fuck you up.' He fled, crying and screaming empty obscenities.

His dad was momentarily frozen. When he saw me turn towards him, hands clenched, he slipped away to complain to Dunney, whom he recognised from his time at Everton. I went back to my pint, and was soon confronted by the Honey Monster, who was as buried in the booze as I was. 'Fucking get over there now and apologise!' he screamed.

I declined.

Dunney grabbed me by the throat, and pushed me back against the wall. He was raging, oblivious to my warning that he had precisely two seconds to let me go. He was bigger and stronger than me, so wrestling was out of the question. I turned feral, and sank my teeth into his fist as hard I could. He roared, let me loose, and involuntarily looked down to see that I had drawn blood.

I rugby tackled him before he could react, pushing him backwards across the room. Bystanders were bulldozed out of the way, human skittles in a bizarre game of bar billiards. Our momentum took us over some steps and into a secondary tier, where Dunney crashed through a glass coffee table.

Momentarily wedged into its metal frame, and understandably stunned, he gave me enough time to think clearly and malevolently. Violence is strangely hypnotic, almost organic in its purity. Right on cue, my inner voice piped up: 'You're going to have to fight him now. He's a big lad, but nothing to be scared of. Wouldn't harm to give yourself some insurance, though.'

I leaped back to the bar and grabbed a pint glass. Tim Flowers recognised my intention, of smashing it across Dunney's head, and threw himself at me. Reinforcements arrived immediately, and before I knew it I was pinned to the wall by five guys. I was screaming unintelligible threats and, out of the corner of my eye, noticed the lad's dad walking towards me, ready to play the Big Man.

I knew I was getting a crack, because I was defenceless, so followed my dad's timeless instruction and dipped my head so he could only pound his fists on my skull. He hit me twice before I took advantage of the confusion he had created, and wriggled free. It was payback time and he knew it. He turned to run, and I set off in pursuit, only to be met by a phalanx of security guards, who threw up a human shield between me, him and Dunney, who was by this time screaming blue murder.

They had guns. I had beer glasses, bottles, ashtrays, chairs, tables. Anything that wasn't nailed down was getting launched at them. They tried to restrain me, and I fooled them with the old schoolboy's trick of going limp to imply surrender, so they would let me go. Once I felt their grip slacken I was away, ploughing through anyone or anything in my path. A Premier League press officer disappeared underfoot.

Eventually, they managed to bundle me through a set of glass doors, which were locked behind me. I tried to run back into the bar, and started to rip pictures from the wall. There was blood all over the marble floor. I was completely gone, psychotic. In the distance I could hear Dunney screaming: 'Why is this happening?' He was being frogmarched to a secure area, and was so out of control he kicked a plant pot, breaking a bone in his foot.

He would miss two key internationals for the Republic of Ireland, but football was the last thing on my mind. I made a bolt for the fire escape, only to be shoved into the lift and escorted to my room. Two armed guards were posted outside the door, and Tim Flowers went above and beyond the call of duty to save me from myself. He stopped me punching the wall, and slept next to me when I passed out.

We both woke in our clothes, and tried to piece together the fragments of a wild night. Chappy, an emissary from the real world, reckoned I resembled the cartoon character the Tasmanian Devil, in human form. I was a whirlwind of destructive energy. He had pulled some strokes in his time, but had never seen anyone lay waste to a place like I had done, in the early hours.

Remorse sent acidic pulses through my guts. Dehydration scoured my throat. There would be a reckoning, because this was the sort of international incident that demands an official response. Had I found the limits of my usefulness to City? Would they try to cash in on me, before my notoriety impacted on my market value?

Pearce was unequivocal. He wanted me thrown into a Thai jail, to await deportation. Club officials were rather less impulsive, and infinitely more calculating. They extracted promises that all damages would be paid for, and hustled me out of a side entrance and off to the airport. I flew to Manchester via Zurich, to put the press off the scent, and went to bed at home, in a world of pain, at six o'clock the following evening.

I slept solidly for 14 hours, and woke with a start when my brother Andrew burst into my bedroom. My first thought, that we were under siege by the hacks, would have been a minor inconvenience compared to the news he bore. 'Have you heard what's happened in St John's?' he gabbled, his words bouncing around the room like pearls from a broken necklace. 'Someone's been killed in the flower park . . .'

CHAPTER EIGHT
HORROR AND HOPE

Gee Walker is a woman of immense dignity, incredible tolerance, immeasurable moral courage and inspirational goodness. No mother should have to bear her burden, of a lifetime's longing for a wonderful son, murdered when his life stretched invitingly before him.

I wept when I read her account of walking through a trail of blood in the hospital corridor. She was struck by its stickiness, and collapsed when she realised it had been shed by her son, Anthony. He was dying, and she was prevented from comforting him in his final moments by detectives, concerned by the possible contamination of evidence.

Those words carry such weight that they should, by rights, tear a hole through this page. As a parent, I'm haunted by the image of a mother's unimaginable despair. As a human being, I recoil at the horror of her son's murder. As someone whose name is associated with such a terrible, racially motivated crime, I continually ask myself whether I could have done any more to prevent it.

Anthony Walker's life ebbed away at 5.25am on Saturday,

30 July 2005. He was 18 and had effectively been braindead for just over five hours, from the instant an ice axe was driven 6cm into his skull by Paul Taylor. My brother Michael was fighting with Anthony in McGoldrick Park when the fatal blow was inflicted.

Taylor happens to be my cousin. I appreciate the damage caused by his abusive childhood, but cannot forget or forgive his actions. I had dark forebodings that he was destined to cause immense harm in this world, but was unprepared for the extent of his malignancy.

I used to see Anthony around the estate. I didn't know him well, but he seemed a lovely kid, diligent and a good basketball player. His sister Dominique was a couple of years below me at school. The Walkers were close and loving, and stood out simply because they were the only black family within about a four-mile radius.

I had a premonition something was wrong, very wrong, when my brother Andrew burst into my bedroom that morning. He had tried to call his twin, but Michael's phone was off. That didn't make sense, because, like most teenagers, he lived on his mobile. It began to have sinister connotations when I attempted to make contact. It had an international ringtone, and rang out.

He had no business to be abroad, and had left no word about his whereabouts. I made some calls around the estate. Details of the murder were starting to seep out, and police were mobilising a manhunt. Someone wrongly suggested the cousin of a mate of mine had been involved, but no one really knew what had gone on.

My phone rang. It was Michael, maintaining he was in France on a fishing trip. He claimed to have heard nothing about what had happened in the park, where Anthony had been ambushed beside a low wall, a matter of yards from where Lee Kinch was stabbed by Tommy One-arm. I knew he was lying, and the implication made me nauseous.

It didn't add up, and within a couple of minutes my phone rang again. Michael haltingly confessed he was at the scene of the crime. The court would later be told he fled, covered in Anthony's blood, having tried and failed to extract the axe, which had pierced his skull and was embedded in his brain. Three men were eventually convicted of helping him and Taylor abscond to Amsterdam, via a Dover to Calais ferry.

That would all unfold, as justice took its course. Trapped in the moment, it felt as if I'd had the wind kicked out of me. I struggled to process the enormity of the situation, but knew I had to do something, anything, to make Michael see sense. My solution was delivered in a stream of consciousness, unsubtle but urgent.

'Turn yourself around and get back here. Whatever you are doing, whatever has gone on, I don't want to know. Someone is dead. This isn't going away. I don't give a fuck who you're with. Fuck them off and get right back here. This is mad shit, Michael. This is real. You can't go on the run for ever. You've got to speak to the police.'

He rambled about our cousin being the killer, and rang off. I turned to Andrew with a sense of dread. Our worst fears had been realised. I'd barely had time to gather my thoughts when my mobile rang yet again. It was Stuart Pearce, ordering me into the club to apologise for the Thailand fiasco. I told him to fuck off.

At that moment, I didn't want to play football again. All the old certainties appeared to have unravelled. My instinctive determination to man up and crack on with life seemed naive. I was 22, had a few quid, and no real ties. I felt a fleeting yet powerful urge to disappear to a desert island. I wanted to run away.

My career was an irrelevance. I closed my eyes, covered my head with my hands, and screamed, silently. My default position was to beat myself up, to blame myself. I never worried about our Drew. He was too smart, too gentle, too thoughtful, to get himself in bother. I knew Michael was different. I'd tried to help, but allowed him to drift.

His phone was diverting continually to voicemail, but a couple of days after our initial exchanges I received another call, from an unidentified number. It was Michael, asking for £1,000. I refused, and repeated my lecture. He wouldn't tell me where he was and sounded desperate, gabbling about not being prepared to go to prison.

I resented my impotence for years afterwards. Could I have prevented Anthony Walker being killed? Arguably. Could I have prevented Michael from ruining his life? Definitely. Could I have stopped Paul Taylor doing what he did? Doubtful. If he hadn't attacked Anthony, he would probably have killed someone else, or been killed himself.

If Michael had come to live with Andrew and me, as I'd wanted, he might have been better placed to work through his problems. If he had knocked on my door, and asked for money instead of taking it illegally, I'd have willingly handed it over. If I had been more forceful with him, when I began to pick up whispers he was involved in bad stuff, I might have made a difference.

If . . .

My mind went back six months, to a white Transit van parked up on the nearby Mosscroft estate. I'd got word Michael was in there with about 10 of his mates, smoking weed. There was talk he had been involved in robberies, burglaries, dealing, but it was couched in gang code, delivered with a nod and a wink. That's the way St John's worked.

I had mates who were up to no good, and had no fear of the local hard cases. I'd known them since we were kids. Each of us knew of our capacity for violence. I made my break with them when I committed to football. They wanted to keep me at arm's length, and preferred to feed me half-truths. At least this time, I had concrete information.

The back doors of the van were thrown open. I recognised a few of the faces and smelled trouble, in addition to narcotic sweetness. Part of me recognised the futility of anger. I rationalised that Michael would have to learn his own lessons. It wasn't my job to step in. I was his brother, not his parent. It wasn't as if I had a shortage of shit to wade through in my own life.

I was about to discover the road to hell is indeed paved with good intentions. He was flesh and blood, even though he had lived with Mum all his life. He was six years younger, and I knew he had been allowed to roam free. He had been slow at school, and his trial would hear that he had a mental age of no more than 13.

'Fuck these dickheads off and get out,' I ordered.

He tried to protest, but sensed I was in no mood to be defied and got into my car. I phoned Mum to tell her Michael was going to be living in my spare room. When I got him home, I told him to wear what he liked from my Reebok-sponsored stuff in the wardrobe, and gave him a fistful of notes to spend on himself. He didn't get away scot-free, because the reprimand was vehement.

'What the fuck's going on? I'm not stupid. Come on, Michael, there's more to life than this shit on the estate. You can't go on like this. You're 17. You're knocking around with a bunch of scumbags. Look, this is where it is at. You need a job. I can help you get it together. I know you need mates, but no more dickheads.'

He talked about joining the army, or going to college. I could never recreate the intimacy of his bond with Andrew, but we began to reconnect. Unfortunately, football intervened. I had away games in the Premier League and UEFA Cup. I asked my mates to keep an eye out for him, but gradually he slipped back into his old ways. He began by staying with Mum over the weekends, and then went missing for a few days. Within a month, I'd lost him.

That was then. This is now. The media are camped outside Nan's house. They're laying siege to Mum's house, unaware that, unforgivably, she is still on holiday in Turkey. They don't know where I live, yet, but they have their uses. I agree to a police request to make a televised appeal for Michael to give himself up.

That address, into an ITN camera, was an out-of-body experience. I spoke from the heart when I said that 'those responsible for the senseless death of a kind, decent young man must be brought to justice'. I offered my 'sincere condolences' to Anthony's family, and demanded their right to closure. I told Michael to contact police 'because you know it is the right thing to do'.

That night Gee Walker spoke for the first time about her loss, at an anti-racism vigil at St George's Hall in Liverpool city centre. Thousands shared her grief. The following day Michael and Paul were apprehended in Amsterdam. They were officially arrested at 6.20pm, when they arrived back on home soil, at John Lennon airport.

I've subsequently read a lot about estates like St John's. It is a generalisation, but sociologists speak of a cycle of low aspiration and minimal achievement. Typically, nearly half the residents rely on benefits. Social problems are exacerbated by loan sharks. According to a thought-provoking piece in the *Economist*, these estates form a new type of white-dominated ghetto, where racism is endemic.

Football broke the chain and broadened my horizons. I was at Everton with black lads from Toxteth, Netherley and Norris Green. There were still kiddie rivalries, and they'd give us a chasing if they saw us in town, but skin colour was meaningless to me because I knew them as people. I shudder to think of the racial abuse the Walker family endured on a daily basis, because ignorance elsewhere was pervasive.

There was a kid at our school, who had an Irish father and a Cypriot mother. He had a slightly darker, Mediterranean complexion, and tanned easily, but used to be taunted as a 'nigger' or a 'Paki'. It was insane; a combination of closed minds, wanton stupidity and a fear of difference. The impact of cultural paranoia and a lack of integration was underlined when an Asian family took on the corner shop in St John's. Within a matter of days someone smeared the word 'Pakis' in huge letters across the main wall.

A certain type of stranger still assumes I am racist because of my background, and the details of the court case. I find that abhorrent, an insult I resent with every fibre of my being, but I can follow the twisted logic. It wasn't Michael Barton and Paul Taylor in the newspapers, or in the dock. It was Joey Barton's brother, Joey Barton's cousin. It created an impression I had to address immediately, not least with my team-mates at Manchester City.

Despite my meltdown with Pearce, the club were hugely supportive when they grasped the magnitude and complexity of my problem. They did, though, have the right to expect me to be remorseful. My mind was frazzled, but I had an obligation to apologise personally to players and officials for my behaviour in Bangkok.

Standing before the squad, in a conference room at our training complex, was nerve-shredding. It was honestly the first time I realised how many black colleagues I had. They had read the papers, watched or listened to the news. What would they think of me? Would they find me guilty of racism by association? Would they still want to share a dressing room? Football issues were trivial by comparison.

My apology was another surreal experience. It felt as if I was looking through a lace curtain. I was determined to lay my feelings bare, to explain myself as best I could, but everything was indistinct. I still wonder, to this day, how I got through it without breaking down. The moment of truth arrived when I stopped speaking.

I heard the applause, and saw Andy Cole and Trevor Sinclair heading towards me. Trevor got to me first, and hugged me. It was a good job I was all cried out; otherwise the hard man would have wept like a baby. Acceptance for who I am, for all my faults and insecurities, felt good. I was still buzzing later that night, when I took a call from John Wardle, the City chairman.

I had always admired his directness. He shared his fears about my self-control and the strain of dealing with the murder. He insisted I had to overcome my aggression, and suggested I spend a week at the Sporting Chance clinic near Liphook in Hampshire. It promised 'physio for the mind, body and soul' and he sealed the deal by offering to reduce my fine for the Thailand incident by £60,000, from six weeks' wages to four.

My immediate priority involved dealing with family

matters. Home was a pressure cooker. I was living with Andrew, Nan, my Auntie Julie, Dad and his partner Kate. Each had their own trauma to deal with. Drew was closest to Mum, but I wanted nothing to do with her. It would be the best part of two years before I could bring myself to speak to her.

Nan had been driven out of her house by photographers. The murder summoned nightmare memories of the violent death of Julie's husband, Joe, in the toilet of the Bluebell pub. It would be seven years before Dad felt able to share the depth of his disgust with Mum's side of the family.

Something had to give, and it was me. Looking back, I think I slowly cracked up. I had behaved like an arsehole, and walked straight into the most socially significant case since the Stephen Lawrence murder. It was international news. I was aware it would probably be held against me for the rest of my life but events were entirely out of my control.

I have made some horrendous decisions, but have generally taken responsibility for them. The closest members of my family couldn't give me any support. I can't remember my exact words, but I ranted about the unfairness of the burden they had placed on me. I was the lightning conductor. I was the one dragged before the cameras. I was the one being branded as a closet racist. It was easier for them. No one knew them.

The energy flow changed, fundamentally. I became the head of the family. I loved my dad to bits. He'd been there to protect me as a kid, but our roles had been transformed. I ripped into him. He was well into his forties, going out drinking and generally fucking about. What the fuck was he up to? I could see I hurt him, but with hindsight it was a cathartic experience for both of us.

I felt I had to free myself from anything that was holding

me back. I still regret the selfishness of letting childhood friendships lapse in order to limit the negative connotations of my background, but the cull was necessary until I was able to better understand myself, and those around me. I didn't sell out, but I stepped back.

It was the perfect time to meet Peter Kay, a tall, gaunt man whose blond bouffant hair hovered above his high forehead. He was a former drug addict and recovering alcoholic, who had established Sporting Chance with Tony Adams, the former Arsenal captain, in a single room near Victoria station in September 2000.

We did not exactly get off on the right foot. When he initially attempted to make contact, at the behest of John Wardle, I slammed the phone down on him twice. He introduced himself by name and, thinking of the comedian Peter Kay, I was convinced it was a wind up, conceived by the lads. It needed a call from John to persuade me otherwise. I was struck by Pete's serenity when he picked me up from Southampton airport at the start of my first visit to the clinic. I was suspicious, reticent, uncertain. I cowered intellectually, and isolated myself, personally. For the next 48 hours I veered between blandness and banality, even making a point of eating alone, but he was scrupulously non-judgemental.

Peter told me later that he sensed the weight of the world on my shoulders. I was monosyllabic, deliberately distant, wallowing in my own shit. He exuded an aura of friendship; any hint of doctor–patient frigidity and I would have remained tightly wound, non-committal. He had a mentor's subtlety, an ability to listen and a refreshing awareness that he didn't have all the answers. He encouraged me to read, to investigate, to contemplate but above all to share.

The dam broke, and something sour and secretive flooded

out. I found it liberating to be confronted by my weakness. I spent the third day unloading on him, after a sleepless night in which I tried to make sense of kaleidoscopic images of chaos, confusion and suffering. He coaxed me along, allowed me to go at my own pace. I had never related to anyone on such a deep, meaningful level.

That evening I had dinner with athletes from all sports, both sexes, whose problems were created by alcohol, drugs, depression, gambling and, in my case, violence. No man, or woman for that matter, is an island. I learned I was not alone. I learned to laugh at myself. I learned to value vulnerability as a gift, rather than a curse. It wasn't a crime to cry.

Nothing, though, could prepare me adequately for Peter's candour in the car the following day. He had been a stranger 72 hours earlier, but shared the formative secret of being raped at the age of eight by an older man. He explained, with a strange, affecting tenderness, his subsequent sense of guilt. His self-esteem was shattered, and he developed into a distant, introverted youth.

He would sing to himself, or hum a favourite tune, whenever memory ambushed him, and became reliant on stimulants to deaden the pain. His first marriage foundered, and he lived in a squat, drinking two bottles of Scotch and ingesting three grams of cocaine a day. At the age of 31, he went into a coma for three weeks, following an operation to remove two-thirds of a diseased pancreas.

He wept gently as he relived his near-death experience, and laughed when he realised the appropriateness of the venue for that night's rehabilitative experience, an Alcoholics Anonymous meeting in World's End in west London. I observed rather than engaged; the feelings were familiar but the rituals were foreign. The celebration of fallibility was counter to everything I had been brought up to believe in.

It was incredible. We talk about reality checks, but what is real? People spending money they don't have, online or in the shops, to save face? They're just deluding themselves into debt. Here were people who had the courage to say, 'You know what? I can't be arsed bullshitting because my life is so bad. I just want to talk.' Their honesty was real.

It is very rare to find someone who is prepared to be honest. Here's a test: walk up to an acquaintance and ask, 'All right, mate?' I guarantee they'll reply, 'Yeah, fine', in a reflex action designed to make both of you feel comfortable, socially. Perhaps I am wired differently, but I'd get on with someone who'd reply, 'Do you know what? I feel like shit.'

Convention tells us that everyone has a right to an opinion. They do, but equally I have the right not to listen to it. Don't waste my time and I won't waste yours. That honesty brands me as abrasive, or confrontational. Football is notorious for people spouting superficial bollocks, pretending to like one another while they are desperate to stab one another in the back.

I went to AA for a couple of years after that initial visit, which prompted me to lean over and whisper to Peter: 'Fucking hell, am I an alcoholic? I can really relate to what these people are talking about.' I understood their expressions of loneliness, isolation and frustration. They felt like shit, and shared the reasons. That started my process of renewal.

I let the voices and images of that evening seep into my subconscious for a couple of days. The stories of booze-fuelled mayhem and anguished remorse were too relevant to ignore. Stopping drinking was almost an act of putting one and one together and making two. In my case the equation was simple: alcohol plus emotion equalled aggression.

The emotion was going to be an issue, because I was still coming to terms with that, but I could at least eliminate one element of the problem. Drinking was a recurring theme in my existential crisis. To use one of Peter's favourite phrases, if you go to the barber's every day, one day you are going to get a haircut.

He left me with a deeper understanding of myself, and a promise that we would speak daily on the phone, if the need arose. 'It doesn't have to be you against the world,' he told me. He held out his arms to hug me as we prepared to part. Not for the first time that week I amazed myself, by holding him close.

Football seemed an irrelevance, but also central to my being. If that sounds confused, I was. I had become so used to abuse from opposing fans that there was something almost soothing about their renewed viciousness. I valued, more than ever, the escape valve of match day, when emotions were familiar and the private rituals of preparation made sense.

Amazingly, given everything, I slotted back into City's first team as if I'd spent my time off on a sunlounger. That gritty little bastard who refused to allow rejection by Everton to knock him off course was still alive and kicking. No one was going to write me off, and Peter remained an integral part of my self-help programme. Even the bad times were good.

We played golf together at Worsley Park near Manchester in the autumn, and I was as conscious of the need to be on my best behaviour as any prospective son-in-law meeting his girlfriend's dad. Sod's law dictated we were playing behind two American women, who turned the game into a still-life painting. They held us up at every hole, and refused to allow us to play through.

This was the acid test of my new-found tranquillity. My guru was alongside me. I was breathing deeply to dissipate the tension, but by the 15th I'd had enough. I turned to Peter: 'I've got to level with you. I'm absolutely raging here. I'm dying to say something to these women and I don't think I can bottle it up any longer . . .'

He looked at me straight in the eye and replied: 'Raging? I'm fucking fuming. I've wanted to hit balls at those two for the last couple of hours!' We burst out laughing, aware of the absurdity of our internal struggle to be measured and considerate.

We spent the rest of the round discussing emotion. I explained the concept of negativity as my spur, and Peter countered by accentuating the positive. He spoke of love being fuel of the highest octane. He promoted the freedom produced by openness and the joy of taking time to build relationships on firm foundations. He opened the door into a world of infinite possibility.

That door slammed shut temporarily in December, during Michael's trial. I didn't attend court, because I would have been an obvious distraction and couldn't see any benefit in my presence, but I pored over the evidence. It was distressing because of its familiarity and horrifying in its intensity.

Anthony, a devout Christian who harboured ambitions to be a lawyer, spent the evening babysitting his two-year-old nephew Reuben with girlfriend Louise Thompson. He and his cousin Marcus Binns offered to walk her to a bus stop close to the Huyton Park pub. The court heard how Michael, dressed in a hoodie with his face obscured by a scarf, abused them, shouting: 'Walk, nigger, walk.'

He subsequently insisted to me that he didn't say those obscene words, but he still climbed into a car with Paul Taylor and ambushed Anthony in the park, a short cut to an alternative bus stop. Louise and Marcus ran to find help while Michael became involved in a wrestling match on the ground he showed signs of losing. This prompted Taylor to strike the fatal blow with the mountaineering axe.

He later told police he was aiming for his arm, rather than his head. Michael told the family they wanted to rough Anthony up, warn him against coming on to the estate. He could quite easily have been killed because the axe missed him by a fraction of an inch. As he told me later: 'It came in from the side. I felt a gust of wind go past my head and the next minute he was lying on me.'

I realise this is a moot point, since nothing can bring back a loving son, or heal the scars inflicted on a family who somehow found, in their hearts, the power of forgiveness, but why did Taylor use such a terrible weapon with such awful consequences? The simple answer is to condemn him as a manifestation of evil. The more challenging solution is to investigate his formative influences, and to examine his mutation from wild teenager to compulsive thief, and eventually, murderer.

He knew nothing other than degrees of violence from his earliest days. He survived by native cunning, intimidation, and the brutal application of a gang culture. The impression of toughness, ruthlessness, was paramount. Michael's suggestibility gave him the opportunity to spread the blame, but both deserved their punishments: minimum sentences of 23 years for my cousin and 17 years for my brother.

They remain out of sight, out of mind, for everyone except the families fused by needless tragedy. Michael was a magnet for trouble during his first year in prison, in which he was disciplined for fighting, stealing, possessing illicit alcohol and making a model gun out of matchsticks. It has been a gradual process, but from being viewed as 'high risk' he is now making a positive contribution as a mentor to other inmates.

Anthony lives on, in spirit, through his foundation, which has the complementary aims of celebrating diversity, promoting personal integrity and developing racial harmony through education, sport and the arts. His mother, a college lecturer, remains a beacon of hope and tolerance. Two weeks after Anthony's death, Gee Walker launched a basketball tournament in his memory.

The trophy is inscribed with the words: 'Don't feel ashamed of your race. Feel guilty only if you stand by and do nothing to unite and bring change to the human race.'

CHAPTER NINE
BOOK CLUB

Les Chapman is an institution, and I can confirm generations of Manchester City players believe he should be housed, securely, in one. He is one of those classic football characters, a court jester who provides regular infusions of light relief in a game that takes itself way too seriously. He is kit man, cabaret artist and stand-up comedian.

Chappy made 670 appearances in the Football League over 22 seasons, and managed Stockport County and Preston North End before spending another 22 years on City's backroom staff, where his zany humour gave him neutrality and kept the dressing room ticking over. He's now a club ambassador. You don't have to be mad to have such a career, but it helps.

He developed half a dozen personas, including a Lancastrian version of Adolf Hitler. Chappy would strut around the training ground in full uniform, screaming at the top of his voice while his stick-on moustache was being dislodged by a stream of spittle. That performance was postponed, for obvious and understandable reasons, when we signed Eyal Berkovic, but

Michael Tarnat and Didi Hamann, our resident Germans, loved it.

Chappy was even in character when he applied for the kit man's job. He based Billy Swift on his uncle Stephen, a patient with mental health issues he used to visit as a child. He turned up at the old Platt Lane training ground in an ill-fitting polka dot suit from Oxfam, which was offset by flat cap, short, gravy-stained tie, and plastic trainers.

He squinted through National Health horn-rimmed glasses, and was so slack-jawed he could drool to order, but it was such a surreal place when I was an aspiring pro that he wasn't especially conspicuous. We often trained to the accompaniment of religious maniacs and winos bombarding us with empty cans of Tennent's Super.

Chappy's logic, on this particular morning, was pretty sound. Footballers love a wind-up, and he intended to use his act to prove he had the requisite personality. He wandered around, apparently aimlessly, before positioning himself on the touchline. His cunning plan had one flaw: when he began rambling about losing his pet dog they called security.

He was escorted to the gate, stammering loudly, before switching out of character. Somehow, he persuaded them to let him stay for the job interview, which consisted of a single question from Joe Royle, the then manager. 'Were you that mad fella on the side of the pitch?' he asked. Everyone fell about laughing, and the rest, they say, is history.

I loved him. He was warm, intelligent and sufficiently well versed in the insecurities of the game to realise he carried no threat to the players. The contrast between his eccentric public antics and his solicitous private asides is significant, because it reveals football's strange schizophrenia. You can show off, but you'd better not show too much.

Chappy's best-known character is William MacSwift, a wild-eyed, tartan-trewed Scot with wig and tam-o'-shanter hat. MacSwift was developed at Preston, where, as the late John McGrath's right-hand man, Chappy would often dress as a punk rocker on away trips. His speciality was leaping unexpectedly out of the bushes, in full costume.

One day, when he had been promoted to Preston manager, he decided to go a fateful stage further, and, after leading the players on a lap of the local park, dropped off the back of the group. He dived into the undergrowth, stripped off completely, smeared mud over his body and plaited his hair with twigs. Chappy emerged, screaming, only to find his timing was awry.

Instead of his first-team squad, he was confronted by a pair of senior citizens, innocently walking their Labrador.

Successive City managers adored him. Kevin Keegan loved his capacity to accept dares, for suitable reward. Five hundred quid from a whip-round among the players was usually enough for him to put on a boilersuit and leap into an ice bath from the roof of a one-storey hut. He would snort pepper and drink a vile concoction of oils and vinegars from the salad bar to get him through to payday.

I'd gone by the time Sven-Goran Eriksson arrived, but by all accounts he was so enraptured by Chappy that he had him take Friday team meetings in character. Football clubs can be dismal places, especially when results are poor, and he had a unique ability to make people feel better about themselves.

Managers, though, are judged infinitely more subjectively by players. We obsess over them, share their faults and foibles on the network. There are very few secrets. One manager became infamous within the game for what can best be described as his creative accounting. Since I have given too much of my money to the legal profession down the years, I had better say, for the record, I have never played for him.

His speciality was making late substitutions, on the understanding his assistant would later collect a percentage of the player's match fee. This was extended to include a cut of the bonus accrued by his academy director, payable when a homegrown product made his first-team debut, however short his time on the pitch.

This manager's biggest earner, though, involved the recycling of former players. The scam was pretty simple. He would recruit trusted retainers from former clubs, since he had a shrewd idea of what they would be earning. They would invariably be seen as logical signings, given that all managers have go-to guys. The tariff for the transfer was precisely half the wage rise the player received as a result of the move. It would be paid monthly, invariably in cash.

Of course, it was in the manager's interests to look after his boys as generously as possible. He consciously operated to the detriment of his employers due to a deeply ingrained sense of greed and a cynicism bred by his expendability. Insecurity militates against loyalty and, some would argue, basic decency.

Again, I had better make it crystal clear I found Stuart Pearce to be a man of the highest integrity. But the tide went out pretty quickly on him, once the prevailing respect for his achievements as a player ebbed away. He was initially very popular with the fans, but tried a little too hard to play to the gallery to be entirely convincing to the senior pros.

He had typically English traits, haring along the touchline to retrieve errant footballs, celebrating passionately and winning every header while being yards from the action. I was accustomed to such animation and quite comfortable with it until he made a point of placing his good luck charm, a Beanie Baby horse borrowed from his daughter Chelsea, beside the water bottles at the edge of his technical area. That left me susceptible to the logic of Claudio Reyna.

'Do you like that sort of stuff?' he asked.

'Yeah, it shows he cares.'

'Nah, that's bullshit. Do you ever see Wenger chasing around like that? People who know what they're doing, people who are absolutely in control, don't run up and down, throwing balls back in.'

I had never thought about it in those terms before. Why would I? I was brought up to duck teacups and take one for the team. Claudio came at it from another angle, as a hugely experienced player who had captained his country and would go on to play a key role in establishing City's New York franchise.

He was spot-on, because who really benefits from the posturing and chest-thumping associated with the English Way? It might make the individual feel good, and provide a suitably theatrical cutaway for that night's TV highlights package, but it is an indulgence.

Claudio believed in the limits of managerial influence. His theory was that, assuming training is well structured, tactics are sound and preparations are precise, the manager's job is peripheral once the match kicks off. Living the game, following each cough and kick, might make the gaffer appear admirably engaged, but his gestures are of minimal importance.

I understand the concept of taking the temperature of the game from the technical area, but as a player you don't need someone screaming at you to press, or screen, or track back, or pick up at set pieces, provided you have got your head where it needs to be. If your mind is so unfocused that you are failing to do the basics, you are simply not up to your job.

Football managers get too emotionally connected to what is going on around them. They have a highly developed sense of their authority, so it is easy for them to be drawn into the sort of incident which ended with Alan Pardew head-butting Hull City's David Meyler when he was at Newcastle. Screaming at referees and treble-teaming the fourth official in a juvenile attempt at intimidation rarely works.

I can appreciate someone like Jurgen Klopp, arriving at a new club, in a new culture, seeking to generate solidarity through theatrical commitment, but too many managers, like his predecessor Brendan Rodgers and Roberto Martinez, his erstwhile counterpart across Stanley Park, are sophists. They're clever in framing their arguments and presenting their philosophies, but are deceptively insubstantial.

On balance, I prefer the clinical approach of coaches in both rugby codes. They look for the opportunity to make subtle adjustments by sitting in the stands with their analysts. Rationally, I understand such pragmatism, but try that in football and the fans' first instinct is to ask, 'What the fuck's he doing up there?'

A manager should keep his distance. He has a bigger picture to observe, and technology can connect him to a trusted lieutenant on the touchline. To extend that military analogy, a general does not go into battle alongside his troops. He secures the high ground, takes an overview, and makes cold, minutely calculated life-and-death decisions.

I believe in planning for chaos, preparing for the most daunting eventuality. The range of human weakness spans the managerial meltdown, the inexplicable error, and the rush of blood which results in a red card. Don't stop with plan B. Use up the entire alphabet, if that means covering all the bases. Substitutions should be structured, but not preordained.

I make notes the night before the game, when thoughts are logical and uncontaminated by emotion. They're a reference point. I'll remind myself, if X happens I'm going to think about Y. If Y happens I'm going to think about Z. I'm not arguing that I am going to make the perfect decision every time, but the process gives me a better chance of doing the correct thing, more often than not.

Conversely, some would say perversely, I feel strangely compromised when I see my manager scribbling on scraps of paper during the game. He doesn't need a photographic memory, but if he can't remember three key points – the limit of relevant, easily digestible information – at half-time, he is in the wrong business.

Baseball folk talk about the Major Leagues as 'The Show'. Football has taken on that theatrical dimension, even though we all hide behind what I like to call the wizard's curtain. Players and managers are masters of distraction; when people come too close to the truth of who we are and what we do, we create a diversion.

A protection mechanism ensures players don't share deep conversations. When a coach does great things it is generally because he has an ability to bond his athletes at a level beyond the superficial in an industry that operates at a dismally shallow level for at least 90 per cent of the time. The real gains, that final 1 per cent, come from the magnitude of a common cause.

As a player, I'm inspired by those moments of authenticity, when someone decides to cut through the bullshit smeared across most things to do with the game. Those moments may come in a match, or in a training-ground situation, but when they arrive I consciously think, 'That's real, that's right, that's different.'

Generally, the only time you are given true insight is when things go wrong, really wrong. That strips away trivialities, and you see a perfectly defined snapshot of what people are about, in terms of their character and where they are in their lives. It might be the smallest thing, an angry word or an unguarded response when we are under the cosh, but it reveals so much.

As for the pantomime stuff, players banging their chest and kissing the badge, guilty as charged. The ties are stronger when I'm in more fervent environments, like Marseille and Newcastle, but I invest emotionally in the clubs I play for. I don't just turn up. I can't. I need to feed off the energy of a place, feel at one with the people I play for. I am an all-or-nothing kind of person, and I struggled at QPR because those feelings were not reciprocated.

It is important to differentiate between that visceral, highly charged approach and the detached, deeply selfish behaviour that shapes so many careers. In retrospect, I'm not proud of having handed in a transfer request at City in January 2006, so soon after the club had supported me in the aftermath of Michael's trial, but it had the desired result.

These things tend to have well-rehearsed choreography. City rejected my request, and turned down a verbal £4.5m offer from Middlesbrough, whose manager Steve McClaren had identified me as a potentially dynamic influence in his midfield. Word magically filtered out that a fee of £6m would concentrate certain minds, but negotiations continued simultaneously with my agent. I signed an improved four-year deal in the summer.

I was established as a name, a face, and didn't sense the

dangers. I slipped back into having the occasional bender, in which drink conspired in the illusion I was invisible and invincible. I wasn't about to back down in a confrontation. One of my late-night adversaries surprised me by calling me the following morning, to apologise. I learned later he had been advised to do so for the state of his health by a well-connected individual who had form for stuffing victims into the boot of untraceable cars.

Liverpool is a village, so it was probably predictable that my next problem, at the end of September, should be caused by a return to my boyhood club. Everton fans had no compunction in regaling me with the details of Michael's murder case. The abuse was constant, uniquely vicious. The home players did their best by acting in concert, to try to wind me up.

It was especially sweet, then, that Micah Richards stole a point by securing a 1-1 draw with virtually the last kick of the match, in the 94th minute. I gave my shirt to a City fan in a wheelchair, and was goaded into baring my backside at the remaining Everton supporters. I was smiling as I walked for four paces with my shorts at half-mast, before our goalkeeper Nicky Weaver ushered me back to the dressing room like a disapproving dad.

It was daft, impulsive and light-hearted, but that didn't stop the outrage machine creaking into action. The home fans who prompted a futile investigation into the incident by Merseyside's finest should have been done for wasting police time, and the jobsworths at the Football Association inevitably decided to throw their weight around, as guardians of public decency.

I was charged with improper conduct, and with bringing the game into disrepute. Ten days later I entered the parallel universe of the FA's old headquarters at Soho Square where, after a functionary took fully 10 minutes to work out how to use a DVD player, the three-man disciplinary panel gravely examined the evidence of my own arse.

They were the usual combination of timeservers, who couldn't follow the logic of a kid's comic but conducted themselves as if they were law lords. They imposed a £2,000 fine and invited my observations. I could have gone to town on them, given it was a colossal waste of time, money and professional expertise, but I restricted myself to a couple of acidic asides about their pomposity. I had a career to develop.

Steve McClaren had become England manager in August, following the WAG-fest at the 2006 World Cup. It is difficult to explain how you learn such things, since it involves a form of osmosis in which media whispers become conventional wisdom, but I became aware in the autumn that I was on his radar. I had to keep my nose clean.

My first Premier League dismissal had come two years previously, when the unassuming Rob Styles issued me with a second yellow card following an argument in the tunnel at half-time at Tottenham. We were trailing 3-0, but somehow came back to win 4-3. My second red card, just before Christmas 2006, was fair enough. I launched myself late, and two-footed, at Bolton's Abdoulaye Faye, and hoped it would be seen as a forgivable flash of excessive zeal.

I was playing well, and a month later David Moyes was ready to meet the £5.5m buyout clause in my contract. The attractions of Everton were obvious, despite my burlesque show at Goodison Park earlier in the season, but I decided against pursuing the opportunity because I reckoned the uncertainty of attempting to bed in at a new club could threaten my England chances.

I am goal-oriented, to a fault. I stayed with City because I calculated the team could have been designed for me to show what I could do and impress. Claudio Reyna and, initially, Paul Bosvelt were effective holding midfield players, which gave me licence to get forward into the box. I also had an ulterior motive: I reasoned that if I excelled internationally it would bring me to the attention of Champions League clubs.

The other variable was the haphazard nature of the England system which, at all levels, is harder to get into than get out of. Just as I feel I deserved many more full caps, on the basis of consistency of performance, I should have had a much more fulfilling career at age-group level. The reason it took so long for me to break into the Under-21 squad beggars belief.

I was the classic late developer, overlooked by FA coaches who had a vested interest in promoting their protégés from within. I was a Premier League starter, excluded because they preferred to pick lads who were benchwarmers in the Championship. It took Trevor Sinclair, during a trip with the senior squad in 2003, to shift opinion by asking David Platt and Steve Wigley, who oversaw the Under-21s, why I hadn't been picked.

Their intelligence didn't even extend to my date of birth. They said I was too young since I was '17 or 18'. Trevor informed them I was '20, and playing fucking brilliantly'. When Steven Gerrard weighed in with an endorsement, they decided they'd better check me out. I made my debut, against Macedonia in Skopje, the day after my 21st birthday.

My internal monologue, before my first training session, may not surprise you: 'I'm going to show these cunts what's going on here. I'm going to take control, show them I'm the best young player in the country. I've been waiting four or five years for this, and they're going to realise they've made a right rick.'

Fair play to Platt. He announced my selection and admitted: 'I don't know him well enough. I walked off the training pitch thinking, "Bloody hell." It's hard to step into international football. You need character and personality. What he has is great energy, more awareness on a football pitch than I gave him credit for. He has also shown me he has great personality. He surprised me.'

I was booked on my debut in a 1-1 draw, but did well enough for Platt to ask me to play out of position, in right midfield, in order to do a marking job on Cristiano Ronaldo in the pivotal qualification game for the European Championships, against Portugal at Goodison Park, four days later.

We started poorly, conceding a soft goal from a free kick by Ricardo Quaresma, who had just signed for Barcelona and was reckoned to have greater potential than the teenager who had cost Manchester United £12m. I first became aware of Ronaldo at Sporting Lisbon, so I knew how good he was, especially in a 3-4-3 rotational system which demanded complete concentration. I grafted on him, smashed him, subdued him so effectively that he switched wings for the second half.

We needed to win to make the finals. I equalised with a low, close-range shot just before half-time, after Franny Jeffers scuffled for a Shola Ameobi header from Paul Konchesky's free kick. That was as far as the fairy tale extended; Tottenham's Helder Postiga punched in a late free kick and we were out. I picked up another caution, and was suspended for the meaningless final group match in Turkey.

I was too old to be retained, seething because systemic laziness had denied me my due. I was convinced I belonged at international level, and had plenty of time to think through the permutations of selection, until McClaren's promotion altered the dynamics of the situation. Steven Gerrard and

Frank Lampard were first choice in midfield, but I felt I had more about me than the supporting cast, which included Scott Parker, Owen Hargreaves, Gareth Barry, Jermaine Jenas and Michael Carrick.

Had things panned out differently, I could have made the obsessive debate about the mutual suitability of the Gerrard–Lampard axis redundant. From what I gathered, Steven agitated to get Liverpool to sign me in 2004, because he felt we had the potential to forge a partnership. I met with Gerard Houllier at Melwood, and agreed everything verbally. A deal was close to being concluded when he was sacked that summer. It was never revived.

There is no point in dwelling on lost possibility, but had that move gone through the temptation to recreate the chemistry of my proposed pairing with Steven at international level would have been overwhelming. As it was, I had to wait until February 2007 for news to break of my selection for the senior squad's friendly against Spain at Old Trafford.

I take people as I find them, and have never forgotten John Terry's immediate gesture, in calling to congratulate me. He took his responsibilities as captain seriously, told me I deserved the recognition, and promised to do all he could to facilitate my transition. He has had serious issues to address in his life and career, but I have always admired him as a player and a leader of men.

There was, though, an elephant parading around the team room when I checked into the England hotel. It was carrying a banner that read: 'We got beat in the quarter-finals. I played like shit. Here's my book.'

My observation on the literary efforts of my new teammates, following the 2006 World Cup, was manna from heaven for the media, who, if they're honest, find covering

England a bit of a chore. They leaped to the convenient conclusion that I was disrespecting Gerrard and Lampard, when my criticism had been obliquely directed at Ashley Cole and Wayne Rooney, who apparently published his first autobiography at junior school.

Wayne took offence when I suggested, in a radio interview with Sir Clive Woodward, that England lacked world-class players. We spoke for an hour, working through our issues. I admire him as a warrior, respect his willingness to sacrifice himself for the group, and can only dream of being as naturally talented as him, but wasn't about to change an honestly held opinion.

Steven took my observations in good heart, pointedly leaving a copy of the first of his two autobiographies outside my room. My initial meeting with Frank, in a lift, was awkward, but he softened once I explained the context of my comments. I had always admired his work ethic as a strangely underrated player, and was aware of his reputation as a smart political operator, so there was no point in being unnecessarily antagonistic.

Urban myth, of course, is resistant to the reality that he accepted my explanation at face value. I am meant to have made a point of sitting as close as possible to him during my first team meal. He is supposed to have responded by rising, and moving to the end of the table. Sorry to spoil a popular story, but my rumoured response – 'Don't worry, Frank, I wasn't going to eat your dinner, you fat cunt' – is fantasy.

To be perfectly honest, I didn't hang around long enough to discover the truth of the theory that the England squad was too riven by cliques to be functional. The lads were fine, at the glib level at which we all operate, but the principal pre-match training session was a disappointment because it limited my opportunity to make a favourable impression.

The team was preordained. We concentrated on shadow play and walk-throughs, preceded by a brief possession session and topped off by shooting practice. I felt like I was just another body, a human mannequin. A 13-year-old kid could have coped comfortably with what was asked of me.

Andres Iniesta, who scored the only goal of the game, a volley following Rio Ferdinand's misdirected clearance, invested huge significance in the night I won my only England cap. He identified Spain's victory as the moment they grasped the scale of their potential. He would score the winning goal in the World Cup final little more than three years later, alongside nine other players who appeared at Old Trafford.

I played the final 17 minutes as substitute for Lampard, against a side with the world at its feet. That's not a great sample size, but I will go to my grave knowing I could cope at that level. There is more time on the ball, and I possess the necessary tactical acumen to respond to the additional subtleties of the international game.

The major factors complicating representative football at the highest level are the lack of familiarity between teammates, the political power of the clubs, and the incompetence of the FA. Why rebuild Wembley? When the team toured the country, fans responded because they felt like a truly national team, rather than the property of suburbanites in the M25 corridor. It worked again, on a smaller scale, before Euro 2016.

I knew I wasn't going to dislodge Gerrard or Lampard, but could do a job if called upon. Self-awareness is essential in professional sport, and whenever I have gone into overload, in testing situations, I have coped really well. To be brutally honest, too many of the players in England's so-called golden generation had character flaws.

They actually formed the 'me' generation. Germany won the last World Cup because they had a collective, rather than an individual ethos. No one prepared better. Each player, every unit within the team, knew their job, and the job of those around them. They were ruthless, calculating, single-minded. They didn't concentrate on silly little dances when they scored; they got on with it.

I know my comments about the book club went down badly, but I was making a serious point about motivation. I wasn't blind to the benefits of a more substantial international career but, for too many players, representing their country was purely a selfish act. Playing for England meant manipulating a move, getting a new contract, securing a new endorsement deal. It didn't mean serving a higher cause, reaching and rewarding a bigger audience.

When you watch the All Blacks you know the shirt is not a PR product. It is symbolic, sacred, the manifestation of pride in a small, isolated nation. I love the story of former captain Sean Fitzpatrick chinning a young player who absent-mindedly allowed his shirt to fall on to the dressing-room floor. That signalled the importance of respect, and higher standards.

I am a huge admirer of the intensity of rugby league. It is a game built on the bedrock of close-knit communities. I would much prefer the earthiness and competitiveness of a Super League Grand Final, or the quality of an NRL game in Australia, to the corporate indulgence of a Champions League final.

Ask the hard question: do we really want to be successful in international football? I'm not sure we do, because we play at it. England teams are the equivalent of the socialite who is seen at the best parties in a smart suit, looking presentable and acting as if he owns the place. He's a familiar figure, but the people who matter quickly forget his name.

You've got to be a horrible bastard to be a winner. I say that knowing, full well, that some nugget will wrongly assume the worst and observe that I am a horrible bastard and a loser, since it was no one's fault but my own that I never played for England again.

I waited three weeks, until City's next home game, a 1-0 defeat to Wigan, to celebrate my cap with my cousin Josh and our girlfriends. We were drunk in Liverpool city centre in the early hours, fancied something to eat, and directed our taxi driver to the nearest McDonald's drive-through on the way home. Things spiralled out of control quickly when he refused.

The girls got out, while we argued for a refund on the £30 fare, paid up front. The driver locked Josh and me in the back, sped off, and called a 'Yellow One alert', a scramble code to alert other drivers he was in trouble. Fearful we were about to be beaten up, Josh smashed the driver's Perspex safety screen and ripped out his radio cord.

We had no option but to run, pursued by other drivers, a couple of whom were wielding baseball bats. I was recognised, and when the police made their inevitable visit I refused to reveal my companion's identity. They duly charged me with criminal damage. Since I was on bail, the FA called to confirm I was ineligible for consideration for impending European Championship qualifiers against Israel and Andorra.

I was acquitted 14 months later, when Josh told the court of his involvement, but that was that, as far as England was concerned. I was resentful the FA declined to offer me the benefit of the doubt, but knew the game was up when Fabio Capello, McClaren's successor, praised my form, but essentially dismissed me as an accident waiting to happen.

He had a point.

CHAPTER TEN

CRIME AND PUNISHMENT

There are bad ideas, brain-fades and flashes of genius, such as asking me to conduct a post-match interview when my emotions are exploding like popcorn kernels in boiling oil. You do not need to be a behavioural scientist to work out that frustration and candour are a dangerous combination.

Anger is an authentic emotion, and only becomes an issue when it mutates into rage. My preoccupation, following a 1-1 draw against a primitive Watford team in my penultimate match of the 2006/07 season, was to prevent resentment spilling over into something infinitely more destructive. The last thing I needed was Paul Tyrrell, Manchester City's press officer, pleading with me to do media chores.

Paul is a good guy, a pal to this day, but those in his role tend to be marginalised as far as players are concerned. He had no idea of the reasons for my irritation. It had been a terrible game, which confirmed my fears about the consequences of Stuart Pearce's loss of control. Our recruitment had been poor, standards had been allowed to slip, and I felt my career was starting to suffer.

I still had hopes of returning to the England squad at that stage. Players in better teams, who couldn't match my influence at club level, were once again ahead of me in the queue. I was wasting my time. I fronted up to the media because I thought being open and honest would shock the club back into life. I was leading scorer that season with seven goals, for heaven's sake. Ridiculous.

I knew the routine. A few gentle half-volleys, so the press guys have at least got something in their notebooks to regurgitate, always precede more probing questions. The second stage of the interview gave me the chance to say what I saw. I reckoned that, at the very worst, it would act as my calling card. Not quite a come-and-get-me plea, beloved of Fleet Street veterans, but a subtle wink at potential suitors.

'I can't get away from the fact we are buying stopgaps who have not cut it at the highest level. We are bringing in average players on top money and they are not producing. We have to sign quality players, not ones who have scored six goals in six games in the Pontins League or in Belgium or somewhere like that.'

Now I had their attention. You know when you are being quotable, because there is a mood shift. The journos' attention span becomes a little longer, and considerably more intense. It was time to kick the argument upstairs, to the City boardroom:

'I have to be brutally honest. I wouldn't pay to watch us at home this season. If I was a City fan I would be humming and hawing about whether to buy a season ticket next season. It is a lot of money for a season ticket at our place and they are not getting value for money.'

Bingo. The club went bananas. Pearce banned me from doing any more interviews, a damage limitation exercise which suited me perfectly. I named no names, but the players I felt were cheating, cutting corners, got the message. It was only later I discovered they were saying, 'Who the fuck does he think he is?'

There was a smoking club of about five or six, which included Didi Hamann and Ousmane Dabo, a lumbering midfield player who had arrived from Lazio with an inflated view of his own importance. I had a problem with them, because I felt smoking set an unprofessional example to the younger players, but that was a statement of principle on health grounds, rather than a personal attack.

Dabo, though, evidently felt otherwise. I had no issue with him, since he was no longer a threat to me. I'd been hyper-alert initially, because he played in my position and I still couldn't shake off the fearful, insecure young lad who whispered in my ear that I was on the edge of ruin, but he was so far off the first team he was irrelevant.

My mood wasn't improved by a 2-0 home defeat by Aston Villa, but the focus shifted to the season's last milestone, the Manchester derby. I missed that game, and would never play for City again, because of Dabo's determination to turn an otherwise low-key training session into his version of the May Day parade.

He began by leaving a tackle on me, a little livener that put me on my guard. He then came in late, so I gave him a dig back at the next opportunity. Neither of us was inclined to give ground, and I began to think, 'So you have got some bollocks after all. Why didn't you show that a little sooner? If you'd suggested you've got a bit of character you'd have played a few more games.'

He was pursuing a risky strategy. He was bigger than me, a little taller, and older. He had never seen me fight, though

I'd had enough altercations for him to realise I'd be no push-over. He obviously thought I needed putting in my place. Fair enough, since my mood swings were extreme, and I struggled to hide my dissatisfaction. But if you go for the king, you'd better make sure you take him out.

It could have been stopped at source, had Pearce stepped in and said, 'Oi, fucking behave yourselves,' but the confrontation acquired a dangerous dynamic. Dabo's running commentary was in French, and I didn't need an interpreter to understand its virulence; a look at Sylvain Distin's furrowed brow was all I needed. I responded sarcastically, telling him what a world-class player he was, but when that didn't register I simply repeated, ad nauseam, that he was shit.

Pearce stopped the session on the advice of his coach, Steve Wigley, when our tackles became increasingly reckless, and Distin walked Dabo to the dressing room in an attempt to calm him down. I followed him, about 10 paces back, and wasn't blameless since I kept on chuntering. He turned suddenly, sprinted at me, and gave me that primal choice: fight or flight. Instinct and experience told me to stand my ground.

As so often in such circumstances, time telescoped. In that split second, I thought of two other training-ground incidents. The first was a similar practice-match situation involving Nico Anelka, who tangled with Steve Jordan, fell on top of him, and split his lip with two punches. The second spat, about six months previously, involved me and Paul Bosvelt. It was a heat-of-the-moment quarrel, since we remain good friends.

Bosvelt, too, ran at me. He slapped me across the face, because he thought I had been cheeky to him. It took me by surprise, and Pearce evidently thought I needed to be taken down a peg or two because he declined to intervene. The lads got in between us, holding me back to give him a chance to tell them he felt I had disrespected him. I had not forgotten that belittlement, which bordered on humiliation.

Dabo wasn't going to get the chance to emulate it. He stopped about a yard in front of me, basically within punching distance, and I saw his right hand go back. Without thinking, I threw a jab, and caught him on the chin. The blow was quick, on the money, and left him stunned. He wasn't a natural fighter. I'm from the streets. There's your difference. I might be slight and wiry, but I've always been able to handle myself. He didn't know my formative influences.

If he had run at someone like that in a pub in Huyton, he'd have been lucky to get out with stitches, if he got out at all. He followed through with his slap, clipped me on the side of the face, but when you've been first to the punch it minimises the impact. I hit him again, and followed him down to give him another whack, because from where I come you never wait for a fighter to confirm whether he wants to continue.

Paul Dickov and Danny Mills jumped in, pulled me off him, and dragged me away. Physios immediately tended to Dabo, who took a couple of minutes to come around. He saw the blood, realised he'd been hurt and lost face. A manic, macho urge prompted him to lash out. Pearce was among those holding him back. I told him, quite calmly, 'Let him go, gaffer. Let's finish it man on man. That's no problem.'

Dabo is shouting and bawling, but I'm at my most rational. I'm not fearful of his aggression, because I know, deep down, I have his number. I am lucid, almost an observer. I didn't want to fight a team-mate, because no one wins, but he resorted to violence first. Had he kept on walking, this would have all petered out in raised voices. Remorse comes later when you realise you have inflicted damage on someone's son, someone's loved one.

If I had been as cowardly, and as out of order, as Dabo later claimed, why would Distin, his best mate, have sat next to me in the changing room and admitted he saw fault on both sides? Sylvain is a lot bigger than me, a physically imposing guy, and if he was really upset he could easily have rectified things on his friend's behalf.

Pearce sent me home, to await further instruction from the club. I did so, and poured my heart out to Peter Kay. Dabo went home, posed for photographs with medical tape over a badly swollen eye, apparently at the behest of his girlfriend, and sold his story. A perfect storm, of prejudice and wounded pride, rolled in.

His story was flawed, since his injuries were hardly consistent with being attacked from behind, as he claimed, but, inevitably, my reputation went before me. I accepted my culpability and, since I didn't have Dabo's number, I texted Sylvain and asked him to pass on a message, offering to drive to Manchester to meet him, to sort things out man to man.

Maybe the message didn't reach him. He pushed the police to press charges, and they duly obliged. My initial intention was to argue that I'd acted in self-defence, but once the judge suggested a guilty plea would lead only to additional community service, and the imposition of a concurrent custodial sentence, I took the line of least resistance.

Footballers are natural pragmatists. I regarded City's decision to fine me £100,000 and suspend me for the final weeks of the season as prejudicial because it created the impression Dabo was an entirely innocent party. I was cast as the instigator, the transgressor. Pearce made a strategic error by admitting the club only took action once Premier League safety had been confirmed.

I exploited the situation that summer, but please don't dismiss me as yet another greedy, feckless player striking out for all he can get. Forget fluffy images of fealty. You have to understand the survival mechanism that is engaged when your future is on the line. It is naive to ignore the reality that everyone associated with you is looking out for number one.

I was under no illusions. I was a commodity with an identifiable market value, to be coveted, nurtured, or traded. City had to assess the balance between my positive influence as a player and the liability I had become off the field. I was a serial offender, and the prospects of long-term rehabilitation weren't great, because I was progressively more aggressive as my frustration festered.

Predictably, short-term self-interest dictated events. I told Alistair Mackintosh, City's chief executive, that I was determined to leave. John Wardle, his boss, confided that Pearce was about to be sacked. New investment, which turned out to be from Thaksin Shinawatra, was coming in. Sven-Goran Eriksson was lined up as the new manager. They wanted me to stay for at least another season. If they felt I would be flattered by their candour, they were wrong.

Fuck them. I was the difference between City staying up, and a bad, bad team getting what it deserved – relegation. How dare they side with someone who had contributed nothing to the season? I was in the wrong, but Dabo was equally culpable. They had betrayed me, and I would not forgive, nor forget.

The £5.5m release clause in my contract was my trump card. Mackintosh offered to double my wages, but it was clear that money would not be a problem, since Newcastle and West

Ham were ready to intervene. City tried to intimidate them by insisting any fee would have to be paid as a lump sum, rather than in instalments, as is traditional.

Newcastle settled me in a rather more salubrious cell to that which I would become accustomed, a suite at the Malmaison hotel in the city. They joked about posting bouncers on the door, to ensure I would not leave until I had signed for them. I met Sam Allardyce, and liked his vision of a team that matched pace with solidity, passion with gumption.

It's funny how things work out. Football is intricately interconnected. Sam had been City's initial choice to succeed Pearce, but Shinawatra insisted on Sven. Sam featured in Chappy's Preston promotion team, and entered club folklore when he lost a sumo wrestling match against Ronnie Hildersley, a slightly built midfield player who began at City, on the beach in a post-season lads' holiday in Spain.

Apparently an arresting sight in a thong, and basted in suntan lotion, Sam was buried up to his neck in the sand as a forfeit while his team-mates played punk rock, which he hated, on the team's oversized ghetto blaster. He became so hungry he ate 11 fried eggs in a single sitting when he was released.

Meanwhile, back in what passes as the real world, Willie McKay, who was acting as Newcastle's agent, was conducting a surreal, day-long negotiating session. He was keen to get my agreement on a double-my-money £60,000-a-week deal, sweetened further by such bizarre add-ons as a £50,000-a-year offer to a mate of my choice, who would act as my driver. Unfortunately, I had given my word to another agent, Mel Stein, that I would talk to West Ham and their manager, Alan Curbishley. To say they were keen was an understatement.

Think of me as the owner of a house, where two potential buyers are in a race to exchange contracts. Each is happy to repeatedly gazump the other, and so the price relentlessly inflates. It is a strange, ludicrously privileged, position to be in. The figures quickly lose their relevance, because they are so contradictory to everyday experience.

Put yourself in my position. This is a chance to establish a lifetime's financial security. It gives me what Mickey Duff, the late and legendary British boxing promoter, used to refer to as 'fuck-you money'. You might prefer to couch that concept in rather more polite terms, but you can't avoid its compelling logic.

The deal eventually hinged on a £350,000 loyalty payment, owed to me by City. Don't worry, by the way. I can hear your muttering from here: loyalty? For doing a job, fulfilling a contract? At a time when you have been agitating for a new job? How can the bastardisation of such an admirable principle be justified?

City and Newcastle argued over it for several weeks, once I had come to the conclusion that Sam was in the process of building a top-four team and the Northeast was my preferred destination. I was on a stopover in Dubai, en route to a holiday in Mauritius with Georgia, when I got word from West Ham that Curbishley and Eggert Magnusson, the Icelandic biscuit baron who was to prove a calamitous owner, intended to fly out with a contract.

That was the tipping point for Newcastle. Like a good poker player, they knew when to hold, and when to fold. They agreed to pay me the £350,000, and pay City the £5.5m up front. I was in City's debt because they had given me the chance to play professional football, but I hadn't been a bad investment for them, since I cost nothing as an academy graduate. I could at last refocus my energies on football.

Or so I thought.

I was flying in pre-season training, and Sam sounded me out about becoming captain. He had partially funded the rebuild by selling Scott Parker and Kieron Dyer to West Ham for £13m. Mark Viduka arrived on a free, Alan Smith and Geremi offered new options in midfield and attack, and the defence was augmented by Jose Enrique, Habib Beye and Abdoulaye Faye.

I led the team in our second friendly, a 1-1 draw at Carlisle, until the 69th minute. Then, for no apparent reason, as I made a straightforward turn, it felt as if my right foot exploded. I've got a high pain threshold, and can usually run off a knock, but this was agony. A scan revealed I had partially fractured the fifth metatarsal, and that was me done for three months. Since the injury was sustained in relative isolation, I blamed everyone and everything.

It was only when I thought rationally that I identified the orthotic insert in my boot as the probable source of the problem. It was the result of a visit to a specialist in Stoke on the insistence of Mark Taylor, a long-term associate of Sam Allardyce. He is now Performance Director at Sunderland but was then operating as Newcastle's Head of Sports Medicine and Science.

I was put through a series of tests on the treadmill when it was discovered that my left leg was slightly longer than my right. The aim was to make me more efficient, but I felt uncomfortable running with the insert in the boot, almost as if I was wearing high heels. I accepted advice to stick with it, but quickly resented the consequences of a decision taken by others.

Discomfort is more manageable than impotence. I could deal with the solitary grind of rehabilitation, and became as obsessive as any gym rat, but my sudden marginalisation stirred deep and dark emotions. I challenged the manager, and angrily asked whether I had effectively been a guinea pig for his belief in sports science.

The episode had a fundamental impact on me, since it confirmed my determination to challenge authority and exacerbated the frustration which eventually led to prison. I was so desperate to restate my relevance as a footballer I falsely claimed I was ahead of schedule, and returned way too early. Even without the insert, I could barely run when I made my full Newcastle debut in a 3-1 home win over Tottenham.

I felt sluggish, unbalanced. The team stuttered, declined. I picked up an ankle injury and pointedly played it down. I branded Newcastle fans as 'vicious' for giving manager and players fearsome stick during a 3-0 home defeat by Liverpool. My diet consisted of regret and anti-inflammatory pills. I could no longer sustain the deception that I had dealt with my alcohol problem. I would go out with the express intention of getting drunk, and talk to myself in the mirror when I got home. I deluded myself that I had weaned myself off Peter Kay's wisdom.

He saw it coming. He used a wonderful analogy with me, of the brain as a muscle, which needed to be worked on like any other. If you go to the gym, and do biceps curls or chest presses for months, your muscles will be strong. You will be lithe and lean. You'll look and feel good. Stop going to the gym and you will gradually regress. You will slip back into old ways, and look shabby. You'll turn in on yourself.

Basically, I had stopped going to the mind gym. My thoughts were cloudy, my actions undisciplined. All it needed was a trigger point, which happened to be Newcastle's 1-0 defeat at Wigan on Boxing Day. I was left out after my substitution in the previous game, a 2-2 draw against Derby, was cheered. Michael Owen had been out of the team for six weeks. We worked up a persecution complex sitting in the stands, and I confronted Allardyce afterwards.

I told Owen I was going home to Liverpool to get slaughtered. I had lost self-esteem. I was trying to make sense of a world I felt was imploding. My body was starting to betray me. My mind was muddled. I had shut down to everyone but Pete, though I made it hard even for him to find the keys to my behaviour. I was slipping towards the edge of the abyss. I should have picked up the phone to him, but I was too proud to reach out for help.

The next thing I knew I was in the police cells, being shown CCTV footage of a thug throwing himself at someone with such vehemence and violence he could have killed him. It was me, captured at 5am in Liverpool city centre on 27 December. The court heard I had drunk 10 pints of lager, and another five bottles of beer, but that was an ill-educated guess. I really didn't have a clue.

The Golden Arches beckoned, once the nightclub closed. I was with my brother Andrew, Nadine, my cousin, and a few of their friends. It was nearly five in the morning. Everyone was pissed and peckish. The McDonald's queue was long and the behaviour was predictable. I was given immediate grief by a bunch of lads who decided, suddenly, that I should be playing for Everton.

I ignored them, endured the usual bollocks about being too big-time to respond. When Nadine told them to shut it, they flipped. She was called a footballer's slag, an easy shag. Unforgiveable, unacceptable. When I told them never to speak to a woman in those terms in my presence, they bristled.

'What the fuck are you going to do?'

Pete's quiet voice in my head, desperately diluting the alcohol, told me to walk away, along Church Street, one of the main thoroughfares. Regrettably, the fuckwits decided to follow us, out of the restaurant. I tried to reconnect with reality by phoning Georgia, who was sensibly asleep and didn't answer, but the mouthiest twat in the group decided he was a hero, and kicked Nadine. The die was cast.

Nadine's attacker wasn't particularly bright. A mate from the estate, who employed him on a local building site, told me later that he quickly realised he had made a big mistake. As he turned to face me, I hit him. I was off the scale. I threw a flurry of punches, connected with several, and was a YouTube favourite before the case reached court. How does that work, by the way?

Normal rules did not apply. His mates announced their intention to stab me. A bunch of schoolboy scallies, alerted by the commotion, recognised me and decided they were hard enough to intervene. Andrew tried to hold me back, but had no chance. I went for the gobbiest kid, punched him once and dropped him, chipping his tooth.

I didn't realise at the time that he was only 15. I was more concerned with my brother, who threw himself at another lairy bystander. I'm sorry, but if you are off your head at that time of morning, challenging allcomers, you deserve everything that's coming to you, even if you are not old enough to have taken your GCSEs. Abuse people and shit happens.

Obviously, I've replayed the incident continually, in my mind. Could I have avoided it? Would I do the same, if it was repeated tomorrow? If I'd been sober, would I have been able to de-escalate the situation? The reality is, it doesn't really matter. I'm pissed out of my head in the city centre at 5am. I've let my family down. I've let my manager down. I've let myself down.

The police had a real-time view, on CCTV, and arrested me within minutes. I awoke in a holding cell, on a bench with a thin plastic mattress. I was covered by a grey horsehair blanket, and wanted to throw up when they served me tea, a sandwich and a packet of crisps. I was isolated, instantly sober. I stared at the walls and wondered, 'What the fuck have I done?'

Absurdly, I was initially preoccupied with letting Michael Owen down. Equally absurdly, we had agreed to share a helicopter into training that day. I knew I had been involved in a fight, because my hands were scuffed and sore. The bizzies told me I was in for the duration, because the court wouldn't sit on 27 December, or the 28th. I contacted Sam Allardyce, who promised help, but I knew I was going to jail, because I had already been bailed in the Dabo case.

The consequences began to overwhelm me. I could forget about a six-month loan move to Juventus in January, which had been mooted by Claudio Ranieri, who wanted me to add dynamism to the team he was re-establishing in Serie A and the Champions League.

I was asked to give a witness statement. I refused to comment, but the CCTV footage I was shown shook me to the core. Was that really me? How had it come to this? When the courts opened for business, in the brief festive break, I was consumed by a dismal sense of dread. Forget my football profile. I was just another St John's failure to be processed and punished.

Newcastle had wooed me with the promise of a driver, and a suitably flash car. I ended up sharing a meat wagon, with men dismissed as the dregs of society. I was no longer a name, but a number. My designer gear, which mocked my pretensions, was replaced by harsh prison-issue clothing, boil-washed to within an inch of its working life.

Voices, from blank faces I did not want to recognise, spoke of due process and deliberation. I was led along a landing at Walton jail, which would later be condemned in an inspectors' report as 'dirty, overcrowded, chaotic and unsafe'. A grey cell door slammed. I was scared, lonely, but not alone.

CHAPTER ELEVEN
INSIDE OUT

Des O'Connor and Carol Vorderman inadvertently helped me through the inevitable existential crisis. I was watching them co-host *Countdown*, the TV game show, after a fitful first night and an endless first morning in Walton jail, when my cellmate returned from his duties and switched channels without a word.

The challenge was primal, as far from mental gymnastics with numbers, vowels and consonants as it gets. In such a harsh, enclosed environment you are quickly categorised as victim, survivor or enforcer. Aware I could not be seen to be intimidated, I got up from my bed and, equally silently, switched it back. I felt my fist tense, imperceptibly, and turned to face my foe.

'What the fuck do you think you're doing?' he said.

His eyes locked on to mine, as he mentally examined his options. It was like watching a cat calculate the odds on winning a fight for territory. Eventually, after several seconds that passed as slowly as centuries, he dropped his gaze, shrugged, and mumbled a frustrated obscenity. He was gone the next day, and replaced by a terrified kid on a drink-driving charge.

New Year's Eve, listening to the dull thud of distant fireworks and the din of inmates who had obviously succeeded in distilling illicit hooch from fruit and potato peel, was bizarre. People are still plugged into the outside world, and actions inside can have external consequences, so I remained wary and introspective. My powerlessness put the fear of God into me.

I was released on bail after six days because Peter Kay convinced the judge I needed intensive counselling. The conditions were onerous, a benign form of house arrest. I had to agree to live with Pete and his wife, which he admitted put a strain on their relationship. He was assigned as my perpetual chaperone, and I was allowed out only between the hours of 7am and 7pm. I was banned from drinking alcohol, and from entering licensed premises.

Just in case I was under the illusion there was widespread faith in my ability to stay on the straight and narrow, we had to fight through a scrum of photographers at the prison gates. Since we had been ordered to be at Pete's place in Southampton within six hours, I had time only for a five-minute reunion with Dad, and a sweep through my bedroom for kit and clothing.

The car journey south was solemn. It offered time and space for honesty, humility, long-overdue gratitude. I apologised for my degeneration, and told Pete, without shame or exaggeration, that I owed him my life. That set the tone of our conversations for the following five months, which were profound and punctuated by gradual legal concessions on how I could live that life.

Georgia would have been within her rights never to have spoken to me again, yet she visited me in Southampton. Our relationship deepened, when it could so easily have been destroyed. Her understanding was another source of salvation, a contrast to the enduring suspicion of the police, who would turn up, unannounced, at the Sporting Chance clinic to check my progress.

It took another fortnight for the judge to be convinced that I needed the physical and psychological release of returning to football. Newcastle owner Mike Ashley offered me his helicopter, since my curfew ensured Pete and I needed to fly to and from training. It seemed a generous gesture until I received an eye-boggling invoice which confirmed it was business as usual.

Ashley had overseen the sacking of Sam Allardyce soon after my release on bail. His choice of successor, Kevin Keegan, was ominous, given the complexity of our relationship at Manchester City. He was the Messiah. I was a very naughty boy. He quickly pulled me to one side and promised a clean slate, provided I had given up drinking.

I was determined to be clean, one day at a time.

The next allowance permitted me to stay in Newcastle. Pete's responsibility eased, to one day with me each week, provided I remained in the company of a club-appointed security guard. I nicknamed Big Dave, my new companion, Baloo after the bear in *The Jungle Book*. He had a quick wit, and stood for no nonsense, but I still couldn't visit football grounds because of the ban on licensed properties.

Freedom in the form I most cherished, being able to play, followed soon after. Keegan was as good as his word, and he put me on the bench for a visit to Arsenal on a Tuesday night, 29 January. I had to sit on the coach while the team meeting took place in the hotel, which was off limits because it had a bar. I was only allowed to go in the dressing room, or on the pitch.

We were well beaten, 3-0, but Keegan lanced the boil by putting me on for David Rozehnal in the 57th minute. I got what I expected, and probably deserved – a thunderclap of booing and abuse. Anyone who expected me to walk on egg-shells didn't know me that well; a trademark tackle prompted Samir Nasri's off-the-ball retaliation, which merited a red card according to Kevin's combative post-match interview.

Even my harshest critic had to concede my mental strength. I played well in the remaining 12 games after that, despite being in limbo, awaiting trial. The boys were planning holidays in Cancun and California, the Maldives and Marbella. My tour operator would be Her Majesty's Inspector of Prisons. My next match would be playing for the drugs-free wing, on the artificial pitch at Walton prison.

Since my solicitor warned me to prepare for a 12-month stretch, I was relieved when sentenced to six months, after accepting the charge of affray and assault. The judge, Henry Globe QC, condemned a 'violent and cowardly act' but took into account two character references. Peter Kay stressed my acceptance of the need for 'total abstinence' and Kevin Keegan assured the court he had seen a 'massive change' in me.

I would be out in three months with good behaviour, but the sense of permanence was striking once I returned to Walton. The four-hour processing procedure was infinitely more rigorous. I was given a small plastic bag of toiletries and dressed in convict chic – shapeless grey trousers, a thin blue tee-shirt and a dark sweater.

I was hyper-alert once again, sniffing the air like a rabbit deciding whether to make a run to the safety of the burrow. A prison officer, acting on behalf of the governor, offered me the chance of a place on a secure wing. He admitted they had a vested interest in minimising the possibility of unfavourable publicity, in the event of me being attacked, seriously hurt, or worse.

The governor shuddered at the thought of a potential compensation case involving the football club, but I resisted his initial solution, calculating that association with paedophiles and perverts, clustered for their own protection, was potentially calamitous. I accepted the alternative of a place on the drugs-free wing, because it offered better access to the gym in return for submission to regular drug testing.

There were no guarantees. I was still an easy mark for someone seeking to make a name for himself. I had no way of knowing how black inmates would deal with my link to such a high-profile, racially influenced murder as that of Anthony Walker. A desperado's arsenal ranged from razor blades to infected syringes. In my favour, familiarity offered some security.

Walton doubled as the St John's branch of Friends Reunited. I met at least a dozen former schoolmates in the first couple of days, and Dad's pals made a point of introducing themselves, but there were some people I wanted nothing to do with, at any price. One was Kevin Corke, my second cousin, who was serving life for the murder of Tommy Harrison, stabbed fatally through the heart in the street following an 18th birthday party in Huyton. Tommy was the cousin of Mash, Matthew McElhinney, one of my best mates. Corke's accomplice Carl Taylor, brother of Paul, Anthony Walker's killer, was in for manslaughter. When they tried to ingratiate themselves with me, I told them to do one.

A friend of a friend, Michael Kinney, ran the gym. He saw to it that I made the inmates' select team, which played with and against the screws a couple of times a week, in addition to having a runout for a team cobbled together from the recovering addicts on my wing. That ensured time off from my job in the metalwork shop.

Another warder, a keen badminton player, picked up a whisper that I had been Knowsley Under-14 champion. He needed a practice partner of suitable quality, so that long-forgotten claim to sporting fame earned me the priceless privilege of being released from my cell, my pad to use prison slang, when everyone else had been banged up.

My first cellmate, a speed freak called Chopper, was a chain-smoker. My second, a lad named Billy, secured my transfer to his non-smoking pad by threatening to put his companion in the prison hospital if he did not apply to move elsewhere. His hyperactivity was best explained by his professional speciality, stealing from drug dealers.

Unsurprisingly, he had been battered, burned, stabbed and shot. He was a warm and funny guy, a cross between Fagin and Arthur Daley, but his psychotic streak was soon revealed, when I had to pull him off an innocent inmate he suspected of being involved in a drink-driving case which led to the death of a six-year-old girl, Demi Leigh Royle. It was a hugely distressing case, which caused an outcry on Merseyside. The van driver, who narrowly missed Demi Leigh's mother, Hannah, and a pram containing her nine-month-old sister Izabella, fled the scene. He was sentenced to nine years for causing death by dangerous driving.

Billy read reports of the trial with unconcealed rage. He had been consumed by hate for drink-drivers ever since his five-year-old sister had been severely paralysed by one, who ran her down outside the family home, and was convinced the driver would serve his time in Walton. The hunt was on.

Billy made it his duty to interrogate any new inmate on our wing, until word reached him that one arrival's story didn't seem to stack up. He sprinted along the landing, unconcerned by the possibility of mistaken identity, and was laying into a terrified kid before I managed to intervene. He was initially too scared to speak, but it soon became clear he was in for an unrelated piece of petty criminality.

Billy attempted to make amends by giving him a cache of chocolate. That was in keeping with his unorthodox entrepreneurial spirit, since he taught me how to reinvest my weekly wage of £7.50 in Sunday church services, when all manner of illicit deals were done. Chocolate and cigarettes were purchased, legitimately, for use as currency in a black economy where people bartered for drugs, drink and DVDs. The going rate for a smuggled iPhone was £1,500, paid by associates on the outside. An inventive inmate spotted a gap in the market for phone chargers, cannibalised from stolen electrical plugs.

I didn't need a phone, because I took a conscious decision to isolate myself, and didn't want to risk having my sentence extended if I was caught with one. I took out a subscription to *The Times*, and found alternative entertainment in Billy's tall tales and football theories. He shared his greatest luxury, tinned hot dogs, which he boiled after blocking the cell sink with toilet paper. Given the stodge of prison food, and believable stories about rats in the kitchen, they were delicious.

He urged me to find my place in the system, which I duly discovered scanning the racing page. I had a eureka moment studying the form, and realised the prison lacked a bookie. I borrowed Billy's chocolate stash to establish a float, gave us insurance by skimming the original odds, and recorded all bets in a notebook. Before long we were an illegitimate version of Cadbury World.

I diversified, using my inside knowledge to create a range of markets for that summer's European Championships in

Austria and Switzerland. It didn't matter that England had failed to qualify. I offered odds on opening goalscorer, number of cards, timing of goals and the final result. When confectionery supplies ran low, we accepted toiletries, bedding and food privileges as stakes.

The screws inevitably discovered our scam, but were sanguine about its success, since they trusted us to prevent inmates getting too deep into debt. In hindsight, I should have been more aware of the probability of jealousy. I was stripped of my gym privileges for eight days when someone posted a photograph of me working out on social media. It was quickly picked up by the papers.

I had my suspicions, since I saw someone with a mobile in there, but wasn't about to grass him up. The publicity, together with my refusal to co-operate with internal inquiries, went down badly. Word clearly went out that I was to be put in my place. As a result, my cell was 'spun', smashed up during a search for an illegal phone, twice in a week. I knew the score: avoid confrontation, clean up the mess, and move on.

I missed fragments of normality, such as Nan's Sunday dinners and the smell of a freshly mown training ground, but it was easy to see why so many inmates become institutionalised. The rituals of prison life became deeply ingrained, from the 7.30am turnout to the regular meals and evening association at 6.45pm before lockup at 8pm.

Each wing at Walton had its own unwritten rules, its distinctive personalities, perils and pressures. Disputes were usually settled in the showers. Yet it was a Category B prison, 'a 21st Century Community Prison', to quote the blue sign on the approach to the entrance. I assumed I would return there after being ferried to Crown Court in Manchester, where I was given a four-month suspended sentence in the Dabo case.

If only. I was taken to Strangeways, high on security and low on creature comforts, because it was the jail closest to the court. The name of Manchester's Category A prison, and its association with such infamous alumni as Ian Brady, the Moors murderer, and Harold Shipman, the GP convicted of killing 15 of his patients, was enough to chill me to the bone. Opened in 1868 and wrecked during the 1990 riots, it had a notoriously high suicide rate and more than 200 lifers in a population of 1,300, spread over nine wings.

They had nothing to lose. I had been deposited at the far end of the criminal spectrum, where an additional 10 years for attacking someone like me with a primitive blade, or napalm in the form of boiling oil derived from stolen butter, was an irrelevance. The welcoming committee, shouting through barred windows as I was walked through the yard to my cell, was sinister in its uniformity.

'You're getting slashed in the morning, Barton.'

'You're getting cut.'

'You're going to die, you maggot.'

Was I scared? Too fucking right I was. I had endured death threats before, and logic told me that someone who intends to stab you doesn't have too much to gain from warning you beforehand, yet this was a war zone. Everyone and everything was a potential threat. I knew I could not back down, and also knew the likely consequences of defiance. I was in no position to appreciate the irony that the skill set of violence and truculence which put me in prison in the first place offered the best chance of protection.

I was allowed only a small bag of possessions, and assigned to the main wing, the so-called council estate. This was the animal kingdom in extremis, a place that operated an excessive form of natural justice. Alarms would sound regularly during the day, as fights sparked intermittent lockdowns. But first I had to survive the longest night of my life.

It was late when I was ushered into my cell. A lad of similar age, but built like a brick shithouse, was in pole position on the bottom bunk. The top bunk is dangerous, since the mattress can be kicked off from below by the dominant prisoner. Fall to the floor, and you are likely to be jumped on and beaten, or raped.

Everyone jostles for position in those first few minutes, hours and days. Fear leads to some pretty strange behaviour. 'All right, mate?' I said in a desperate, transparent attempt to break the ice. He didn't reply, and continued to watch TV as if he was in a trance. I struggled to suppress a mounting sense of panic. He was black, which set my mind whirring madly.

He was obviously not the most upstanding member of society, since Strangeways wasn't built for life's innocents. He was awaiting his chance. He knew of me through the 'Joey Barton murder' and would seek revenge. I elicited a grunt when I repeated my opening gambit half an hour later. He was in his own little world. My palms were damp with perspiration, though the cell was cold and claustrophobic.

I was convinced that it would all go off, probably in pitch darkness. Maybe he was one of those who had issued bawled promises to slash and scar me. Maybe he was constructing a warped fantasy of beating me to a pulp, or shagging me into submission. I immediately resolved to lie on top of the bedsheet, to give me better self-control if he decided to kick me out of bed.

Sleep was impossible. I listened to his breathing and monitored his every movement. My mind was like a tumble dryer, endlessly processing different scenarios. I clutched a can of beans, one of my few permissible rations, to my chest; he was getting smashed as hard as possible in the face with it if he decided to come for me. We would see where we were after that. I was prepared to do anything to survive.

The first rays of light, which I guessed shone through at around 5am, felt like molten gold. The dawn chorus at Strangeways is not a barrage of birdsong, but the impatient yelping of Alsatians and the heavy boots of their handlers, patrolling the landings. It was a reminder of the need to remain alert. Sure enough, when the cell door was opened at 7.30am, my cellmate walked out without a word.

Football had taught me to examine the angles, determine the danger posed by those around me. I was exhausted; my eyes stung and my limbs ached. I catnapped for an hour, then tried to formulate a plan. When I was taken out of my pad to complete the paperwork, I got to work on the screw who accompanied me. 'Lock me back up in that cell tonight and it is all kicking off,' I warned him. 'The atmosphere is horrible. Someone is going to get hurt. It is either going to be me, or the other lad.'

This warder evidently didn't need a badminton partner, or an insight into his favourite footballer. He was sour, indifferent to my anxiety. I gabbled on about wanting to see the governor to arrange a transfer, but he dismissed me as just another scrote with ideas above his station. 'Nah,' he said. 'You're doing what you're told.'

I had no option but to confront my fate. My taciturn cellmate was still out when I returned, so I sat in a chair, opposite the door, and waited. I had retrieved a can of pineapple chunks from my bag. It had more heft than Heinz, but still my imagination ran riot. Matey Boy would arrive, tooled up by unseen accomplices. This was his chance to be The Man, to impose a little fear and loathing of his own.

The door opened.

'All right, mate?' he said. That had to be a bluff, to put me off guard.

'Yeah,' I replied. 'You?'

'Yeah, yeah. Sorry about last night. My bird had been on the phone, and she'd been giving me grief. My head was scrambled. So when you let on to me I was just worrying about what was going on at home. I didn't want to speak to anyone.'

My imaginary assailant, my murderous juicehead, turned out to be a decent lad from Chapeltown in Leeds. He came armed only with the best wishes of Micah Richards, his mate and my former team-mate at City. We talked football and mutual acquaintances for one of the weirdest hours I have ever spent. The crisis wasn't over, but it suddenly appeared more manageable.

All sorts of things went on in the wing, so I had to be on perpetual guard against head-bangers. One particular screw's obsession with a local Premier League club gave me the chance to duck and dive. He could no longer afford a season ticket, so once I had him hooked, I offered to arrange a pair for him, plus some pocket money.

Unsettled by the seemingly endless silence, I wondered if I had overplayed my hand. He exhaled before asking me in a stage whisper what I needed from him. 'Get me shipped out to the drugs-free wing,' I suggested. Within 24 hours he had been as good as his word. I had a job as a gym orderly, with responsibility for cleaning equipment and organising sessions. He could retrieve his club scarf from the wardrobe.

My new cellmate was a farmer who had taken out a burglar with an unlicensed shotgun. It was difficult to work out what he had done to deserve to be in prison, other than be a convenient target for societal revenge. His punishment for doing the wrong thing, at the wrong time, in the wrong setting, seemed harsh and counterproductive.

Billy, my mentor at Walton, would have been proud of the way I played the system. I extended certain gym sessions in return for a bit of extra food, or something else with which to barter. I developed my options by taking a second job at the serving hatch in the kitchen, doing the dishes and picking up gossip.

It's mad how people adapt to their surroundings. I was taught to play backgammon by Johnny, an American expatriate who had lived in Monaco for most of his life. A financial advisor, he was serving eight years for embezzlement; up to $40m had apparently gone missing. He claimed the only culture shock was a lack of cold, crisp French white wine.

His friend, housed in the pad facing his at the end of the landing, was Marius, a softly spoken Czech who weighed in excess of 20 stone and had more tattoos than Lemmy from Motorhead. He was held in the highest esteem, and not simply because of his uncanny dexterity on a short-tennis court. He was an assassin, extradited back to the UK when CCTV footage linked him to a gangland hit.

He was at the head of the prison hierarchy, a man to be feared, since he had a perilous degree of pride in his status as short-tennis champion. The game is played with smaller rackets, softer balls and lower nets on a court that is around half the traditional size. Serves are underarm, volleys are not permitted, and the ball must bounce once before it can be returned. The winner is the first to reach 17 points.

Marius moved well for a man of his bulk. He had an instinctive feel for the pace of the ball, and the depth of the angle. I picked the game up pretty quickly, but he was far too good for me in our first match. As if to prove the managerial lament that I had rabbit droppings for brains, I challenged him again, and beat him.

This did not go down well. Marius started shouting and banging his racket against the wall. Not for the first time in my life, I had overestimated the limits of self-preservation. He calmed down pretty quickly, but I was still wary several days later when he asked me to pop into his cell to sign something he wanted to send back to his family.

I tried to style it out, and suggested I'd be honoured to welcome him into my pad. Nothing doing. It was precious cargo, a special book he held close to his heart. He was serving 28 years, and I wasn't keen on him rubbing me out as a professional courtesy, so I asked a couple of guys to watch my back, just in case the door to his cell slammed shut behind me.

It was dark, eerie, almost a literal interpretation of a man cave. Marius wasn't daft: he could read my mind, even in the half-light. I think it amused him. I signed his book, made small talk for as short a time as possible without implying disrespect, and got the hell out of Dodge. The lads on the landing saw my face as I emerged and pissed themselves laughing.

My farmer friend had been reassigned, and I scuttled to see my new cellmate Mick, a Huyton lad who'd had the misfortune to be apprehended with a car boot stacked with AK47s he was running for a Lithuanian gang. He controlled the prison laundry, a coveted role which gave him great scope to operate a grace-and-favour network. His little luxuries included a wide-screen TV that could have done service in the local multiplex.

A tabloid invention had him bullying me until I broke down in tears. Another red-top freak show proclaimed Georgia as 'the bravest WAG in Britain'. The article used saccharine language but implied she was a potential victim of domestic abuse by quoting an unnamed 'pal' as saying: 'She wants her head looking at, shacking up with that thug. Blokes like him never change.'

The usual suspects were mobilising. A third tabloid used a rent-a-quote Tory MP to condemn my release after 74 days. Funnily enough, he stopped short of suggesting the other 24,999 prisoners allowed out early due to the end of the government's custody licence scheme should have served their sentences, in full.

The cardboard warriors at the FA re-emerged to charge me with violent conduct for the Dabo incident. By the time they banned me for six matches, with another six suspended for a season, Newcastle United were in meltdown. Keegan resigned the day before the result of the FA hearing was announced.

Society was never going to provide an unequivocal welcome for the young man with a pudding-bowl haircut and a black bag slung over his shoulder, who emerged from the gates of Strangeways prison on the morning of 27 July 2008. No one really wanted to pose the question whether incarceration had done its job.

I had, in effect, been rehabilitated during those first six days on remand in Walton. I resolved, there and then, never to return to jail once my dues had been paid. Only a fool or an amateur dramatist would describe prison as a positive, life-affirming experience, but it gave me an invaluable insight into the human condition. Adversity was an ever-reliable tutor.

Can I guarantee I will never relapse? No. Did prison alter my outlook? Yes. My love intensified for the woman with whom I realised I wanted to live, for the rest of my life. My bonds to a small circle of family and friends drew tighter. I learned that some relationships are sacred, while others disappear, like dust borne on a gust of wind.

CHAPTER TWELVE
HERO

When the going gets weird, the weird turn pro, and turn up at St James' Park. The chaos I discovered on my return to Newcastle United from the peculiarly comforting certainties of the drugs-free wing at Strangeways was straight from one of Hunter S. Thompson's mescaline-fuelled fantasies. Mike Ashley's 'Cockney Mafia' were intent on making their bones.

They were an eclectic bunch, fond of a bracket to express their titular significance. Dennis Wise, a professional irritant, was executive director (football). Tony Jimenez, an obscure property developer, was vice president (player recruitment). Derek Llambias, an equally obscure casino executive, was managing director (sanitation).

I might have made up that last embellishment, but truth was stranger than fiction. Here was a football club being run contrary not just to convention but to common decency and common sense. Human beings were regarded as blots on the balance sheet, inanimate objects to be shifted like cheap tee-shirts.

I'm resigned to my expendability, but even I was surprised to receive a call towards the end of the summer transfer window, informing me that the club had agreed to sell me to Portsmouth without consultation. I was ordered to travel to London to meet Tony Adams, Harry Redknapp's assistant, who was overseeing their end of the deal.

It didn't add up. I had made a two-minute comeback as substitute in a 3-0 defeat at Arsenal on 30 August, having worked hard, alongside the youth-team squad, to regain fitness after missing the first team's pre-season training camp in Majorca. Kevin Keegan spoke enthusiastically on the journey home about his plans for me, once the FA had thrown their dollies out of the pram.

I liked Tony, having known him through Sporting Chance, and paid him professional respect by listening to what he had to say. Something was not right, since I was unconvinced by his response to basic questions about the short- and medium-term goals of the club. He seemed to lack insight. His team-building strategy was as vague as his assessment of the extent of the owners' ambitions.

It took time to discover Pompey's progress was built on financial quicksand, but I was immediately spooked. My gut instinct was to call Keegan, and confront him about his apparent betrayal. I must have learned something on those long nights inside, though, because I opted for a more measured approach, through his assistant Terry McDermott. He had been hugely supportive in the lull before my imprisonment.

Terry recognised my vulnerability, sensed I needed the security of a family environment, and regularly invited me to his house for gammon, egg and chips. He was a football nut, and the evenings would inevitably end with him bringing out his medal collection to stimulate stories of legendary

European nights. They were told with special relish, since he knew full well I was a bluenose.

Our relationship broadened to include shared evenings on the road, assessing players and opponents. Cynicism is a default position for a footballer, but I trusted him implicitly. His bafflement when I told him about the Portsmouth episode was persuasive. He was adamant he knew nothing about any deal, and promised to call Keegan because he understood I could only make my decision if I had access to all the facts.

Kevin called 10 minutes later. He, too, didn't have a clue. He reiterated his faith in me, both personally and professionally. I had nearly three years left on my contract, and he urged me to stay. To be frank, he was pushing on an open door. I told the Newcastle hierarchy in no uncertain terms that I was going nowhere.

At the very least, they were guilty of unbelievable naivety. Anyone who has been in football for more than five minutes understands that players are inveterate gossips. It took about that long in the dressing room before training the following morning to learn that Michael Owen and Alan Smith had also resisted pressure to leave the previous day.

The manager had been cut off at the knees, since he had briefed the press he had hopes of bringing in four additional players in the window. His authority had been blatantly undermined by the unwanted departure of James Milner, and attempts to sell three more senior pros behind his back. His resignation was regrettable, inevitable, and entirely honourable.

He would be vindicated in October 2009, when a Premier League arbitration tribunal ruled in his favour against the club, which was found to have made untrue statements and given profoundly unsatisfactory explanations for its conduct. He was awarded £2m, in addition to appropriate interest, for the systematic abuse of his managerial ability and experience. The cost to Newcastle United's credibility was incalculable.

It had hardly been enhanced by the identity of his successor, Joe Kinnear. The public perception that he represented the crazier element of the Crazy Gang at Wimbledon was hardened by his infamous, 52-expletive, 'you're a cunt' rant at the press. It was football's equivalent of a Chubby Brown stand-up set which, to be honest, went down brilliantly in the dressing room.

I got on well with Joe, despite his eccentricities. My first game for him, following my FA suspension, wasn't exactly the stuff of Geordie legend, since it coincided with Sunderland's first home win in the Tyne–Wear derby for 28 years, but I warmed to his withering honesty. It was a strange time, and the club was in a very strange place.

I tore my medial knee ligament in a 2-2 draw at Wigan in November, and JFK – as he was inevitably christened following his potty-mouthed tirade – wasted little time in calling me into a meeting with Ashley. He wanted to take the temperature of the dressing room, and evidently thought of me as a kindred spirit.

To be honest, I wasn't sure how to take that.

'What's going on here, then?' he asked, brusquely, before I'd barely had time to settle in my seat. This was his version of consensual management, which cannot be found in the self-help section of your local bookstore. Never mind the bollocks, give me the truth.

He wanted to know the underlying problem; so, embracing his spirit of bluntness, I told him. He needed to cull a couple of the more temperamental foreign players, and warn the rest that cliques would not be tolerated. Ashley had to see sense in the transfer market, and sanction the purchase of seasoned English players, who'd give consistent seven-out-of-10 performances.

Charles N'Zogbia, about as useful in a dogfight as Charles Aznavour (ask your nan, kids), went to Wigan in an exchange deal involving Ryan Taylor. I'm not entirely sure whether wires were crossed or JFK regarded his birthplace, the Republic of Ireland, as a foreign land, but Shay Given was shipped out to Manchester City for £6m.

Kevin Nolan came in from Bolton on a four-and-a-half-year contract. The board had obviously not done their homework on him, since he is the strong-willed, highly driven sort of player who is unafraid of calling out his supposed elders and betters. It was all a bit higgledy-piggledy, but I still believe had Joe stayed in charge we would have avoided relegation.

He underwent a triple heart bypass operation in mid-February, and Chris Hughton became caretaker manager for the second time that season. I didn't play a single game for him, because I had broken my left foot on 28 January, in my first game back at City following my move. It was a freak injury, sustained when I sought to turn, but my rehab went well and I was training with the first team when I turned again, and felt my foot go pop.

An immediate scan suggested severe bone bruising, but a clean break would have been better, as I would have been able to get it pinned and allow nature to take its course. As the weeks out of the team extended to months, the pain refused to go away. Whenever I tried to run, it felt as if a nail was being hammered into the sole of my foot.

It's up to you whether you believe this, but there is a fair amount of guilt floating around in such a situation. I felt as if I was not earning my money, and the imminence of relegation challenged my professional pride. The emotional stakes were raised when Alan Shearer was brought in, on a whim and a prayer, with eight games remaining.

Superman had arrived to save the day. I had played golf with Al a couple of times, and shared a few pints without admitting I had once successfully badgered Dad to buy me his Blackburn Rovers shirt, with a red number nine on the back. I understood the hero worship, the schoolboy crush on the local lad who wheeled away from the Gallowgate with his right arm extended to the heavens in triumph.

I identified with what he represented as a player, and appreciated his disciplinarian approach as a manager. He stressed the club's social significance, and warned us about going out on the town when we were playing poorly. His mistake was to accuse the group of lacking fitness. His imposition of morning and afternoon sessions, so late in the season, was counterproductive.

His choice of Iain Dowie as assistant, which led to the ridiculous spectacle of a limited former player attempting to lecture Michael Owen on the finer aspects of goal scoring, completed the alienation. It took four games of Shearer's tenure, defeats against Chelsea and Tottenham punctuated by draws against Stoke and Portsmouth, for the mood to become funereal.

I was in the gym on the Monday morning, following the goalless home draw with Pompey, when Shearer approached to ask how I was getting on. I was working on the strength and flexibility of my ankle with one of the physios because, as I explained, I couldn't deal with any physical loading on my foot. I told him I was 'kind of' getting there.

'Look,' he said. 'We need you back. I've got no legs in the middle of the park, no mobility in there. I'm desperate for you. If you've got anything, then give it to us now. We need a bit of fire.'

I responded to the aura of a hero, rather than the desperation of a novice. I liaised with the medical staff and levelled with the manager. I would be half-fit, at best. I would have cortisone injections to numb the foot. They would reduce the pain, but compromise my quality. I promised to run around, get the rest of the team at it.

I had thought the lads would pull us out of trouble, but it didn't look promising. I told Al I didn't realistically fancy our chances at Liverpool, but if I got 70 or 80 minutes under my belt I reckoned I would be better placed to help us eke out the two wins we required in the final three games, against Middlesbrough, Fulham and Aston Villa.

So much for Joseph Anthony Barton and *The Art of War*.

When I look back at footage of that Anfield match I notice two things: the omnipresence of Xabi Alonso and the fact I am soon running with a limp. Cortisone combats inflammation, but its anaesthetic effect wears off after a while. That's when the body does its best to compensate, by producing adrenaline as a natural painkiller.

Xabi and I had history. He blamed me for knocking him out in what he thought was a deliberate clash of heads in one of our earliest contests, and I blamed him for stealing my move to Liverpool. All that remained to be agreed with City was the fee, when Rafa Benitez took over from Gerard Houllier. I was in Dubai when I was informed he had instead decided to sign a kid from Real Sociedad who had just broken into the Spanish national team.

That turned out to be £10.7m well spent. Xabi is one hell of a player, whose passes have great range and accuracy. Whenever we played, I sought to get the game on my terms, which were relentlessly physical. He didn't mind that, since he had been prepared for the remorselessness of English football by John Toshack, who made him captain of the Basque club at the age of 20.

The game at Anfield was less than 10 minutes old when he elbowed me in the back of the head as he ran past me to close down our fullback. I turned to the referee and wondered whether he had seen it. It was Phil Dowd, so he hadn't. I knew I would get a chance to even things up, and was prepared to wait as long as necessary.

Thirteen minutes remained. Liverpool were two up, cruising, and playing keep-ball. The Kop conducted an incessant, infuriating chant of 'Olé, olé olé!' The smug mood must have lulled Xabi into a false sense of security, because he retained possession near the corner flag fractionally longer than was prudent.

That gave me the opportunity to fly in, and disguise my malicious intent as best I could. The crowd bayed, and Alonso milked the moment with a barrel roll. I expected a yellow and was shown a red. That meant a three-match ban, the end of my season. I had let a lot of people down, not least the physios who had given me a chance to make a difference.

Shearer blanked me as I left the pitch, and was steaming when he entered the dressing room. I couldn't argue with him when he ranted at my idiocy. I didn't demur when he accused me of betraying my team-mates. But then he stepped over the line, and into mutually dangerous territory:

'You're a shithouse. You're a fucking coward. You tried to break his leg.'

This was personalised abuse, not professional analysis. I've never hidden my animosity towards Alonso. We'd had it out on many occasions, but kept it in check. Sure, I'd gone in late. He would be feeling it in the morning, but it wasn't a tackle designed to jeopardise his career. I have never tried to top him.

I told Shearer to fuck off.

The Duke, Mark Viduka, was sitting next to me. 'Leave it, leave it,' he hissed.

'No,' yelled Shearer. 'Let's hear what you have to say. The floor is yours.'

I'm conscious of the silence, the fascination of players watching the scene unfold through eyes shuttered in self-defence. Fuck it, he's getting it. I am only following orders.

'You don't want to deal with the truth. All you want to do is listen to the sycophants who surround you, telling you how great you are. Someone needs to tell you that it is not all about you. You were a great player, but that's done. Let's deal in reality, because I can deal with that. I've been a stupid cunt. What about you? Have you ever done anyone? Do you remember kicking Neil Lennon in the head? You're a cheat.

'You are miles off the mark, miles off. To be fair, that's where you've been at since you walked into this football club. I've been watching everything that's gone on. Keeping people out for afternoon sessions when it is about energy conservation and uniting the group? Is that a fucking wind-up? The training has been all wrong.

'I loved watching you as I was growing up, but you are no hero to me.'

Dowie decides to intervene, and squares up like a fighter in a fairground booth. I can't remember this, but the lads assured me afterwards I said, 'Hang on, you. You keep it shut, boxing-glove head.' That was his training-ground nickname, because, let's face it, he's never going to be accused of being a natural beauty.

I do recall the rest of my retaliatory volley. I called him a head on a stick, a cart horse. Dressing rooms are evil places in such circumstances. I was about 20 feet away from Shearer, and four of the senior pros eased into no-man's-land between us, just in case hostilities escalated. We shouldn't have spoken to one another in such terms, but swapping insults, however personal, is better than trading punches.

I was scapegoated, as expected, in the subsequent press conference but was caught off guard coming out of the cinema the following evening. I returned a missed call from a club official, who told me I was suspended until the end of the season. I was banned from the training ground; if I needed treatment, the physios had been instructed to work on me at home.

I was persona non grata at the three remaining matches, so completed my community service instead. I cut lawns, cleaned toilets, humped furniture and picked up litter in the local park. My only football involvement was coaching a group of underprivileged kids. I wanted Newcastle to stay up, but was made aware that Portsmouth, West Ham and Bolton were interested in taking me.

The Sky cameras loved the tears, tantrums and broken tiaras of that supine single-goal defeat at Villa Park, which meant we went down by a point after 16 seasons in the Premier League. The rebuilding process would, by its nature, be private and profound. Shearer preferred to return to punditry where, to be fair, he has excelled after losing his creosote conformity.

Chris Hughton stepped up once again, but Ashley didn't seem convinced, and asked me to play golf with him. He wanted to be my partner in a fourball match against Smudger Smith and Llambias, but I insisted on playing with my teammate; we beat the owner and his chum quite comfortably. We all understood the subtext, a chance to set a new agenda. I explained the need for stability, and the flaws in the Superman experiment. In as many words, he was told to trust an experienced core to support a rookie manager.

The agenda for a pivotal team meeting after an embarrassing 6-1 defeat at Leyton Orient in a pre-season friendly was set by a group that also included Nobby Nolan, Steve Harper and Nicky Butt. Immediate promotion would be achieved through self-policing; anyone who wanted to leave was advised to make arrangements asap. Cheats would be exposed and excluded.

The delicacy of the balance of power created complications. I apologised to Chris and his assistant Colin Calderwood for storming out of a training session following a disagreement about our defensive shape, which I insisted left us vulnerable to free kicks swung in from wide areas. He said he appreciated the gesture, but dropped me to the bench for the opening fixture of 2009/10, a 1-1 draw at West Bromwich Albion.

We were both victims of the subsequent scramble. He was rightly aggrieved, and understandably suspicious, when he was reminded of his caretaker status and ordered to reinstate me. I resented the implication that I'd conspired in my recall because, despite our occasional differences, I regarded Chris as a man of the greatest dignity, the highest integrity.

Ashley had evidently pulled on his hobnail boots after removing his golf shoes. The message came down from on high that they wanted me off the wage bill. If only it were that simple.

I did my best for Hughton, playing some part in six of the first eight games, but came off in the 59th minute of a 3-1 home win over Plymouth when the pain from my foot became too much to bear. I had become morose and withdrawn at home, crying my eyes out as I tended the foot for hours in a Game Ready ice machine. My brain was so scrambled I contemplated deliberately breaking it, to force the issue.

Experts seemed unable to help until I met James Calder, a London-based specialist. He recognised the bone in my foot had been under such stress that it had stopped regenerating. I required a new form of operation, in which he would drill holes in the bone to stimulate the healing process. He would be learning on the job, along with surgeons from Australia and the United States, who monitored the procedure on a video link.

I was wheeled into theatre on the promise I would be back playing in two months. That estimate doubled by the time the anaesthetic had worn off. I ended up being out for six months. I became deeply depressed, seized by a dread my career was over. Peter Kay was there for me, as ever. Jamie Murphy, the physio who shepherded me through the darkest valleys, was my confessor, tutor and, above all, my friend.

There were too many days when the curtains remained drawn, and I endured a form of mourning, but all things must pass, as George Harrison sang. I played in the final nine games of the season, including the 2-1 home win over Sheffield United on Easter Monday, 5 April, when promotion was confirmed with five matches to spare.

The highlight of the run-in was the 2-0 win at Plymouth Argyle that clinched the title. The Toon Army stormed the pitch at the final whistle, and lifted us all shoulder high; it was a surreal out-of-body experience, like drifting along on an inflatable lilo. The eight-hour coach journey home the following morning, necessary because flights had been grounded due to the Icelandic ash cloud, was equally bizarre. Most of us were drunk; the lightweights lay down in the aisle and tried to sleep.

I was delighted for Chris, who had been promoted from interim manager the previous October. His man management was occasionally questionable, but he gradually came to terms with the dynamics of a combative, committed group, tight-knit and raucous. A phenomenal rapport had been established between some combustible characters.

Malingerers and those with ulterior motives had been forced out. Senior players had been as good as their word. Nobby led by a captain's example. Even Andy Carroll, one of the worst trainers I had ever seen, was a force of nature when it mattered. We believed. There was an affinity with the aims of Chris, Colin Calderwood and Paul Barron, our goalkeeping coach. The madness had subsided.

Or so we all thought.

On the eve of the new season we were consumed by a dispute which set off a train of events that ultimately cost Chris his job. The argument soured, expanded and eventually brought several more of us down. It was triggered by the structure of a bonus-payment scheme, but boiled down to points of principle and Ashley's perception of power.

Negotiations dragged on for a month between the players' representatives, Nobby and our vice-captain Steve Harper, and the club. No Premier League squad had ever gone into a season without agreeing a performance-related deal, yet the night before our opening game at Old Trafford the situation was deadlocked, and inflamed.

Let's shelve, for the moment, the question of whether such an arrangement was strictly necessary, when basic wages were so high. I have some sympathy for that view, to be honest, but this involved custom and practice in modern football. Harps had called around the league, to check that our demands were at an acceptable level.

I consulted with the PFA, who confirmed that every member of the first-team squad had to sign the agreement for it to be valid. This was a problem, since I was in a militant mood. I didn't want to get dragged into the politics, but when the owner insisted we had to agree to his terms before a ball was kicked, I had little choice.

Chris retained our respect, but he was frantic, adamant we had to sort things out that night. I was incredulous, increasingly irate. I told him: 'We're playing Manchester United tomorrow. We don't need this shit. I don't need this shit. It is interfering with our preparations. Is this what we've come to?'

In hindsight, his alarm was understandable. Ashley regarded the episode as a critical test of his manager's credibility. If Chris could not enforce the owner's will, his power over his players was, to all intents and purposes, negligible. The strain was etched on his face the following morning, when he called a squad meeting and reiterated that bonuses had to be agreed before we made our bow on *Monday Night Football*.

I made a decision there and then. Fuck Ashley. I wasn't going to sign, regardless of the consequences. We were dealing with a tyrant who was trying to impose his will on us, an individual who uses financial pressure to force people to do as he wishes. Someone had to stand up to the bully. It might as well be me.

I've got enough money. He's a very rich man, but only a man. I've met him one on one and he is not as horrible as he appears when he goes through intermediaries. I had a vision of thrashing it out with him *mano a mano*, but the reality of the situation was that we were locked in yet another meeting at 4pm, four hours before kick-off.

I took the floor: 'Do you know what, lads? This will be worth about 85 grand a man, if we stay up. I'm not going to sell my soul to him for that. I want to stay in this league for what it means to me as a player, for the justification he can never understand or put a price on. This is about how we value ourselves as a group. It's not about money. I'm not signing.'

The debate swirled, from the potential impact on younger, lower-paid players, to the lunacy of the timing of such a manufactured crisis. Eight to 10 of the lads supported me. I tried to explain to Chris that our decision wasn't a personal snub, but the logic of the argument didn't register. He understood the decision's gravity when it was communicated to Llambias.

To no one's great surprise, we lost 3-0 to United. The agreement remained unsigned, and relationships festered. Speaking later, to those with better access to the corridors of power, Ashley had his Margaret Thatcher moment that night. Instead of vowing to smash the unions, he resolved to break up the players' leadership group.

We found our defiance liberating. Team spirit soared. We knew we were not going to get a bonus, but that was the point. We wouldn't let him undermine us. We were going to do well in spite of him. In fact, we were going to do well to spite him. Ashley might have owned the football club, but he didn't own us. It was a while before the guilt kicked in.

Chris bore the hangdog look of a man on borrowed time. He told me subsequently he made a point of wearing his best suit to West Ham on 23 October, because he was convinced he was about to be sacked and wanted to look presentable. A 2-1 win ensured his survival. To use his words, 'I took my coffin' to the Emirates a fortnight later, in expectation of summary execution.

We won again, beating Arsenal by an Andy Carroll goal. According to that day's papers, he and Nobby had marked the previous weekend's 5-1 win in the Tyne–Wear derby by embarking on a 14-hour drinking binge. I hardly helped by losing control in the following match, a 2-1 home defeat by Blackburn, which led to a three-game ban for punching Morten Gamst Pedersen in an off-the-ball incident.

I was still my own worst enemy. When Chris was finally sacked on 6 December 2010, the day after a dispiriting 3-1 defeat at the Hawthorns, I had every reason to examine my conscience. The club statement pointedly spoke about appointing a successor 'with more managerial experience'. It praised his 'exceptional character and commitment' without removing the implication he had not been strong enough to control his players.

Had I done the right thing, in the wrong way, by so blatantly confronting Ashley? Had I been seduced by my supposed influence? Had Newcastle somehow become a personalised vanity project? Had I overestimated what a football club means? Such challenging questions can only be answered through quiet contemplation.

CHAPTER THIRTEEN
THE PEOPLE'S GAME

On the advice of Steve Black, my friend and spiritual ally, I seek serenity in Liverpool's Anglican cathedral. My favourite place to sit and think is an alcove, close to the tomb of Frederick Arthur Stanley, 16th Earl of Derby. Legend has it that anyone who finds the minuscule bronze mouse hidden on this monument to a Victorian man of means must rub its nose and make a wish.

I am tempted . . .

His legacy, as a former Governor-General of Canada, includes the Stanley Cup, ice hockey's greatest prize. Stanley Park, the green lung between Everton and Liverpool football clubs, is named after him. He belonged to an age of poverty and paternalism, which coexisted in a city developed by the despair of the slave trade and the desperate ambition of Irish and Italian immigrants.

Pay £5.50 to reach the top of the cathedral's sandstone tower, and the panoramic landscape spread 154 metres below you takes in the Irish Sea and River Mersey, industry and distant hills. Gentrified streets, elegant rows of smart three-storey houses, were once slums which spread from the dockside before they were cleared into the hinterland.

Liverpool is a place of impulse and contradiction, emotion and discord. It is no wonder I feel so at home there. It is a political city, an opinionated city. People will happily engage you in conversation about football, or the issues of the day. I was weaned on stories of the Toxteth riots, and opposition to the poll tax.

I am resolutely agnostic, and find it difficult to reconcile the purity of unquestioning faith with the commercialism that means this building, the world's largest completed Anglican cathedral, lacks only a rollercoaster ride to relieve visitors of their loose change. Yet its scale is so imposing I can understand how supplicants are drawn in by a belief in a higher power.

It has become a cliché to speak of football grounds as modern cathedrals, but, like most clichés, the observation contains a grain of truth. There is a similar sense of worship, of population by ghosts. They are places where men and women congregate, to share and celebrate their dreams. They leave behind something of themselves, an intangible residue of raw emotion.

St James' Park is the classic cathedral on the hill. It dominates the Newcastle skyline. Sam Allardyce sold me its sanctity. He promised passion, a life lesson. I was touched immediately by the yearning of the fans, the longing for their loyalty to be at least appreciated, if not reciprocated. It sounds crazy to say this, but I have always seen myself as an extension of the people I play for.

I've fallen out with fans on more occasions than I care to remember. I've spoken my mind and delivered uncomfortable truths. I told QPR supporters I joined their club solely for financial reasons. It didn't make me try any less on the pitch, but I will never repeat the mistake of allowing money to be the single factor dictating an important decision.

It was strange. I was uneasy at QPR, because I suspected the fans would see through me. It made me realise what my underlying motive was, at that time, to be in the game. I needed to refresh myself. It was almost as if I had to fall out of love with football to fall madly in love with it again. I needed to sweep away all the crap that had accumulated around me.

People might struggle to understand this, because of the constant controversy and initial underachievement through injury, but even failure at Newcastle had its compensations. I have not forgotten the telling mixture of anger and hope prompted by our relegation. The sense of solidarity was special and somehow sacred.

Liverpool, my birthplace, is defined by football. Manchester, the city in which I grew up as a footballer, has two great clubs, surrounded by many others in Greater Manchester. In Newcastle there is only Newcastle. The Toon is the Toon. Even now, when I return, I am struck by the generosity of memory, the warmth of the welcome.

Football is still the people's game.

It is not the property of capitalist monsters who treat it as a plaything or a profit centre. I have the privilege of playing the game, for silly sums, but when I can no longer cut it I will revert to being a fan. I'm already discovering the joy of taking Cassius to matches. It is my game, his game, your game, our game. It represents our communities. We are the people who will prop it up long after the TV money has gone.

Players deserve to share the rewards of prosperity. I'm not justifying some of the scary numbers out there, but people aren't taking out TV subscriptions because they are fascinated by owners and their boardroom bullshit. They enjoy what we do, even if danger signs of disillusion are easily detectable. A balance needs to be struck before a wedge is driven between those who play and those who pay for the emotional release football can still provide.

A tipping point will come, when the finances of the game become unsustainable. I'm not Nostradamus, so I can't identify precise timings, but it is the nature of markets. They expand, explode and expire. There are already indications of an impending crash. More and more genuine football lovers are alienated by the elitism and arrogance of Premier League clubs who are quite happy to be marketed as tourist attractions.

Fans can make their presence felt. They are a positive force for the common good. Think of the impact of the boycott organised by Liverpool supporters in protest at ticket prices, the movement towards fan-owned clubs. Look across the Football League, and applaud well-organised campaigns against awful foreign owners at clubs like Leeds United and Charlton Athletic. Revolution is in the air.

Eventually, the corporate pigs who have grown fat at the trough will impose one price rise too many. People will say enough is enough. They will take up arms against the notion that it is necessary to push the game out of reach of those who sustained it when it was not so fashionable or profitable. They will reclaim their birthright.

What is football? As far as I'm concerned, it is players playing, and people watching. No one cares about the corporate conceit, the garbage that swirls around the hospitality industry. That is business, while football is art and science, poetry and theory.

Football is nothing without the fans. An empty stadium is as cold as Lord Derby's tomb. Empty seats are gravestones.

Football is nothing without footballers who reflect the passion they generate. Empty-hearted mercenaries, who apply the kiss of death to the badge of whatever club they happen to be earning from, inspire only anger and frustration.

The FA have lost sight of their responsibilities as guardians of the game. They have allowed themselves to become a pale imitation of the monster they spawned. The Premier League is cleverly presented and commercially astute, but tear off the mask of modernity and it is a vampire, which will suck the lifeblood out of the English game unless a stake is driven through its heart.

Economies have been ruined across European football by greed and larceny. Serie A bears the scars of neglect and nefarious activity. Ligue 1 in France has been enslaved by PSG, and their Qatari owners. Portugal's Primeira Liga is little more than a factory farm. Despite the defiance of Diego Simeone's Atletico Madrid team, La Liga is warped by the commercial, cultural and political influence of Barcelona and Real Madrid.

The bleakness of Blackburn, Chelsea, Manchester City and Manchester United buying the Premier League was at least neutralised last season by Leicester City. But the majority of our biggest clubs are global corporations, distanced from their communities. Foreign owners are going to ruin football as we once cherished it. Without wishing to belabour the point, as someone who has earned well from the game I understand people concluding that I am part of the problem.

I could quite easily keep my nut down, say nothing, and pick up a few quid. That isn't me. I've seen, on the streets where I grew up, what happens when it is every man for himself. You have to leave something for others. You can't just take, take, take, because bad things, or bad people, fill the resulting vacuum.

Why should my kids, their kids, and their kids' kids be denied the opportunity that we were given to fall in love with the game? If we keep going as we are they will be priced into indifference. Football has become a vehicle for the egos of owners who don't recognise their real role, as custodians of the game. Heritage must be cherished and protected with equal ferocity.

Sport often holds up a mirror to society. I learned about Jesse Owens and Hitler's Olympics as a child, without fully understanding the context of the story. It took time to appreciate the principled defiance of Muhammad Ali, and to grasp the significance of the silent, black-gloved protest of John Carlos and Tommie Smith at the Mexico Games in 1968.

The lack of jobs in Liverpool was a preoccupation in my formative years, the early nineties. War in Yugoslavia was a grainy, distant experience. It came to life much later, through the personal experiences of Serbian and Croatian team-mates. Football was the platform for ethnic and political tension which was to cost so many their lives.

Politically, I buck the trend, because as I have got older I have become more left wing. I grew up in a Labour heartland, where it was accepted that prominent sportsmen, like Robbie Fowler and the Wigan rugby league players, had the right to champion causes and provide social commentary. Margaret Thatcher was the devil, Neil Kinnock well-meaning in a bumbling sort of way. Tony Blair caught my attention when Noel Gallagher turned up at Number 10.

As you will have guessed, I wasn't exactly a responsible adult when I started to earn decent money. I didn't have the deepest understanding of economic issues beyond a vague belief that I had the right to spend what I earned on whatever I wanted. Some of the things I bought still make me shudder. As I have accumulated wealth I have moved left of centre, because I still identify with anyone under pressure to survive. That's not a party political stance, but a human point of view.

With Labour the dominant force and Grandad loving a political debate, it is likely I subliminally absorbed their principles from a young age. I haven't always voted for them, and won't do so simply because that is expected of someone with my heritage, but the selfishness and superficiality of their opponents is striking.

Footballers, as a breed, are pretty uniformly right wing, so that makes for some interesting conversations in the dressing room. Try explaining to a bunch of Premier League players that money gives you a certain status, but it doesn't make you happy. That's a tough gig, since they either look blankly at you or enquire what planet you beamed down from.

What I am saying, without being self-righteous about it, is that we have to be more mindful of what we leave for others. I'm not advocating the collapse of capitalism, but the imbalance between the accumulation of obscene wealth and the wider benefits of social progress is intolerable.

Look at the publication of the Panama papers earlier this year. That exposed the elite as venal, fearful people who will do anything to preserve their wealth. The rich are becoming richer. At least Lord Derby, their antecedent, did something positive with his money. He helped build the cathedral in which he was laid to rest.

Mike Ashley will argue he has spent a lot of money on Newcastle United. But he is a businessman, who has made it known he will sell it for the right price. I stood my ground against him, after effectively telling him we didn't need a manager, didn't need his lapdog Llambias, and didn't need him or his money. In hindsight, that was too much for him to take. It smacked of a peasants' revolt.

Had I known at the time that I was triggering the avalanche that would bury Chris Hughton I might have behaved differently. But Chris was doomed, in any case, because of the nature of the beast he was dealing with. Look at the incredibly ruthless business model Ashley operates at Sports Direct.

He admitted to a panel of MPs that workers at the company's Derbyshire distribution centre were paid below the minimum wage. He conceded that a policy of fining staff for being late was unacceptable. Union officials spoke of a 'climate of fear'. An employee was said to have given birth in a toilet at the warehouse, due to fear of losing her job if she called in sick. Workers reportedly likened conditions to a 'gulag'. To be fair, Ashley promised changes to what were described as '19th-century working practices'. But should I have stood up against him? Of course. I am proud of having done so.

I didn't want to leave Newcastle United. I loved it there. I loved living in the city. I plan to be back there in some capacity in the future, when Ashley has gone. The reaction when I returned to play in Steve Harper's testimonial was ridiculously humbling, because I didn't produce the type of performances in my four years at the club that would have justified the acclaim.

Someone whose judgement and experience I trust told me I made a connection with the fans because I stood for something beyond my footballing ability. I was out of order several times. I said and did the wrong things. But my values were their values. I played, and knew what pulling on the shirt meant.

Standing up for my principles has, without a shadow of a doubt, cost me professionally and financially. You can be a dickhead and use a pile of cash as camouflage or you can front up and push for something in which you believe. Given the value I attached to the zebra stripes, I'm black and white in more senses than one.

Ashley's choice of Alan Pardew to succeed Chris was cunning, because of his working-class, building-site background. He is one of the better managers I have played for, but I don't feel the fans ever related to him. He justified their prejudices, because he looked like a stereotypical southern wide boy. He fancied himself a little too obviously for their tastes.

The average Geordie who works his bollocks off can't bring himself to give a good-looking Cockney lad the benefit of the doubt. He is much more comfortable with the grittiness of one of his own. That's why Alan Shearer is idolised, and Pards was mistrusted. Rightly or wrongly, he was seen as Ashley's ambassador and apologist.

He wasn't exactly welcomed with open arms by the players. We were seething at the way they had got rid of Chris and, once we got wind of Pardew's impending arrival, during an afternoon conditioning session in the gym at the training ground, there was a full-scale rebellion. We weren't having him at any price.

Llambias was responsible for an unforgettable 'I am Spartacus' episode when he swaggered into the dressing room. 'I've heard a few of you have got a problem with our appointment,' he said, with a confidence that suggested he considered himself the owner's Rottweiler, rather than his poodle. 'Who are you? Let's be seeing you.'

I stood up straight away: 'Me.'

Smudger was almost on tiptoe: 'Me.'

Harps did an impromptu impression of a Schmeichel starburst: 'Me.'

The skipper, Nobby, wasn't about to be left out: 'Me.'

'Well, then,' said Llambias, as it soon became standing room only. 'What's your problem?'

I didn't speak to him with the respect he obviously expected, as managing director. I treated him as a cross between an imbecile and a naughty child.

Llambias was a cheeky bastard, and he was getting told. I could not have had less respect for him. I called him out as a casino manager who knew nothing about football. He thought he could treat people as playthings, just because he was given power by his mate. That's not how my world works. In my world, you earn your stripes.

He had sacked a noble man, who held himself with incredible dignity in the face of adversity. He had humiliated someone we cared about, someone who had conducted himself with an enlightened professionalism that contrasted with the malicious amateurism of his employers. Chris Hughton got them the promotion they needed to maximise their investment, and he was rewarded with contempt.

Alan Pardew had done nothing to deserve his job. I went back through his career, recycled the rumours about his personal life which spread like wildfire on the network of friendships between players at different clubs. He was arrogant, a wannabe playboy in a toyboy's Ferrari. I knew all this would get back, but at that point I simply didn't care. Others piled in behind me, but mine would be the first name mentioned when Llambias scuttled off to tell tales.

I admit I judged Pardew prematurely, superficially. No one who saw his excruciating dad dance on the touchline at Wembley, in celebration of Crystal Palace taking a lead they soon squandered to Manchester United in the 2016 FA Cup final, would ever accuse him of being shy and retiring. But there is a difference in substance between the private man and the public figure.

He handled himself very smartly when he arrived. He visited Nobby and Harps, who were astute politically, in their homes. Smudger and I had intensive individual discussions for a couple of hours in his office. I levelled with him, told him what I thought of him as a man and a football manager. He spoke candidly and passionately about what he expected of himself and what he would demand from me.

I was impressed. He had answered my assumption that he lacked substance. As I turned to leave, I told him: 'I didn't want you as manager. The group doesn't want you as manager. We admired Chris, and respected his values. But you've been honest with me. I'll give you the time of day. As long as you're straight with me, you'll never have an issue.'

He shook my hand, and gave me his word. We never had a problem from that moment. I scored in his first match, against Liverpool, and dedicated the win to Chris and the staff who had lost their jobs. Pards understood the gesture and offered his complete support when we had to deal with one of those synthetic controversies that have punctuated my career.

It was a niggly match, in which I had a running verbal battle with Fernando Torres. I motioned towards my groin and told him he lacked *cojones*, the bollocks to make the most of his talent. That impulsive act was wilfully distorted, so I had to answer baseless accusations of homophobic abuse. Welcome to my world, gaffer.

I also used the Liverpool game to publicly criticise Ashley. It would have been easier to tug my forelock and turn a blind eye to the human wreckage he leaves in his wake. He obviously wanted me onside, and I could definitely have got an improved contract out of a bogus show of unity. But that isn't me. It will never be me.

Pards went out of his way to connect on a human level. His man management was excellent, and complemented by his coaching ability. His sessions were measured, interesting and intelligent. That combination of qualities translated into the development of a resilient squad who gave a fantastic set of supporters something to shout about.

The disenchanted group that Llambias tried to lecture would probably not have come back from 4-0 down at half-time, at home to Arsenal. I scored two penalties and the noise that engulfed us when Cheick Tiote equalised with three minutes to go was loud enough to be heard in Holland, across the North Sea. It was some goal, a 20-yard shot that fused power, timing and technique, and some celebration. We went nuts. Had the game lasted five more minutes we would have scored the winner.

It was the perfect way to end a bittersweet week in which Andy Carroll was sold to Liverpool. The fee, £35m, was huge, but Ashley and Llambias couldn't wait to cash in. It went against everything we had been told, about building a young and hungry squad. I was doubly annoyed because Andy and I combined really well.

Andy was a local lad, well liked, and I very much doubt that he wanted to go. He asked for a new contract at Newcastle to reflect his importance to the team, and the financial deal he was being offered by Liverpool. He was rebuffed, and given little option but to make a transfer request. It was another reminder we all have our price, our limits of usefulness.

I was playing really well, at one with the fans. I had 18 months remaining on my contract, one of those traditional bargaining points, and Llambias was eager to secure a deal that guaranteed my market value. My future paled into insignificance when I took a call from Georgia during winter training at a warm-weather camp in Portugal. She had miscarried in the early stages of pregnancy.

It was one of those moments when football and life intertwine. It had been our secret, and so many emotions swirled around. A surge of grief and devastation was quickly consumed by worry. My instinct was to jump on the first plane home, a plan Pards fully supported. Georgia insisted she was fine, getting all the support she needed from her mum. She persuaded me to stay on.

I felt powerless and it was only when I got home that I realised I should have been more insistent about returning to be at her side. The fear of not being able to have children was immediate and understandable. We were both ready for kids, and saw the doctor, who explained it was one of those things rather than the precursor of serious problems. We agreed that whenever she was ready we would try again.

How she had stayed with me was a source of wonder, given that our first date – a meal as part of a bigger group of friends – had to be abandoned when I got into a fight with a cokehead, who cold-cocked me with a punch to the face when I walked back from the toilet. The dispute, believe it or not, was triggered because he insisted our tables were too close together.

He was a huge lad. I managed to get him in a headlock and we spilled out into the street. I steered him into the shadows, out of sight of any CCTV cameras, and knocked him down three times because I turned it into a boxing match rather than a brawl. He ran away, promising to return the next day to shoot me, a plan he revised when he received a call from an old friend suggesting it wouldn't be in his best interests to do so.

Some of the lads on the estate told me later they had promised to intercept him. I laugh about it now, but, to them, that sort of threat was normal, rational. They became involved out of a strange loyalty to me, as one of their own. They were in their early twenties, and had been using knives since they were 15 or 16, so the mind boggles about what they intended to do to him.

Georgia had obviously gone by the time I returned to the restaurant. I thought I had blown my chances, but I am nothing if not a trier. She was attractive, intelligent and funny. I hung in there until we clicked. We moved in together and she transferred to Newcastle University, where she got her degree in fashion design, when I moved to the Northeast.

Nan is a great judge of character, and she fell for her almost as hard as I had. Georgia was nervous about meeting her for the first time, justifiably since I had told her all about the family's queen bee. Nan weighed up everything, from the modesty of Georgia's car to the values of her family, and the respect she showed in making a point of not staying overnight with me in her house.

She announced herself satisfied that Georgia was not a 'sunbed clone', to use her phrase for some of my previous girlfriends. It is wonderful to watch them together with Cassius and Pieta, and Nan never stops telling me how good she is for me. She's right, as she so often is.

Football, like many businesses, operates on the assumption that it exists in isolation. I was being pressurised into signing a new contract, but the original offer of a two-year extension, on the table when we were dealing with the miscarriage, was resubmitted towards the end of the season, with a wage decrease factored in.

I was settled, privately euphoric and simultaneously

petrified. Georgia was pregnant with Cassius, and we were trying to protect ourselves from further devastation by keeping the news to ourselves. This was our chance to put down roots, to plan family life from an unusual position of certainty.

I was ready to give Newcastle what theoretically would be my best years, and would have taken less money had Llambias made the conciliatory gesture of making it a three-year deal. When he refused, I decided to see out my existing contract. I wasn't stupid, since I knew I would be a decent proposition as a free transfer. This went down predictably badly.

Pards managed the situation as best he could, but was pressurised from above. Matters came to a head during the summer window, when Nobby Nolan dropped a division because Sam Allardyce gave him a five-year deal at West Ham. His departure could only have been a business decision, since he was a brilliant captain, a unifying force in the dressing room who had scored 30 goals from midfield in the two previous seasons.

Nobby had two years left on his contract, and Newcastle preferred to receive around £4m instead of paying him what he deserved. He told me he had felt disrespected because a contract offer from Newcastle had been withdrawn. He was a calming influence on me, and I was his deputy. When Fabricio Coloccini, who spoke little English, was named as Newcastle's new captain I knew my days were numbered, and that the club was changing around me.

I was officially recognised as vice-captain, but when Coloccini missed a pre-season friendly against Leeds United at the end of July 2011, I was overlooked again. That was a deliberately provocative act, since it belittled me in the eyes of my team-mates. I went mad, told Pardew to fuck off, and refused to shake his hand before the game. He took offence, and everyone else took to the trenches.

I was ordered to train alone, and made available as a free transfer. Derogatory stories mysteriously began to appear in the local press. It bore all the hallmarks of the sort of campaign that drove Kevin Keegan out of St James' Park. I know people think my skin is tougher than tungsten, but it is a basic human instinct to want to be appreciated. Being the victim of character assassination is unpleasant.

I know what I am about. I know why I am portrayed as I am. I've lost count of the times I've turned up to do interviews, where people are seeking soundbites to justify what they intended to write about me in any eventuality. I understand that is the way the media works, but it gets to me occasionally because I know it does not provide a true representation of who or what I am.

I'm not saying I didn't help them put me in the box they assembled for me. There are elements of my character that enabled them to construct the caricature. But an easy angle should not excuse distortion. I'm seen as a one-dimensional thug when, like all of us, I am a multifaceted individual. There's a lot more than meets the eye.

As a footballer, I can control things by how assiduously I prepare, and how well I perform on the pitch. As a man, a human being, I have minimal influence on the image of me, created by passing strangers who have access to a public platform. Peter Kay taught me to deal with the frustrations of that so vividly I can recall his advice in its entirety:

'Look. You can be the nicest person in the world, and try to please everybody. There will always be someone who turns around and calls you a shit. All you can be is yourself. People are going to judge you because you are vocal and opinionated.

When you say something, it reverberates, so you must expect to be judged.

'You can either say, "This is the price I must pay for the path I have chosen", or you say nothing. If you take the latter option your life will be easier in one sense, but much more difficult in another, because only you will know, deep down inside, that you have chosen to cower.'

I wasn't going to bow and scrape to the likes of Llambias and Ashley. I was at war with them, and had the means to answer back on my own terms. Newcastle United sent me a legal letter, warning that I would be in breach of contract if I used my Twitter account to comment on club affairs, but it was too late.

The genie was already out of the bottle.

CHAPTER FOURTEEN

THE MEDIUM IS THE MESSAGE

The first telephone call, made by Alexander Graham Bell to his assistant on 10 March 1876: 'Mr Watson, come here. I want to see you.'

The first words recorded on the phonograph, an invention announced by Thomas Edison on 21 November 1877: 'Mary had a little lamb.'

The first song in space, whistled by cosmonaut Yuri Gagarin aboard *Vostok 1* on 12 April 1961: 'The Motherland Hears, the Motherland Knows'.

The first message transmitted from the surface of the moon, by Apollo 11 astronaut Buzz Aldrin on 20 July 1969: 'Contact light . . . OK, engine stop.'

The first tweet by @Joey7Barton, at 9.20am on 26 May 2011: 'This is the 1st official tweet by me. I know a few have tried to be me but this really is . . .'

Doesn't really have the ring of history, does it? It barely deserved the response, of 52 retweets and 16 likes. One tart observation, 'Who would want to be you?', set the tone for the madness to come. I have in excess of 3 million Twitter followers, though if I described that term as slightly Orwellian, given its implication of slavish devotion, I'd probably get slaughtered as a pseudo-intellectual.

For the record, I have variously quoted authors, inventors, politicians and philosophers because I happened to be reading them at the time, and they matched my mood or stimulated my interest. The accelerated development of social media co-incided with a period of my life when I consciously decided to push my boundaries. I had time on my hands and brain cells to spare, since I was sober and no longer a city-centre accident, waiting to happen.

I wasn't under any illusion. The average person on the street had a really negative opinion of me. Harsher elements of my character, a necessary evil that enabled me to survive St John's and football's rat runs, were refracted through the prism of the mass media. To address the misconceptions I had to approach things differently.

Peter Kay, typically, was the catalyst. He challenged me to challenge myself. What was I actually interested in? What did I want to get into? I became a knowledge junkie, and started by studying the contrasting characters of Churchill and Roosevelt, through the political and military strategies of the Second World War. I read voraciously and the identity of the historical figure with whom I most identified may not surprise you.

It was Genghis Khan.

He is portrayed as the epitome of evil with good reason, considering that he was responsible for the massacre of millions, yet his achievements would have been impossible had he been the savage barbarian he is popularly depicted as. He united the Mongols, ruled over a vast empire, delegated responsibility to his generals and set up lines of communications in an era in which messages were delivered on horseback.

He introduced a uniform system of writing, practised meritocracy and encouraged religious tolerance. He opened up the Silk Route and expanded trade and cultural contact with Christian Europe and Muslim tribes in Southwest Asia. Before his death, and burial in an unmarked grave in Mongolia, he appointed his successor and assigned special responsibilities to his sons and grandsons. That is an incredible feat of leadership.

Similarly, Churchill, the classic wartime leader, fascinated me because of the contrast between his inspirational public persona and his darker, deeper, more fallible private side. He was disliked on an individual level by those closest to him, but understood the power of solidarity and the human spirit.

I've little time for mundane people who are afraid of engagement and prefer to coast along the middle lane of life. I tried to get there once, but found my niche on the margins. It is important to interact. If you have an opinion, express it. But if someone asks you to share your views, make sure you've got credibility through research and reason.

I used to randomly pontificate on things I didn't truly grasp simply because I'd been asked to do so. I knew, deep down, no one really gave a shit what I thought, and they were probably waiting to catch me out, but I figured the worst thing they could do would be to ignore me. This may be counterintuitive to some of my critics, but social media stopped me becoming a rent-a-quote mediocrity.

I'd been alerted to Twitter by Andy 'Tagger' Taylor. He was working with Newcastle for Puma at the time, and was evangelical about the potential of a platform which gave me the ability to bypass the threshing process of old-media bias and superficiality. I had quietly joined it in June 2010 without posting, and studied it for nearly a year before taking the plunge. What did I have to lose?

I had a new medium to match a new mindset. It might have been the equivalent of letting a pyromaniac loose in a firework factory, but initial trivialities gave way to something more strategic, as I discovered I could set my own agenda. No more quotes taken out of context to suit a warped narrative. No more leaks about me, full of holes.

This was a rapier compared to the baseball bat wielded by the Newcastle board, who became increasingly distracted by my candour and carefully planned defiance. As my audience grew with a speed that staggered me, I could distance myself from football's exaggerated importance, and address a range of subjects that moved me, from music to social injustice.

I want to stress I am not claiming any credit here, because I remain in awe of the Hillsborough families, whose refusal to yield in the face of institutionalised abuse, criminality and deceit resulted in justice for their loved ones, in the form of a jury's verdict that the victims had been unlawfully killed. But their heroic 27-year pursuit of truth gave me an insight into my sudden ability to assist change.

I used Twitter to support campaigners' calls for the government to withdraw opposition to full disclosure of documents relating to the disaster. It was a small, heartfelt gesture; over the course of a day I posted 40 or so tweets, urging right-minded readers to sign an electronic petition. I lobbied celebrities to amplify my calls, and the 100,000 signatures required to force an emergency debate were soon secured.

I was consumed by a sense of pride, for my city rather than myself, and a feeling of immense privilege when I was invited to be in the gallery at the House of Commons to hear Steve Rotheram, MP for Liverpool Walton, give the speech that held the authorities to account. It is easy to be cynical about the playground pettiness of party politics, but this, surely, was democracy in action.

Inevitably, startled media corporations and football industry insiders tried to put me back in my box. They lampooned me as a Nietzsche-quoting jailbird. They simply couldn't get their heads around a footballer prepared to talk about something other than his latest car, his PlayStation skills, or the banging tunes he picked up on in Ibiza. Truth be told, I enjoyed creating confusion. It was stimulating. They were like ageing, lazy cats, trying to catch a lively young mouse.

Some of my most infamous targets, such as the illiterates on *TOWIE*, the shy and retiring Piers Morgan and the Brazilian captain of PSG, Thiago Silva, were selected mischievously. Others, like Alan Shearer and his deceptively doe-eyed chum Gary Lineker, had deeper significance. Of course, I made rash snap judgements, most notably when I prematurely dismissed Neymar as football's answer to Justin Bieber. It was all part of the fun of the fair.

Already, digital communications are so pervasive that I find myself yearning for the innocence of a handwritten letter, or the clarity of a telephone call over a landline. Twitter has a built-in obsolescence, because, as Stephen Fry suggested, there are now too many people in the swimming pool, but the principle of instant, direct and personal communication is here to stay.

Trolls are becoming increasingly vindictive, an affront to basic decency, and need sorting out. I've got a degree of self-protection, since I have learned to zone out from abuse that comes with the territory. Being booed every time I touch the ball, and being told by knuckle-draggers that I'm a piece of shit, tends to dull the senses.

The dullards who took the piss when I dwelled upon the disciplines of philosophy, and recycled the wisdom of men like Aristotle, Seneca and Plato, spectacularly missed the point. My interest was the result of a deeper way of thinking, inquisitiveness rather than pretension. I have become conditioned to looking beyond the obvious.

Look at a glass of water, for instance. Most people see it literally, as a container filled with clear fluid. I'm now disposed to look at it from different angles. I'll study the sunlight glinting through the glass, and across the liquid. I'll recognise the beauty in the fragmentation of the ice. I'll appreciate the zest of the lemon slice, and the practicality of the plastic straw.

If you are wondering, by the way, I've been in worse places than Pseuds Corner.

The old me demanded information and reached an immediate conclusion. Bang. Now I defer judgement, because I'm interested in other people's take on things. I may not agree with an alternative point of view, but I learn much more by not being so dogmatic. People fascinate me, because of the iceberg effect. There is so much going on beneath the surface.

I always thought I would be smart enough to avoid jail, and can understand people thinking, 'It will never happen to me', because they believe it takes an extreme set of circumstances to end up behind bars. The criminal system is screaming out for reform because it is paralysed by people who thought they were a million miles away from jail, when they were only a heartbeat from being locked up.

Think of a prison as a deep-sea trawler. The lowest of the low get hauled in, but what shocked me was the arbitrary nature of the rest of the catch. It includes victims of circumstance, like the family man who had two drinks too many and hurt innocent bystanders in a car crash. It ensnares dim-witted petty criminals and desperate credit defaulters. Before you ask, I deserved to be in there with them.

My best personality trait is my mental agility. I can condense situations into bite-sized chunks, and deal with adversity or success without getting carried away by either. Most people never have a go at life because they are too scared of failing. They never jump off the diving board because they are afraid of making a splash. Me? I bomb from the top board for bloody Britain ...

I find balance in madness, which helps because things don't always work according to plan. Experiences I felt were grave setbacks, like going to jail, ended up as genuine blessings. What I initially regarded as a blessing, fame, tricked me into making mistakes. I can cope across what we are taught to consider a rigid social structure. Within two or three years of being in a cell I was in the owners' enclosure at Royal Ascot, interacting with the privileged minority.

I am proud of my working-class heritage, without being obsessed by it. I think someone from my background cherishes education and intellectual advancement, because social mobility, to give it its political buzz phrase, is a relatively recent phenomenon. My chance came through the development of football as mass entertainment in an age of huge technological change.

I fitted the prejudicial working-class stereotype, by drinking and fighting. I can remember sitting in jail thinking, 'Fuck this. This is not me. This is not what I want to represent.' I sifted through the wreckage of the train crash and realised the driver was out of control, off his head.

I like listening to people who give a fuck, people who care, like Sir Dave Brailsford, cycling's innovator. I enjoy assessing their journeys and processes. I can relate to some, but not to others. Success doesn't just happen and successful people are not preordained. Some have it tough before they get there, others coast towards it. They find their own way. They have their own treasure maps.

I wouldn't recommend following mine, but I was lucky in finding something to love. Football is my passion. Not in an unadulterated way, like a fan, who has an almost happy ignorance of reality. Things can never be the same once you are inside the game. It is like discovering Mum and Dad arranging your presents under the tree on Christmas Eve. Dreams dissolve in an instant.

But it gave focus to my battle to survive. I learned to enjoy the sunny days, the fleeting brightness, because I came to terms with the fact that there would also be shitty days, when bad stuff happens. I was determined to let nothing pass me by. Imagine reaching 70, 80, and being told you have a terminal illness, knowing you've had your head down for so long you have never enjoyed the view.

I'm not intimidated by opportunity. People tuned in to *Question Time* to watch me, on the most popular political programme in the UK, because they expected to see some sort of performing chimpanzee. They were evidently surprised to discover a footballer whose knowledge extended beyond an appreciation of the sauces on offer at Nando's.

I was writing for the *Big Issue* at the time, exploring an unlimited range of topics which included the future of the NHS, the conflict between Israel and Palestine, the scourge of unemployment, the pernicious influence of Olympic sponsors, and England's chronic cultural fear of ambition. I wasn't a role model, and my views lacked the gravity of a great sportsman like Shaun Edwards coming out in support of the miners, but I understood the power of my profile.

David Beckham can project the shiny One Direction version of football, but that's not my reality. I like to think I prove that big mistakes are not necessarily fatal. I knew I would walk into that TV studio undervalued and underestimated. They'd expect a monosyllabic malcontent who couldn't hold a conversation.

The prevailing view of me in media central was voiced by Jeremy Paxman, when he introduced me on *Newsnight* as 'a man with two convictions for violence and one appearance for England'. Fair do's, though he was, by that time, straying into the realms of caricature himself. *Question Time* obviously suspected I was box office, because they spent 18 months trying to get me to appear.

If this was going to be regarded as my cup final, I decided to prepare for it appropriately. I asked the lady who wanted to book me for the programme to invite me behind the scenes. I had grown up watching the programme, and was aware that a lot of people were waiting to see my facade crumble, but I came away from the live transmission convinced I could hold my own.

I attended the post-show dinner, hosted by David Dimbleby, and sat next to Iain Duncan Smith, who had been the most polished guest, along with Theo Paphitis, the Millwall-supporting entrepreneur. The former Tory leader was pensions secretary at the time, and I disagreed with many of his political principles, but I related to him as a person. The enemy was out of uniform, and although his world view was completely different from mine he gave me an idea of what I was getting into.

It was a good recce mission, as was an invitation to address the Oxford Union. I spoke for an hour on topics as varied as homophobia in football, social marketing, and the merits of my education in the university of life. The experience enabled me to frame my thoughts, and introduced me to the disciplines of proper preparation.

Despite the storied setting, my approach wasn't a lot different from football: I formulated a game plan, based upon a summary of my strengths and a reasoned analysis of the threat represented by the opposition. It made a change to line up against planet-brained students rather than pea-brained midfield enforcers.

I had two coaches for *Question Time*, philosophy lecturer Raj Sehgal and Charlie Lesser, a retired coffee trader who had also enrolled on Raj's course at Roehampton University in southwest London. We had different perspectives on life, and the political process. It was refreshing for me, since my closest professional relationships are, inevitably, focused on the common ground of football.

Realistically, I had to appear on the programme outside the football season, so I agreed to do one based at Heathrow airport. I shared a panel that included universities and science minister David Willetts, shadow Scottish secretary Margaret Curran, UKIP MEP Louise Bours, and some jumped-up journo named Piers Morgan.

Raj commandeered a classroom and set up a mock programme. The only difference was this one lasted three days, instead of an hour. The first day involved Raj, me, and a whiteboard. We explored my beliefs, and drilled down into the issues of the day. The second featured politics students, rounded up with the promise that they could go for the jugular. The third was a caffeine-fuelled wrap-up. It left me wondering what on earth I had let myself in for.

There was an element of educated guesswork in the preparation. Plans for a new Heathrow runway were obviously going to be on the agenda. The seemingly endless Chilcot inquiry was grinding on. UKIP were somehow squaring the circle of reviling Europe and contending in the European elections. I had no intention of making use of my specialist subject, football. A win for me was not making a fool of myself.

The final council of war was convened at breakfast on the day of the broadcast. It included Raj, Charlie, Georgia and Nan, who was appalled when I told her I wasn't going to be wearing a suit. I didn't want to dress as a politician; I had no party affiliation although, like many sportsmen with a high public profile, I had been courted by them all.

I had no need of their regalia, the three-piece suit and colour-coded tie. I wanted to be myself. No one goes to a cricket match dressed as a cricketer, unless they are puddled. You shouldn't go to a football match dressed as a footballer unless you're below the age of eight. I wasn't on there as a machine politician. I wanted to be seen as the representative of a different demographic, and that was that. I hauled on smart casual trousers and a John Smedley tee-shirt.

Some people still expect me to be frothing at the mouth when they meet me. You can see the conflict in their faces, because they are baffled by the contrast between what they have been led to expect, and what is standing right in front of them. They have bought the bollocks, which is understandable because we all judge strangers in isolation.

I might have survived Strangeways, and played in front of a capacity crowd at Wembley, but Joe Barton is no different from Joe Blow. I was petrified when I was miked up and plonked on that panel. My imagination was in overdrive; I had this vision of millions sitting down to watch me star in car-crash TV. This was not a classroom, where I could ask for time to gather my thoughts. It was cameras, lights, action. I was in the modern equivalent of the lions' den.

The 15-minute warm-up section, before we go live from the floor of Terminal Two, doesn't do too much to ease the nerves. It gives me just enough time to agree with Piers that travel companies are exploiting hard-pressed parents, who are prevented from taking advantage of cheaper holidays in term time.

The theme tune strikes up, and Dimbleby is off and running. We're five minutes in, but it feels like 25. I finally get into the conversation, but I don't hear the applause for my disdain for the European parliament because I'm in the zone. It kicks off with the UKIP panellist, a sour woman representing a sad, dangerous party. I make an analogy about four ugly birds. I think it works, but then I worry. 'Shit, you've put your foot in it. You're fucked.'

I question the redaction of evidence to the Chilcot inquiry, and draw comparisons with the Hillsborough families' struggle for justice. Those who lost sons and daughters in the Iraq war have an identical right to the truth. I admit to nimbyism, because I live under the flightpath, and oppose a third runaway at Heathrow. I call for the government to combat obesity by introducing a voucher scheme for lower income families to buy fresh fruit and vegetables.

All too quickly, the credits roll. Everyone seems very happy.

I'm talking to Piers, who is very accomplished, when Dimbleby asks me to sit next to him at the dinner. Shit. This must be the TV equivalent of being summoned to the gaffer's office for a bollocking. He tells me not to be so daft when I try to apologise about the analogy. He thinks I came across well. My fears dissipate, because he has done this for years. He is a better barometer than Mr & Mrs Angry of Suburbia.

It was only when I watched the show back that I realised the audience was not as hostile as I imagined. I wasn't aware that the UKIP representative had stood for office in the Knowsley constituency, my neck of the woods. She took offence, and let herself down by coming out with the usual piffle about footballers' brains being in their boots. Not quite Simone de Beauvoir, was it?

If you're asking for my match ratings, I'd give myself a solid eight out of 10. The papers were full of it. The programme had record levels of engagement on social media. I wasn't custard-pied. I've been asked to do it again. I've no great yearning to do so, but will probably accept the invitation, because it was a great experience.

I'm nothing special; anyone who prepares well, and is socially and politically aware, could do it. I'm a firm believer that anyone can do anything if they set their mind to it. My progress from a social pariah to someone who is at least respected for his sincerity might be extreme, but people surpass what others believe to be their limits on a daily basis.

I am changing, as the world around me changes, but there will always be competing elements in how I am regarded. I was a terrorist in the eyes of people in positions of authority, such as the FA and football club board members, and a freedom fighter in the eyes of those fans who quite liked me for standing up for myself.

It is probably easier to pigeon-hole me as a rabble-rouser, and avoid the reality that I have begun consciously filtering what I have said publicly, over the last couple of years. Very few people see that. I'm still passionate, and occasionally revert to type by responding on the spur of the moment, but I'm no longer the kid who neither knew, nor cared, about the short-, medium- and long-term consequences of his actions.

I understand why many are waiting for the next explosion, the latest indiscretion. This book will probably be used as evidence for the prosecution, as well as for the defence. I've come to the conclusion that honesty is the best policy. Don't laugh at the back, but I've noticed a slight softening in attitudes towards me, following my work as a football commentator.

Radio is a fantastic medium, since it requires buy-in from the listener and gives me scope to share my enthusiasm for the game. It gives me the chance to look at things from a different perspective, and the process is surprisingly intimate. I was especially touched, during a co-commentary stint for the BBC at Leicester City towards the end of the 2015/16 season, to read a tweet from a blind listener, praising me for my insight. The thought that I had acted as someone's eyes and ears was mind-blowing.

I still have an awful lot of living to do, and have learned that influence is most easily extended when you are inside the system. I am a natural outsider, so my challenge is to instil trust in others, so they appreciate I am worthy of the privilege of that influence. That means taking notice of the tattoo I have on the back of my calf.

It is of a wolf, in profile. I've always related to the mythology of the lone wolf, fending for itself. I recognise the strength of the pack, but like to know that I am capable of hunting alone, if necessary. The tattoo reminds me of the famous Cherokee parable, in which a chief tells his grandson about the two wolves that live within us.

'A fight is going on inside me,' he says. 'It is a terrible fight. One wolf is evil. He is anger, envy, sorrow, regret, greed, arrogance, self-pity, guilt, resentment, inferiority, lies, false pride, superiority, self-doubt, and ego. The other is good. He is joy, peace, love, hope, serenity, humility, kindness, benevolence, empathy, generosity, truth, compassion, and faith. This same fight is going on inside you, and inside every other person, too.'

The boy asks the old man: 'Which wolf will win?'

The wizened chief replies: 'The one you feed.'

I am now more mindful of which wolf I feed. We all choose the wrong one, every now and again. We are all likely to make bad choices, fuel destructive attitudes and emotions. I am on patrol all the time, because I know the minute I let my guard drop and think I have both wolves under control, I will be vulnerable.

CHAPTER FIFTEEN
SWEET AND TENDER HOOLIGAN

We were about 10 minutes from Queens Park Rangers' training ground, where I intended to confirm my transfer, when Willie McKay's mobile rang. Sitting alongside him, in the front seat of his car, I could not fail to notice digital confirmation of the caller. 'Sir Alex', it read, and after pleasantries had been exchanged, the agent motioned to me and said, 'He's with me now. I'll put him on.'

I was greeted by a familiar Govan growl. 'How's things? I've seen what you're up to on Sky Sports News. Don't go doing anything silly now. Why don't you come here and we'll have a conversation?' Hallelujah! Finally a big club, and a great manager, had come to their senses. I would give Manchester United's midfield a bit of bite, an injection of urgency.

We spoke about my role, and the extent of my ambition, before he rang off with promises to sort the formalities. 'What are you waiting for?' I asked McKay, as I handed back his phone. 'Turn the bloody car around.' I expected him to be alarmed, angry, because he was representing QPR in the proposed deal. Instead, he speared me with a cheesy, triumphant smile.

'You soppy bastard.'

He couldn't wait to tell me I'd been stitched up, good and proper. The call was from a mate of his called Joe, whose Fergie impression was close to perfection. There would be no curtain call at Old Trafford, the Theatre of Dreams. My destination was a run-down former students' sports ground on the Heathrow flight path, and a club who thought cash would compensate for chaos. The next year would be carnage.

I signed for Rangers on the rebound from Arsenal. Pat Rice, Arsene Wenger's assistant, had told Peter Kay they fancied me. A meeting with me was in the manager's diary for the first Tuesday of the new season. He had the perfect opportunity to monitor my form three days before that, in what was to be my penultimate appearance for Newcastle, a goalless draw against his team at St James' Park.

Maybe word of my potential move had filtered through to the away dressing room. They queued up to have a dig, and referee Peter Walton missed Alex Song's stamp on me. If there was to be no red carpet, I made sure there was going to be a red card by going down like a sack of spuds when Gervinho slapped me. His outrage, on being sent off, was worth my booking.

Rice sent Pete a text soon after: 'Arsene says Joey will never play for this club.' That was a shame, since Neil Warnock at QPR was in another, much lower, league. I know all players are Pep Guardiola incarnate at about half-five every Saturday, but the consensus of my new team-mates was that Warnock was a man manager, plain and simple. The only way he could have been classified as a coach was if you had taken his teeth out and installed a set of seats in his mouth.

The manager was very much a junior partner in the negotiations, which resulted in a four-year contract worth £76,000 a week. I know, I know. It was silly money, but would you have turned it down? The deal was driven on a conference call from Malaysia by Tony Fernandes, who had purchased Bernie Ecclestone's shares that summer and controlled the club with the Mittals, one of Britain's wealthiest families.

QPR had assembled solid senior pros, including Clint Hill, Shaun Derry, Brad Orr, Jamie Mackie, Heidar Helguson and Paddy Kenny, but Warnock allowed the group to be compromised by a couple of overindulged wasters. He let the mavericks get away with murder, ignored the lack of unity, and tried to rule the rest by fear.

I hate such double standards, and the lads were all too willing to moan behind the manager's back, but I decided to speak as I found. Warnock has cultivated a media image as the stereotypical bluff, straight-talking Yorkshireman, but I thought him much colder and infinitely more fragile than he intends to appear.

He tried to get me onside by offering the captaincy, which I accepted with the proviso I would be in his face if I felt it necessary. The owners had great ambitions and grand schemes, which they seemed capable of financing, but it quickly became apparent that the club had tolerated second best for too long. It wasn't fit for purpose in the Premier League.

The physio was overworked, and there were long queues to see the solitary masseur. There weren't even plugs in the baths. The manager was a peripheral presence on the training ground for much of the week, and his coaches seemed complacent, a self-perpetuating boys' club. Very little work was done on the training pitches, even less on team shape or opposition analysis.

The principal problem manifested itself in a 1-0 home win over Chelsea that was to become notorious for John Terry's alleged racial abuse of Anton Ferdinand. I honestly had no idea of what had gone on until much later; I was too busy trying to ensure I stayed on the pitch after being one of 11 players booked in a match Chelsea ended with nine men.

It was a nasty, niggly game, but no one, least of all Anton it seemed, had any inkling of the magnitude of the controversy until the following day, when Sky highlighted the incident in a manner which demanded action. As strange as it sounds, we were all initially preoccupied by the latest spat involving Adel Taarabt.

He threw his toys out of the pram when I prevented him from wrestling the ball off Heidar, who won and converted the decisive penalty. It didn't take a genius to work out why that upset him; it was a live TV game and he had a childlike need to be the centre of attention. Taarabt literally stood and sulked for 10 minutes. He used to do the same when others were given preference over free kicks.

A key figure in the promotion season, he was given reason to believe his intermittently applied talent justified special treatment. His timekeeping was appalling, and his attitude towards the laundry lady was objectionable. He fiercely denied spitting at her, as she and some of the lads claimed, but he certainly tossed towels around the room when his kit wasn't folded to his liking.

It is easy to concentrate on the lowest common denominator, and accuse professional footballers of being pampered, but the vast majority of those I've played with and against down the years are respectful and grateful for the more menial work done on their behalf. Taarabt was a deeply divisive figure, and, as captain, I told Warnock his behaviour was unacceptable.

Yet he turned a blind eye to his excesses, and resentment

grew. Though his unpredictability made him an asset going forward, he was a liability defensively. The team could not afford to carry him against top-quality opposition. Taarabt pushed his luck too far when, on learning he would be on the bench for a game at Norwich City, he suddenly claimed he had picked up a back injury.

He obviously spent his free weekend at Lourdes, since he was miraculously fit when he ambled out, five minutes late, for a 2pm start at training on the following Monday. He went through the motions, pissing about until the boys had had enough. Warnock showed no sign of intervening, so I decided we had to get him out of the group by any means possible.

I made three ridiculously late tackles on him, enough to send the message the party was over. He hit the floor screaming and looked imploringly towards Warnock, who realised he had lost control and had his head down, studying his boots. The senior pros, who often joked that Taarabt must have had some dodgy photos of the manager in a safe deposit box in Hatton Garden, smirked.

No one expected Taarabt to train the following day, and it only took one tasty tackle for him to walk off. Instead of confronting the issue head-on, the manager sent him to a fitness camp in Italy. The next thing we knew, the club received a letter from his solicitor, accusing me of attempting to end his client's career.

Nonsense, of course, but it enabled me to thrash out the problem with Warnock and Phil Beard, the chief executive. I sensed their weakness, since instinct told me they felt threatened by the possibility of Taarabt going public with his unhappiness, but was enough of a pragmatist to realise that he needed to be reintegrated into the group, on at least a superficial level.

The price of the players' co-operation – the employment of an additional masseur – was eagerly accepted without changing the dynamics of the situation. We had reached that mythological point about which everyone outside football speculates, but very few understand. The manager had lost the dressing room. The slow degradation of trust and respect had become critical.

That happens at different rates to different individuals. Think of judgement on a sliding scale, between one and one hundred. Each manager is quietly given a nominal number by his players when he joins a club, dependent on reputation and achievement. An ex-England international, with a good coaching background, would come in at 80. A relatively unheralded lower-league manager, arriving at a big club, would slot in at around 20.

Each day is an examination of leadership, endeavour and character, which might just be the most important attribute of the lot. I tend to agree with one of the most famous observations made by legendary US college football coach Lou Holtz: 'You can tell a lot about a person's character, not by the mistakes he has made, but by how he has handled those mistakes.'

Let's look at our two imaginary examples. The upwardly mobile manager isn't intimidated by the scale of his new surroundings. He communicates well, builds his credit on a daily basis with the thoughtfulness of his sessions and the thoroughness of his preparation. His team thrives. He might have come in as a 20, but his score soon soars, to 80 and beyond.

Meanwhile, the celebrated former player speaks down to his staff. His players see him cowering, or making bad decisions. They start chuntering among themselves when they notice him picking on the younger, weaker members of the group. The team underachieves. He slides down the scale, consistently, until his score reaches the point of no return, let's say from 80 to 20.

A lot of players are sheep. They want to turn up and be told what to do. The best groups have five or six real leaders, who set the tone. One outstanding example was set by Jose Mourinho's first Chelsea team, and their so-called Untouchables – Ballack, Cech, Cole, Drogba, Essien, Lampard, Makelele and Terry. They were fantastic players, who knew how to handle the levers of power.

Rafa Benitez lost the survivors of that group, who responded to the more conciliatory style of Guus Hiddink, just as an earlier generation had to Roberto Di Matteo. I was as surprised as anyone when Mourinho failed to absorb an enduring lesson; he was an alienated, distracted and self-destructive figure when his second spell at Stamford Bridge ended unceremoniously.

Many managers make a point of throwing their arms around their players, but it is not just about being a nice guy. That might be enough to keep someone in a job in the short term, because the players are placed in a form of suspended animation by the lightness of the mood around the place, but it merely creates an illusion of harmony and efficiency.

Sean Dyche, at Burnley, rates highly on my scale. He's a man's man, who demands as much of himself as he does of his players. He makes small incremental improvements in those around him, on a daily basis. He might slip down a couple of points if he started banging tea cups at half-time, but they would soon be recovered because of the intelligence of his strategy and the depth of his character.

Players lead in certain ways. A good dressing room is big enough for the quiet, urgent type and the alpha male who feels the need to strut and shout. Bad teams tend to force people to the front, because they usually contain too many players who are content to live a quiet, comfortable life, regardless of the consequences.

My leadership was at the aggressive end of the spectrum. No shit Sherlock, I hear you say, but I made mistakes because of that. My mantra was that of one of my mentors, Arthur Cox: if it is going wrong then work fucking harder. It wasn't that simple. I learned through bitter experience the delicacy of the balance I needed to strike between being a strident voice and a source of measured advice.

Decisions about managerial futures are much more clinical these days. Chief executives and chairmen at modern football clubs are little different from their counterparts in other industries. They are answerable to investors, slaves to the share price, determined to avoid damage to the brand. They have no compunction in consulting senior players; their doors are ajar, if not obviously open.

Others had obviously been in before me when I was asked to see Tony Fernandes and Amit Bhatia, the vice chairman. The detail in their questions suggested they had been briefed beyond the usual tittle-tattle. They wanted my insight as captain, which I offered honestly, without malice or exaggeration. It felt like a considered process, rather than the random assembly of a firing squad.

Warnock obviously felt differently when he was sacked following a run of eight league games without a win and a scrambled FA Cup draw against MK Dons. He suggested he had been 'slowly poisoned' by shadowy figures inside and outside the club, who supposedly 'manipulated' an inexperienced board through social media.

He has his press pals, and said all he needed to say by pointedly refusing to talk about me. They did the rest. I returned fire on Twitter, likening him to Mike Bassett, star of the mockumentary about a tactically inept England manager who quotes Kipling and tells puzzled players 'just do whatever you want'.

To give him credit, Warnock at least answered the phone when I called to clear the air. I wasn't about to disagree when he insisted he had placed too much faith in his coaching staff. He stressed he was finished with football, but was out of the game for only 41 days before he became manager of Leeds United. That might give you a hint as to why we were destined never to see eye to eye.

Mark Hughes was appointed as Warnock's successor at QPR within 48 hours of his sacking, following a suspiciously swift and successful lobbying campaign. I did what all players do at such a crossroads, and called my mates who had played for him at Manchester City. It is fair to say the read on him wasn't entirely flattering.

I had an overwhelming sense of déjà vu as I settled down to another heart-to-heart in the tiny manager's office in the left-hand corner of the main Portakabin at the training ground. There was no point in being coy; I told Hughes about the divisions within the squad, and was upfront about the issues I discussed with the owners before Warnock's departure.

He was watchful, and spoke carefully, but seemed to accept my explanation and analysis at face value. He rejected my offer to give up the captaincy; it wasn't until he settled in, and started to throw his weight around, that I realised his trust was shallow, at best. He obviously intended to use my prominence within the group to his advantage.

The standard of our training sessions, and the quality of our pre-match planning, improved markedly. Yet my relationship with Hughes worsened when he began to call me out in front of the squad, often without reason. I got where he was coming from; he had survived some hard schools as a player, and wanted to make a point by publicly putting me, as a dominant personality, in my place.

I played along with it to a degree until his idea of internal discipline degenerated into personal belittlement. I wouldn't take that from anyone, even though I recognised weakness and vulnerability in his stage-managed shows of strength. There were times when I gave him too much leeway; he rightly substituted me 62 minutes into one of the worst performances of my career, against Liverpool at Loftus Road.

With me safely sidelined, and booed all the way to the bench, Rangers scored three times in the last 13 minutes to win 3-2. I had a whinge at the fans on social media, which wasn't that smart in retrospect, and was dropped for the following match, at Sunderland. He compounded the snub by making me warm up continually, with little apparent intention of putting me on. The Mackems gave me dog's abuse.

I wasn't in a great place, personally. I had started drinking again, and the reaction of Hughes to a brief, quickly forgotten spat with Shaun Derry during a 1-0 defeat at West Bromwich Albion proved to be the flashpoint. The manager threatened to strip me of the captaincy, but changed his mind after I told him he had lost me, for good.

He obviously had a mole in the dressing room because a little while after I told the lads about his blustering, he challenged me in front of them. I followed him down the corridor into his office, and closed the door behind us. There wasn't room to swing a cat, let alone a decent punch, but we squared up. I could see in his eyes, and his flared nostrils, that he was desperate to get it on. He was aggressive as a player, but as a manager knew he had more to lose.

I stopped just short of following my subsequent advice to Brad Orr, when he was trying to get Hughes to release him from his contract. That would have involved turning over the desk and sending the lot – laptop, scouting reports and the paraphernalia of management – crashing to the floor. We merely shouted and screamed at one another.

I left nothing unsaid. He knew how intensely I disliked him as a man, regardless of our differences in football philosophy. He must have been in shock, since he picked me for the final four games of the season. I played particularly well in a 1-0 win over Tottenham, a match in which Adel Taarabt surpassed himself by getting sent off after scoring the only goal.

No one seems to remember that we survived on the last day because Stoke City drew with Bolton Wanderers, who went down instead. It is remembered for Martin Tyler's orgasmic yelp of 'Aguerrroooooo' when the Argentine forward snatched the title for Manchester City with their second goal in added time, and for the mayhem triggered by my clash with his fellow countryman, Carlos Tevez.

They only run to plastic flags at the Etihad, but the reaction to my sending-off had the whiff of flaming torches, carried by a lynch mob. They called me an animal. I can't say that was unjust, but the slurs didn't take into account my uncanny clarity of thought during one of the most notorious sequences of my career.

I get asked about the incident all the time. I can rationalise it, without excusing it. It conformed to a pattern; most of my major controversies have been preceded by two to three months of intermittent turmoil, usually out of the public eye. It's a bit like a volcanic eruption. Pressure builds, plates shift and then booooom! . . . the pressure is released with spectacular, destructive force.

This will sound borderline insane, but I was completely in control after I responded to Tevez's sly punch to the side of my face by throwing an elbow. When I watch CCTV of the city-centre fight for which I was imprisoned, I am out of control. When I watch the Tevez controversy, I am analytical, detached.

I knew what was coming when referee Mike Dean advanced towards me after consulting with his linesman, Andy Garratt. Shaun Derry was on his shoulder, in his ear, but he was reaching into his pocket for the red card. I calmly handed Dezza the captain's armband when I heard Bobby Zamora hissing, 'Take one with you.' We laugh about it now, but I remember thinking, 'Good idea!'

I bought myself a couple of seconds by protesting, and the dominoes soon began to fall. Aguero was close by, and emotionally engaged because I'd cuffed his mate. I kicked him in the thigh, hoping he would retaliate, but he went down with the speed of an overmatched undercard fighter, seeking sanctuary on the canvas.

Vincent Kompany bustled forward, shoulders braced and chest extended. He was wide open for a punch, but I feigned a head butt to see if he would react. Tyler, a brilliant commentator, by the way, observed, 'This is crazy', but he couldn't read my mind. I was calmly considering the odds of taking on Joleon Lescott before Kevin Hitchcock and Eddie Niedzwiecki, the QPR coaches, could reach me.

Micah Richards, a friend from my City days, helped them hustle me off the pitch. It was only then that I spotted another unused substitute, Mario Balotelli, posturing like the comedy professional he was, and always will be. I headed for him before I realised the futility of fighting with him, since getting him sent off wouldn't influence the game.

Reality, and guilt, kicks in as I walk down the tunnel of my own accord. I've fucked my team. I've screwed things up, yet again. I am in deep, deep shit. As I stand under the shower I do what I tend to do in such circumstances. I distance myself from the inevitable consequences, try to deflect blame.

It is a default position that disturbs me, to be honest. It is self-delusion, a play on the words if, but and maybe. If that lad in Liverpool city centre hadn't kicked Nadine, I wouldn't have battered him. If Dabo hadn't turned and run at me, I wouldn't have taken him out. If Tandy hadn't set fire to my shirt, I wouldn't have attacked him with the first thing that came to hand.

My inner child, the immature character who is scared, vulnerable and fearful, tells me I'm powerless in those sorts of situations. But I am a grown man. I want to be seen as older, wiser, an elder statesman. The more mature, more rational part of my psyche scolds me, tells me I am better than such warped reasoning, such damaging behaviour.

The kid attacks, the man suffers. The kid says, 'Shit happens', the man feels remorse. I can't walk around every day, carrying the burden of that conflict. It is energy-consuming, and I just have to let things go. My problem, compounded by my reputation, is that others have no intention of doing so. They come for me.

Football has an unerring knack of highlighting personality defects. I watched the closing stages of the match at the entrance to the tunnel, where I had an uninterrupted view of Roberto Mancini's meltdown when City were losing 2-1 to ten men. I had never seen a manager lose the plot so completely. He was running up and down the touchline in a frenzy, continually screaming 'you are letting me down'.

Trust me, those sort of slurs are not washed away by

celebratory champagne. Players are used to dealing with pressurised situations, and that sort of weakness is neither forgiven nor forgotten. I am convinced that afternoon, and the scene of his greatest managerial achievement, signalled the beginning of the end for Mancini in Manchester. His players could no longer trust him.

Of course, I had more immediate matters to deal with. I was a mess after the match, and couldn't relate to everyone's relief at avoiding relegation. I even had a go at Samir Nasri for coming on to our team bus to share his joy at winning the title, because we had nothing to celebrate. The owner attempted to console me at the airport by praising my contribution to the season, but I wasn't convinced by the strength of Hughes' farewell handshake.

With good reason, since the club hierarchy met to decide my future before the FA disciplinary hearing into the City clusterfuck. I received an unprecedented 12-match ban and a £75,000 fine, exactly as had been predicted in that morning's papers. I am sure such prescience was coincidental, since briefing is obviously beneath the guardians of Our Great Game.

The rest was as per programme. I was assigned to the bomb squad on my return to training. The club fined me six weeks' wages and banned me from a pre-season trip to Asia. I had more chance of climbing Everest than retaining the captaincy. Hughes took time out from making some weird and wonderful signings to confide that he had sorted me out a loan deal at Sheffield Wednesday.

With as much diplomacy as I could muster, I told him to do one.

Did I need football at that stage of my life? No. Had I fallen out of love with everything to do with the game? Yes. Walk away, then. But why should I rip up a contract that still had three years to run? QPR had been desperate to make a statement by paying me a lot of money. Why make a fuss? I could sit there, let them all vilify me, and still have an easy life.

I'm no one's fool, since I offered Fernandes the option of sacking me. He would be obliged to pay me the £4.5m balance of a £6m signing-on fee, but would save on the basic wages liable as part of the original deal. He refused and was suitably astonished by my contingency plan. I wanted to be allowed to join Fleetwood Town, newly promoted into the Football League.

It was not as daft an idea as it might have sounded. I was good friends with Andy Pilley, the Fleetwood chairman, and with Andy Mangan, a forward who subsequently left, and is in his second season at Shrewsbury Town. I wanted to train hard, and make the best use of my time by reconnecting with old-school, mortgage-on-the-line, balls-out football.

I wasn't there for a long time, but a good time. Initially, I had no intention of playing any games, risking injury when several clubs, including Fenerbahce, were circling, but I was persuaded to have a 45-minute runout in a 4-0 friendly win over Kilmarnock. Micky Mellon, the Fleetwood manager, did a nice line in mock outrage when I subsequently missed a training session to travel to London.

There was literally a sliding-doors moment when I walked into the Chelsea Harbour Hotel. Jose Bosingwa was walking out, having completed his move to QPR. He would last less than a year, and be seen laughing when relegation was confirmed. My meeting with Vincent Labrune and Jose Anigo, respectively president and sporting director of Olympique de Marseille, was as amicable and productive as I could have hoped.

Conversation flowed freely for a couple of hours, despite the limitations of having to involve a translator. They were men of stature, whose intention was to progress from the Europa League to the Champions League. I think the depth of my knowledge of French football surprised them, and I had given prior thought to how I could best suit the team, as a deep-lying midfield player.

We discussed the politics of the far right, but only after I had reassured them that rumours I had a racist tattoo were unfounded. Fernandes subsequently removed the final barrier by agreeing to pay a small percentage of my wages. I thanked him, and suggested he should brace himself, because Rangers would not win a match for the first two months of the season. I was wrong. It was nearer three.

That was none of my concern, in the short term at least. I had the sense that Marseille fans liked their players to be distinctive, so I decided to make a political statement, of sorts, by wearing a black tee-shirt I had received from the Hillsborough Justice Campaign at my official unveiling in the south of France. It featured the names of the 96 victims on the front, and the heartfelt message – 'Don't buy the S*n' – on the back.

That gesture went down well, but I was unprepared for the scene that greeted me when I turned up to watch my new team-mates play Rennes at the Stade Velodrome. There, behind the goal, was a huge banner which recognised my twin passions, football and The Smiths. The message was written in white gothic letters on a red background.

'Welcome Sweet And Tender Hooligan.'

CHAPTER SIXTEEN

LOVE AND LOSS

'And it's a Grand Old Team to play for,
And it's a Grand Old Team to support,
And if you know your history,
It's enough to make your heart go wooooah.'

That, ladies and gentlemen, is the sound of my childhood. It is the terrace anthem that triggers my earliest memories of watching football at Goodison Park, the song which proclaims Everton's status as the People's Club. It hints at deeper passions, broader themes, and goes a long way to explaining why I found it so easy to settle in the south of France.

They know their history at Stade Velodrome, on the south side of the great Mediterranean port. Olympique de Marseille was formed in 1899, 71 years before Paris Saint-Germain, the club that represents the cultural arrogance and economic dominance of the French capital. L'OM are anchored to the people, with a fan base estimated at 14 million which stretches from Normandy to North Africa.

PSG are the plaything of the petit bourgeois, a product of

political expedience and a prime example of the rootlessness of much of the modern game. Purchased by the Qatar Sports Investment company and repackaged into a supposedly global brand, they are too posh to push in anything other than the Champions League. At some point, their importance as a marketing tool will diminish, the money will dry up and the mercenaries will melt away. All that will be left is a void, where tradition and community should be.

L'OM were the perfect club for me when I pitched up there in August 2012, at the start of a season's loan. They are a huge but very human organisation, a unifying force across different creeds and colours in a city that, like Liverpool, has been shaped by immigration. They romanticised me as a rebel and identified with me as a man. It is only now, with the passage of time, that I realise how much of an impact I made on them, and how much they made on me.

The people retain their love for those they adopt as one of their own. I was staggered by the warmth of the welcome I received when I returned to Marseille for this summer's European Championships. Riot police were on the prowl a matter of yards away, as the old port became the focal point of unrest, but groups of L'OM supporters encircled me. 'Come back,' they urged, 'we have no balls in our team.' Such fans remind me how important it is to relate to passion and ambition.

The club drove a hard bargain, so I gained the perspective of accepting a wage cut of around £25,000 a week for the season. Money was no longer the primary reason to play football. The media gave me room to breathe instead of endlessly recycling my rap sheet. They actually preferred tactical dissection of my performances to the usual cop-out, mock outrage.

People were intrigued, open-minded. I responded in kind

by being frank in interviews and embracing their enthusiasm. It made me stand out, because I was surprised by the distance between my new team-mates and the fans. They were haughty, wary. I didn't get it because I thought it was only in England that working-class lads made good, and forgot where they came from.

L'OM reminded me of Newcastle United, but on a slightly bigger scale. There would be a couple of hundred people at the training ground every day. They were young and old, and had come from all over France to pay their respects in return for fleeting recognition from the players. Most would drive straight past them on the way in, or out.

I was one of the few who stopped at the gates to sign something, or pose for a picture. I'd park up, get out of my club car, a Renault Clio, and spend half an hour with the fans. It was the least I could do; I was once that kid, waiting fruitlessly outside training grounds at Bellefield or Melwood on Merseyside. The disappointment of being ignored stayed with me.

Speaking to the fans, through friendly body language as much as the strangled Franglais I used in that infamous press conference after my debut, was part of my spiritual rehab. I formed a rapport with them. My team-mates struggled with such close contact, since they are taught to be suspicious of the politicised supporters' movements in French football.

The ultras are powerful lobbyists, with individual identities and tribal loyalties. The club's third kit is often in their colours – red, yellow and green in the case of the Velodrome's North Curve, which houses Marseille Trop Puissant, Yankee Nord Marseille, the Fanatics and Dodgers. A hard core known as Virage Nord are agents provocateurs, close to the away enclosure.

Similarly, the influence of the South Curve ultras was

recognised by the introduction of an orange change kit. That end of the ground is occupied by Commando Ultras 1984, the South Winners, Amis de l'OM and Club Central des Supporteurs. The groups are left wing politically, to a greater or lesser degree, and traditionally have the right to ask players to attend their functions.

As the resident *rosbif*, and time-serving enfant terrible, I was wanted by them all. I regarded it as a compliment rather than a chore, and wanted to thank them for embracing me as part of their football club. They gave me a greater understanding of the nature of the region, and I tried to put across the lessons of my own upbringing.

They left me in no doubt about my sacred duty, to kick anything that moved when we played PSG, whose investment in David Beckham typified the difference between the clubs. I've never bought into the purity of the Beckham brand, or his supposed world-class status, though his work ethic and ability to reinvent himself are exceptional, even in retirement.

PSG's other symbol of decadence, Zlatan Ibrahimovic, couldn't wait to introduce himself. I gave away about six inches and four stone, so the responsibility of front-screening him required a little devil and a lot of concentration. My plan was to disrupt him by jumping early and inviting physical contact. Once I felt his arms on me, I hit the deck.

The referee bought my ruse, and the Swede became increasingly irate. 'You are shitting your pants, tough guy,' Zlatan hissed, in heavily accented English. He called me a 'pussy', so I highlighted the size of his ski-slope nose. All a bit yah-boo-sucks-to-you, but the cameras caught my gesture. The media made a fuss, and the ultras loved it.

Integration is a tricky process at any new club. You have to be aware of existing hierarchies in the dressing room, and make rapid judgements of character. Since I had a ban to serve when I arrived at l'OM, my initial impact would be through my work rate in training. Only Loic Remy could beat me in the timed runs, which were the biggest outlet for my competitive instincts.

Training had greater subtlety than in England, increased intensity in short bursts because everything was geared to peaking on match day. Christophe Manouvrier, our head of football fitness, initially oversaw additional conditioning work for me since I didn't have that release. He would be my unwitting ambassador, my link to the group.

If he wanted me to do 10 uphill shuttle runs, I would throw in a couple extra for effect, knowing he had moaned about certain players who couldn't, or wouldn't reach his target. If he planned a 30-minute session, I'd stretch it to 45. The plan worked, because when Vincent Labrune, the club president, turned up, Christophe announced I was 'not right in the head'.

That was meant, and taken, as a compliment.

Things had come together, personally and professionally. The climate was great, and we had a Californian lifestyle. Looking down wooded hillsides and out on to the sweeping curve of the bay from the terrace of our rented villa, the rat runs of St John's had never seemed so remote. Yet the estate lived on, in my desperation to better myself.

French football developed my game immeasurably. It was more technical, surprisingly physical. Each team had a Vieira clone, who would seek to intimidate through his power and presence. Roles were much more defined: I was part of the defensive unit, given the responsibility of shielding and assisting the back four.

Playing slightly deeper, as a water carrier in the mould of Didier Deschamps, taught me how to read the game quicker in and out of possession. I began to see different shapes and angles, and learned to recognise small pockets of space in which to work. I even took perverse pleasure in helping to keep a clean sheet, something I thought only appealed to goalkeepers, centre backs and trainspotters.

We led Ligue 1 for a while, and were on pace to qualify automatically for the Champions League. Meanwhile, QPR had sacked Mark Hughes and were being pumped on a weekly basis at the bottom of the Premier League. I was delighted. Take sides against me, when my back is to the wall, and you deserve all you get. Fuck you, if you are suffering. It's your choice.

The English scouts I met in Marseille told me Rangers were missing me, the sweet-talking bastards. I helped them facilitate meetings, and offered insight into both team-mates and opponents. I even acted as unofficial translator, since that embarrassing *'Allo 'Allo!* moment – which reduced my brother Andrew and Tagger Taylor to tears of laughter – had improved my commitment to my French lessons.

No one believes me when I say my Franglais was a misguided attempt to mimic the accent of my interpreter at that press conference. To be honest, having seen the video which went viral, I can understand why. It is just one of life's little burdens . . .

Ambition and avarice recognise no borders, so I became used to being approached discreetly by team-mates, attracted by the money and global exposure generated by the Premier League. The biggest initial English target was Remy, who refused to take a meeting with Harry Redknapp, the new QPR manager, until he had checked him out through me.

In retrospect, I should have claimed commission, since he signed for a club record £8m, and used QPR as a shop window for subsequent moves to Newcastle and Chelsea. I preferred to count my blessings, because I loved the culture and had struck a chord with the fans. We finished runners-up behind PSG, so my ambition of playing club football at the highest level, in the Champions League, was within reach. I had left England under a cloud and saw no reason to go back.

Marseille wanted me to stay. I had dinner with Vincent, the president, and agreed a two-year deal worth 32,000 euros a week, provided I could come to some form of compromise with QPR, who were committed to paying me £76,000 a week over those two years. You don't ever 'earn' that type of money, because it is so unreal, but I was never going to walk away from my original contract, which was Tony Fernandes' solution.

We were at an impasse. Vincent tried to sweeten the pot with European bonuses and, more importantly, he promised me scope to move into coaching, initially through the academy. At some clubs such promises are empty; I had huge respect for him, and trusted him implicitly. He, in turn, recognised my wider importance, because of my popularity with the ultras.

Fernandes was playing the long game. I had to seek him out on my return to England, following a brief holiday, since there was no official correspondence regarding my future. He refused to budge on his negotiating stance even though, logically, my wages would be unsustainable in the Championship. Logic, I was to discover, was conspicuous by its absence from QPR's business plan.

He insisted he was happy to take the financial hit. I countered by pointing out the impossibility of returning to a club where the fans hated me. He sent me a series of texts along the lines of: 'Come back and lead us. It'll be a great story.' My replies were blunt, and to the point: 'Why? You backed Mark Hughes and fucked me off to France. Why should I save your arse now?'

I knew returning to Marseille wouldn't be an easy option. You get a sixth sense for teams on the turn; a few small cracks were beginning to emerge, which would result in l'OM finishing bottom of their Champions League group, and only sixth in Ligue 1. I never got a chance to prove my theory that I could be a galvanising figure in a transitional dressing room, since Vincent tired of waiting and recruited Dimitri Payet and Florian Thauvin.

I simply became less of a priority. Vincent kept me on a string for a while, but gradually it loosened, and eventually became limp. My chance had gone. That hurts, but that is football. It has a nasty habit of reinforcing your relative insignificance. I was back with the bomb squad at Harlington, checking out the liveries on the tail wings of the planes descending into Terminal 5 at Heathrow.

You don't even have the dignity of being invisible in such a situation. People used to go out of their way to avoid me in the training ground, as if I carried a fatal virus. Conversations would be cut short as I entered a room. Staff members would dive into the Portakabins when they saw me walk across the car park. Harry spoke to me briefly before the first-team group went on a pre-season tour, but managed to avoid me whenever possible.

I largely kept myself to myself, and operated a watching brief. My best relationship was with Steve McClaren. Mercifully, he had come in to help with the coaching after being sacked in his second spell as manager of Twente, whose board had revealingly short memories since he had led them to their only Eredivisie title.

Steve, oblivious to the force field of negativity, had an obvious affinity with me as one of the few English players to attempt to make a go of it in exile. He had a sharp football brain and an enquiring mind, which was a change at QPR. I sensed he was not a natural front man, and his sensitivity to public scorn was obvious when we spoke about interpretation of our 'foreign' accents. He couldn't laugh at his, as I did at mine.

It was cards-on-the-table time. I calculated that my stock would rise at l'OM if they stank the place out that season. I had maintained my personal relationships by acting correctly, showing appropriate respect to the club and supporters. A return remained on the agenda, at a date to be decided. No bridges had been burned, which was probably a first for me.

I had to make football's fickleness work in my favour. Invariably, you become a better player when you are not around and things go wrong. It wouldn't take a lot to turn the QPR fans in my favour, provided I put in the effort to get them promoted. I made that familiar journey to the manager's office, even though Harry hadn't spoken to me for three weeks.

'This is where it's at, H,' I said. 'The Marseille deal is dead in the water. I'll stay here for another year. You've got two options. You can isolate me; make me train with the reserves. I promise I won't interfere or give you a problem. Or you can let me play football, and I will give you everything I've got. I'll help you get where you need to go.'

All he needed was a vodka tonic, a camel-hair coat, and he'd have been back in the Winchester with his alter ego, Arthur Daley. 'Brilliant, Joe,' he said. 'Happy days. Good to hear that. If I was you I would have gone back to Marseille, but you're staying. You might as well join back in with the first team then.'

That was that. The following day he asked me if I fancied playing with the kids against Leyton Orient reserves, to get in a bit of match practice a week before the start of the season. He started me in the opening Championship fixture, a 2-1 win against Sheffield Wednesday at Loftus Road, and carried on as if nothing had happened. Harry's ability to move on, without regrets or grudges, is one of his great strengths. I was on a charabanc ride that was to end at Wembley.

To get there, I had to get the fans on board. The reaction to my return, against Wednesday, was mixed. Some booed, hopefully out of habit, and others were more sympathetic. That was vital, since I would have had little option but to head of out of Dodge had the reaction been overwhelmingly negative. At least I had the opportunity to shape my own destiny.

Peter Kay used the analogy of me as a car, to stress how I needed to keep working, not just in football but in life. Take your foot off the gas, he reasoned, and with the best will in the world you will be pulled back into bad habits. Stay on top of things, with a little low-key maintenance and the occasional oil change, and you will save yourself the expense and inconvenience of an engine replacement.

Pete knew all about writing off cars, metaphorically at least. He had been drink and drug free for more than 20 years, helping countless people in his sobriety. But who helps the helper, when the demons return? I did my best, because I would have done anything for a man who was a phenomenally positive influence on my life, but I'm haunted by my inadequacy and ineffectiveness.

I began to worry about him soon after I returned from France, when he confided he'd lost a lot of money gambling online. He knew I couldn't legitimise his lapse by simply paying the debt out of my own pocket, because that was contrary to his belief in actions and consequences. It was a moment of the harshest truth, which remains imprinted on my brain.

We are sitting on a bench in Richmond Park. He listens to me working through a minor problem, and suddenly announces he can no longer look me in the eye. 'I've got to tell you everything that has happened,' he says. 'I can't live with myself if I don't.' For the next half an hour his story, of creeping desperation in the face of another addiction, tumbles out.

I tell him to share with other people in his circle. I tell him we will work something out. I am humbled, because for me he is still on a pedestal. In my eyes he is infallible. He is confessing to being very human. Roles have been reversed, and I must do justice to his guidance by seeking a position of safety, if not serenity.

The footballer's pragmatism kicks in. I ask Pete about his assets. It turns out he has a riverboat, which I buy for way above the odds. I don't like sailing, and I'm easily seasick, but this reduces his expenses and gives him a chance to stabilise his life. It is only after his death that I discover he has also sold the deeds of the boat to another friend.

I will laugh at his subterfuge, because it doesn't interfere with the sanctity of his memory, but before then there will be many tears.

I stayed with him on and off for about five weeks, dividing my time between his flat and Georgia and the family in Liverpool. Pete continued to give his external lectures, and I began to pick up the rhythm of English football once again. I was playing well, and winning hearts and minds at QPR without it being a preoccupation.

I was fully aware of Pete's issues because he had basically drunk his pancreas away as a young man, but something wasn't quite right. I couldn't put my finger on it, other than sensing an atmosphere whenever I returned after a weekend away. By the Tuesday or Wednesday he would be back to normal and ready to share his insight. The fluctuation in tone and mood was unsettling.

On this particular evening, returning from a long weekend on Merseyside, I arranged to see him in a restaurant in Richmond. He was very rarely late, so when he was overdue I called him to check he was all right. He made absolutely no sense, and was in a dishevelled state when he eventually turned up. He claimed he had crashed his car, but it looked as if he had been in a fight, or the bushes.

Everything told me he was pissed, but I could smell no alcohol on him. He began telling me of blackouts, of losing three hours at a time. He had been changing his medication, and thought his new tablets didn't agree with him. I was scared, because he refused to go to hospital, insisting he would sleep it off.

I took him to see his sister Naomi, who lived nearby in Petersham. He was adamant he didn't want immediate treatment, so I monitored him overnight, before she took him to see his doctor the following morning. When I returned from training, his medication had been amended, and he had been ordered to rest. Over the next three days he slowly improved, without regaining his sharpness.

He enjoyed watching us beat Ipswich Town 1-0 with a goal in added time by Tom Hitchcock, the son of Kevin, our goalkeeping coach, but it was a brief respite. He was struggling, so I decided to stay down in London, with Georgia's blessing, in the week leading up to our next home game against Birmingham. He had been there for me when I needed him most. I would be there for him. It was the least I could do.

Getty Images

ed up for England, at last. Training with my fellow authors, Steven Gerrard
Frank Lampard.

PA

meo role, and a cap. Pressurising Andres Iniesta during my one England
earance, a 1-0 Spain win he regarded as the start of a three-year journey to
ning the World Cup in 2010.

Getty Images

Sam Allardyce sold me t
spirit of Newcastle Unite
in June 2007. I'd love to
go back there, perhaps a
coach, in the future.

Dark days. Released on bail from Walton jail, where my survival instincts kicked in.

Getty Images

Paying due respect to the Newcastle fans after my first game on bail, a 3-0
at Arsenal.

Getty Images

ıe moment every footballer
ars. I've suffered the medial
knee ligament injury, in
November 2008, which
ruined my season.

Getty Images

v my chance to even the score with Xabi Alonso, then saw red. My
ling off at Anfield let down my team-mates, but Alan Shearer, a rookie
ıager, let himself down.

PA/Empics

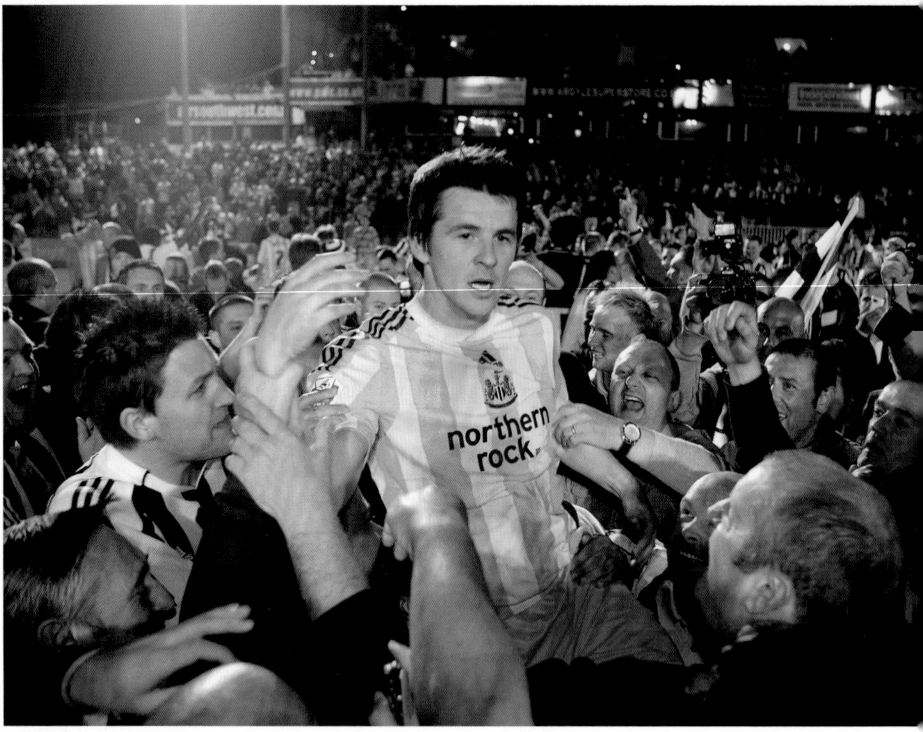

The Toon Army celebrate promotion by carrying us around the pitch at Plymouth. One of the most surreal and satisfying nights of my career.

Getty Images

Another manufactured controversy, this time involving Fernando Torres, w an early test of my relationship with Alan Pardew. I didn't want him to get Newcastle job, but he proved to be one of my better managers.

Getty Images

Neil Warnock – in charge when I moved to Queens Park Rangers, but not for long.

Getty Images

tdown at Manchester City on the final day of the 2011-12 season. Don't be ed – I was under complete control.

Getting up the nose of Zlatan Ibrahimovi during my time at L'Olympique de Marseille, a great club which provided me with a fantastic football education.

A Kaizen moment with Blackie. A unique, very special man who inspires me to continually improve.

Getty Images

Not quite on the shoulders of giants, but we helped QPR owner Tony Fernandes out of a hole by winning the 2014 Championship play-off.

PA

believed at Burnley. This goal, against local rivals Preston, was particularly
et.

sort of picture that becomes
mily heirloom. I hope Cassius
remember the day his dad won
motion, in the years to come.

Rangers had me at hello. What an institution. Celebrating my move to Ibrox with Bradley Orr, Eddy Jennings and Cassius.

Smiley, happy people. At Glastonbury with Georgia.

Pre-season training complete, a final chance to hit the pause button in the beautiful setting of Loch Lomond.

Inside my bub
of strength: a
family holiday
Quinta de Lag
in Portugal.

I am not really spiritual but I had a premonition on the Thursday night, the sort of feeling that stops me from being a full-blown atheist. Pete was perched on the window ledge of his flat in Kingston, chain-smoking, while I sat on the couch. We spoke for a good six hours, fuelled only by the occasional cup of coffee and an inexplicable desire to share.

Pete spoke to me, for the first and only time, about the pain of his recent divorce, and the difficulties of a new relationship. He was frustrated by his health problems, aware of his increasing lack of focus. He was proud of his intellect, stressed out because his memory was beginning to betray him. It was as if he was determined to make the most of one last burst of lucidity.

Our conversation ranged from the importance of reliable male role models to the political jigsaw puzzle of Winston Churchill's life and times. We discussed our strengths and our vulnerabilities. He planned to write a book, this book, and outlined where he saw me in the future, as a leader of men. We hadn't communicated on such a deep level for years.

I told him that, all being well with his health, I would have him in my first management team. He had the ability to make people feel more comfortable in their own skin. That would lead to them doing their job better. His skills were needed, because footballers are emotionally stunted, and liable to struggle in an environment that demands constant improvement and self-justification.

We spoke about where we had come from, what we had overcome. We expressed our pride in one another without embarrassment. We hugged before we called it a night and went to bed. Typical Pete, that. He used to laugh about how uncomfortable that made me when we first met. He explained the psychological aspects of the gesture and the cultural reflexes that made me recoil. It became a symbol of the bond we had created.

I played well in a 1-0 win against Birmingham, hitting the post and delivering the half-cleared free kick from which Charlie Austin scored his first QPR goal. I texted Pete after the game, and didn't get a reply until the following day. I decided to travel down to London first thing on Monday morning, go straight to training, and then stay with Pete after a meal in Knightsbridge with Ian Montone, a good friend who was over from America.

I got off the tube at South Kensington, and noticed a missed call from Naomi, Pete's sister. No worries, I thought, she was probably wondering if I fancied a cup of tea. When I got through to her she spoke haltingly: 'I found Pete dead this morning.' Boom. The weirdest thing was that I was so shocked I never cried. It took me about three days to process the news, emotionally, until I did so. Numbed, I just wandered about aimlessly for an hour.

Surely, it could not be real? I thought back to Thursday night, and that last embrace. I remembered Pete's ability to move from a search for the deepest meaning to ridiculous, close-to-the-bone humour, almost in the same sentence. I had this image of a smiling man, whose ability to remember people's names made them feel as if they were at the centre of his universe.

It's funny how grief makes the brain work. I could not get another image, of Pete at a supermarket checkout, out of my head. I was with Mash, one of my mates. We didn't know where to look when Pete started to ask the checkout lady whether she had kids. In a matter of seconds these passing strangers were swapping stories like old friends. He had this amazing knack of disarming people, bringing lightness into their lives.

I knew I had to remain strong for Pete's family, his mum,

brother Alan and Naomi. They were struggling to make sense of it all. I had spent the most time with him in the last couple of months of his life, so it was up to me to share, as Pete had done with me. They cried and laughed, as we told tales of his random nature.

I was devastated, but tried to think as he would have thought. When I spoke to his mum about him I used another of his analogies, about life being a bus journey. Each of us has an individual bus stop, where we are destined to disembark. We share the journey with special friends; some get off sooner than others. For some, seeing the bus disappear into the distance is a blessed relief.

I took solace in the knowledge that Pete knew where he was going, and when he would get off. I sensed he knew that life wasn't going to get an awful lot better for him, because of his health. He had almost died on the operating table 30 years before. He was told he'd be lucky to live for another five years, and had finally reached his bus stop. Had he remained on board, deteriorating to the point of complete dependency, he would only have suffered.

I still felt his spirit. I wasn't ashamed of crying, but something asked me what I was crying about. I realised it was a selfish act, a concentration on my own sense of loss. What about the positive energy Pete left behind? It was right that we should mourn his passing, but the more I thought about it, the more I felt his life should be celebrated.

I have no rational explanation why, a little later, I chanced upon a letter from Pete while clearing out the locker at my golf club. It was dated Friday, 16 May 2008, four days before I was due to be sentenced. The best way to gauge its emotional impact and its cherished symbolism is to reproduce it here, in its entirety:

Dear Joey,

Tuesday is approaching. Your immediate future will be decided by a court and a judge. I wanted to write to you, explaining that for me Tuesday's decision and verdict is rather immaterial, in as much as it doesn't change who you are.

As you are aware, I have much love and respect for you, and know the man you are. I also know the struggles you have endured in finding out who you are, your values, hopes and aspirations. Regardless of what occurs on Tuesday I would like you to know how proud I am of you, and of the mature being that you are turning into.

I am happy you are a part of my life, and hopefully will always be so. You have qualities that I seek for myself and search for in friendship. I will stand by your side, speak up for you and support you as long as you are willing to do these things for yourself. Your true character has emerged through all this adversity, and I believe, as I know you do, that everything happens for a reason.

Please remember this in times of trouble or trauma, and use the word 'God' in a way that suits you. For some it is from the Bible, others the universe, or from some form of life force which is present within them. Whatever suits you and reaches your spiritual side. The important thing to remember is that we are not God, and there is something out there more powerful than us.

In actual fact, as you know from your own experience, when you let go of a situation, keeping only your side of the street clean, amazing things happen and peace prevails. I truly respect you and believe in you.

Here the letter changes from elegant handwriting, in black pen, to capital letters, in red:

Our deepest fear is not that we are inadequate. Our deepest fear is that we are powerful beyond measure. It is our light, not our darkness, that most frightens us. We ask ourselves, 'Who am I to be brilliant, gorgeous, talented, fabulous?' Actually, who are you not to be so?

You are a child of God. Your playing small does not serve the world. There is nothing enlightened about shrinking so that other people won't feel insecure around you. We are all meant to shine as children do.

We were born to make manifest the glory of God that is within us all. It is not just in some of us. It is in everyone, and as we let our own light shine we unconsciously give other people permission to do the same. As we are liberated from our own fear, our presence automatically liberates others.

It is signed 'Peter', in black pen, almost as if it had been scribbled in haste. A coincidence that I found it when I did? I wonder . . .

Pete died soon after Grandad, who kept everything in. His generation was influenced by those who went into hospital, like his brother, and never came out. He insisted he didn't need a doctor. He showed no emotion. Don't worry about me. I'll crack on. That indomitable spirit, that dignity, was his legacy to me, and the rest of my family.

Pete's legacy is everywhere, captured for posterity in stories that can be kept as cherished secrets, or shouted from the rooftops as statements of intent. He left marker posts in the ground for me to map out my own journey. What could I be? What could I have done differently? What will my legacy be? What will my history say about me?

CHAPTER SEVENTEEN

THIS MATTERS, NOW

Just before Peter Kay died, I showed him a letter from a QPR supporter, which remained unsent for more than a year because the writer needed time to work through his disgust at my meltdown at Manchester City. Dr Raj Sehgal was finally ready to introduce me to the philosophy degree course he ran at Roehampton University.

Pete was so enthused he suggested we study together. It was the sort of extracurricular activity he relished, because it fitted his grand scheme of diluting football's dominant influence on my life. He recognised that the game stirred dangerous emotions, and believed in the perspective of a fully engaged mind.

His cremation, on one of those musty mornings that signal the arrival of autumn, was sad even though I had a sense of a life well lived, and a man well loved. Pete Townshend of The Who sent his condolences. My mentor was a firm friend of his, and had even helped design his kitchen. Such touching vignettes emphasised the void left behind him.

I spent an hour circulating at the family reception, where I spoke to Charlie Lesser. We had become extremely close, because of the impact Pete had on our lives. I told him I intended to do the course, because it was what our friend would have wanted. Charlie offered to be my companion, for a similar reason. I spent an hour with Raj that afternoon, and agreed to sit at the back of lectures for first-year students.

I took notes and was immediately drawn into the subject. It wasn't a dry academic exercise, pontification for pontification's sake, but a living, breathing topic. Historical figures had modern relevance. Beliefs could no longer be blind, because they were examined minutely. I understood why, in the original Greek, philosophy translates literally as 'love of wisdom'.

Raj thought I had been ambling along, intellectually. He surveyed the battlefield of my Twitter account, and recognised someone flirting with self-improvement through informal education. It was a clever analysis, since I had started to lose myself in bookshops; I loved their intimacy and anonymity. Whenever an individual or issue captured my imagination I would follow up recommendations, seek out as much information as possible.

The philosophy course, which I attended at least twice a week after training, gave structure to that process. It offered the opportunity to follow Immanuel Kant's advice: 'Dare to think.' Since I know such lines are foundation stones for the theory that I'm a jumped-up poseur, I'll cite Cicero in my defence: 'It is the peculiar quality of a fool to perceive the faults of others and to forget his own.'

I find my faults unforgettable, since they are many and varied. They manifested themselves in the classroom, where I drove fellow students to distraction by extending debates way beyond their allotted times with my moral meanderings. Some aspects of discussion, like the intrinsic difference between subjective and objective judgement, were relevant to my professional life; others were intriguingly abstract.

I was able to take a sniper's approach to the framing of my arguments, as opposed to the carpet-bombing I had previously indulged in. Raj's appraisal, based on grades over my first year, suggested a first-class degree was within reach if I committed to full-time study. That was obviously impractical, but we came to an understanding that my education will resume when I finish with football, or it finishes with me.

The influence of the course was subtle. I didn't exactly mellow, since I picked up 13 yellow cards over the season, but I saw additional sides of an argument. I needed to, because implosion was imminent. QPR fell out of the automatic promotion places due to a run of only two wins in eight matches. A subsequent 2-1 defeat to 10-man Bournemouth brought matters to a head.

Suddenly the unthinkable – failing to qualify for the play-offs – seemed very plausible. Leicester and Burnley were clear at the top. Derby and Wigan were seemingly irresistible. We were stalling, and vulnerable to late surges by the likes of Brighton, Reading, Blackburn and Ipswich. King-killers were on the loose.

For a change, I wasn't one of them. I respected Harry Redknapp for the respect he had shown me. He confided in me, asked for my views on personnel, playing patterns and tactical tweaks. In short, he was doing everything he should have been doing with his captain, Clint Hill. Harry was in danger of betraying his greatest gift.

He will admit his strength is not in taking training, as Steve McClaren had done to such effect before leaving to manage Derby. It is in gelling a group, assembling the right balance of players and letting them get on with it. I began to room with

Hilly once his best mate, Shaun Derry, left to manage Notts County, so was an obvious sounding board for the skipper's disenchantment.

He is a great lad, a stellar example to younger players through his work ethic. He will definitely go on to be an effective coach, perhaps a manager if he becomes more assertive. He resented Harry's lack of inclusivity, and I couldn't disagree when he complained of being disrespected. It was symptomatic of a wider issue, the negativity of players normally content to go with the flow.

Players can easily get managers the sack. Margins are so fine that indifference or malice can be disguised. All it takes is fractional slowness in closing down a shot, the concession of a small amount of space at a set piece or marginal failure to track a runner. Players can train without due care and attention, or undermine the group by talking behind a manager's back to easily led team-mates.

I would never do that, even if I disliked someone with a passion. I still tried for Mark Hughes even though I suspected he was hell-bent on getting me out of the club. It sounds a bit trite, but I have a strong sense of duty. Something wasn't right when I walked into the upstairs dining room at the training ground and heard a voice saying, 'We've got to mug him off.'

An entire table suddenly went very quiet. Interesting . . .

Experience told me they didn't want me to know the depth of feeling, because they feared the consequences if the manager discovered their identities. I joined them, and asked them to level with me. Perhaps my reputation for militancy counted for something, after all. They shared their concerns.

Harry was too detached on the training ground. He was playing at it, going through the motions. He had his favourites, but no one really knew where they stood. His tactics were shite. These were the generic complaints of a team in turmoil, and I, in turn, risked a heart-to-heart:

'You know what, lads? If I thought changing the manager now would get us promotion, I'd get in there myself. I'd tell him to his face to get out of the club. But that is not the answer. It doesn't matter who we plug in at this stage of the season. Going up is the only thing we need to focus on. Whatever happens after that happens.

'If we don't get into the Premier League, Armageddon's coming. Some of us will pack up and leave, but there is going to be a hole in a football club that has given our families a chance to live in nice houses. Whichever way we look at it, we are duty-bound to have a go for the fella, and for the generations of fans who will be here long after we have gone.'

I thought I had talked them round, though I had no idea what was said when I left to sit and think in a mercifully empty dressing room. I was exposed, whether I liked it or not. There would be no names mentioned, but I had to communicate the level of hostility. I walked down the corridor and asked Caroline, who has been secretary to no fewer than 35 QPR managers, whether Harry was about. I knocked on his door, and entered his office.

He was watching the Racing Channel, and it was pointless hedging my bets:

'Gaffer, I need to speak with you. I don't know how you've managed to do this, but everyone hates you. I've known managers polarise a dressing room, but I have never been in this situation, where no one has a positive word to say about you. That's difficult to do, because even if a fella is a cunt there will be people who like him for his arrogance.

'I'm in the middle here, H. I like you. I actually like you. You have been fair with me. You have done well for me when you could quite easily have bombed me out. When you put me back into the group I promised you I would give you everything I've got. I'm here now because of that promise. It is easy for me to buy into what is going on, go with the flow, and down tools, but that is not me . . .'

It was as if all the air had been sucked out of the solitary window, at the back of the room. Harry sighed, and looked suddenly weary. 'Joe, Joe, Joe,' he repeated. 'You'll know this one day. When you sit in this chair you will know what I'm up against. It is part and parcel of being a manager.'

The words came quickly: 'I swear to you, gaffer, I don't see how it is. It can't be because this is a horrible place to be. I'd hate knowing people feel the way they do, when they talk to me about you. I'd absolutely hate it. Surely, after everything you have done in your career, it can't be like this all the time.'

We spoke about how to improve things, quickly. I asked him to Google Steve Black, a motivational speaker and fitness consultant who mentored Jonny Wilkinson. We had been working together privately, away from the club for a couple of weeks, and I was convinced his positivity and sensitivity would create the best environment for a promotion push. I thought my optimism had registered when I turned to leave, but as I was about to open the door I heard an exasperated cry of 'Fucking hell . . .' It was Harry's way of telling me to fuck off.

I understood, but also appreciated Blackie's relevance. He is a very special man, unique. I'd watched Jonny play for Toulon when I was at Marseille, and marvelled at how self-contained he was in a combustible environment. Eddy Jennings, one of my closest friends, raved about Blackie's work with Freddie Woodman, a young goalkeeper at Newcastle.

Eddy arranged for us to meet in a bookshop near Leicester Square. We realised, instantly, how similar we were, and a half-hour's chat over coffee turned into a five-hour heart-to-heart. Blackie had an energy and a serenity that really registered, but I wasn't prepared for what hit me when we next met.

I expected an amicable meeting over lunch, airily discussing life, yet Blackie pushed my buttons for the first time. I gave a stereotypical football answer when he asked whether I thought I could improve. I told him I was in a toxic situation at QPR, concentrating on trying to stop the inevitable decline. I was 30, and honestly felt my best years were behind me. You hear it so often, from the media and even the clubs, that you blindly believe it.

Blackie didn't mince his words: 'How much better can you get? If you don't think you can get better, day by day, you might as well stay at home. What's the point in turning up if you don't think you can improve?'

There was no point in working with me if that was my attitude. I'd talked about my ambitions to coach and manage, but Blackie insisted I had to concentrate completely on becoming a better player. I was taken aback because no one had challenged me in a professional capacity with such force.

He wasn't aggressive, but I couldn't avoid the reality of what he was saying. I went for a walk along the Thames, to a prearranged meeting with Sir Clive Woodward, and couldn't get it out of my mind. He was talking common sense, but not common practice. I had talent, and needed to work on my strengths. If I worked to my weaknesses I would be mediocre, at best.

Blackie is a proponent of kaizen, the principle of continual improvement developed most prominently by Toyota in Japan. The aim is to improve incrementally, on a daily basis. Every action leads to review and reflection. Lessons are drawn from every experience. It has formed the basis of everything I have done in the last three years and will underpin everything I do in the future.

Blackie's impact on me was immediate. He spoke of me as a true alpha male, strong enough to acknowledge a soft core. He saw someone prepared to lay himself bare, and identified a pressing problem by referring to energy vampires, players who suck the lifeblood out of a team. They take many guises, but are uniformly dangerous.

He sent me into QPR, where loyalties had been abandoned or at the very least stretched, to deliver a direct message: 'Is your attitude worth catching? Infect the group if it is. If it isn't worth catching, because it is harmful to the group, then fuck off. We don't want vampires in the building. We don't need you, because what we are trying to do is hard enough as it is.'

Phil Beard, the chief executive, evidently had an efficient intelligence system. He learned of the sourness of mood, called a meeting of the senior pros, and asked what was going on. Even the quieter members of the group were straight in, leaving him in no doubt about the strength of feeling. I saw an ominous look of alarm spread across Phil's face and realised I had to front up:

'It's too late to change. We could bring Mourinho in, but we wouldn't go up. Any upheaval at this stage of the season and it will all go down the tubes. We can work this around, but we've got to be in it together. We've all got to step up. Being a good leader is not just about reacting when you're asked for an opinion. It is not about criticising, but about having solutions. It is providing an example everyone can follow.'

I mentioned Blackie's inspirational qualities again. Phil met him in Middlesbrough, and offered him a short-term consultancy role without Harry's blessing. The manager didn't even acknowledge his existence for the first week. It took a mad 5-2 home win over Nottingham Forest, which I missed through injury, to tip the balance.

I was at the mouth of the tunnel when I bumped into Jamie Redknapp, who was obviously and admirably watching his dad's back. I had noticed him in the directors' box, sitting next to Amit Bhatia, and explained the origins of the wobble while introducing him to Blackie. Whatever was said must have had an impact because by Monday morning Harry had done a 180-degree turn.

Blackie spent hours closeted in the manager's office. It can't have been easy for Harry. He was 67 and in some pain with his leg. He must have been wondering, 'Am I bowing out of the game here?' He knew how football worked. Someone could quite easily come in with a cattle gun, and put him out of his misery.

Did he want to go on, spending a significant amount of his life dealing with bullshit? He'd seen Sir Alex Ferguson get out at the top and here he was, scrapping in the Championship. Blackie helped him by bringing the principal coaches, Joe Jordan and Kevin Bond, out of their shells. 'You've got to help this fella,' he told them. 'He's hired you to help him. You're his lieutenants. Don't cower. If he does something you don't agree with, step up.'

His simplicity was his genius. He would have a quiet word with out-of-favour players – 'All right, son? What's happening with you?' – to ease their isolation. He challenged those more centrally involved to build credibility on a daily basis. 'You don't need to be great for a season,' he told us. 'All you need to be is great for six weeks. That's all we need.'

The group bonded behind a straightforward slogan: 'This matters, now.'

I felt we were invincible going into the playoffs, having finished fourth. Harry had been transformed. He rotated selection cleverly, and wound us up a treat by suggesting he'd been told we were the team everyone wanted to play. Our semi-final opponents Wigan, who finished the regular season like a juggernaut under Uwe Rosler, were being measured for their Wembley suits.

I bumped into Bondy in the canteen three days before the first leg, at the DW Stadium. 'The fucking gaffer wants to take them on,' he said in a low, conspiratorial voice which signalled his alarm at the prospect of unnecessary risk. 'He's talking about playing 4-4-2. I know you're not in until 10 tomorrow, but there's a coaches' meeting at nine. It wouldn't be a bad idea if you're around. I reckon you might be the only one he will listen to.'

This was a big call. Such meetings are traditionally off limits, but Blackie encouraged me to take up the invitation. He followed me into the coaches' room the following morning. Harry wasn't there but Bondy, who was by the whiteboard, welcomed us. Joe Jordan and Wally Downes, the other coaches, were at their desks.

Joe, in particular, didn't agree with my argument that we had no need to win at Wigan. They were flying but we could break them psychologically by defending intelligently and counterattacking quickly. Margins were fine, but sitting in made sense. Joe took the view that we had better players, players better suited to dictating the tempo.

The dynamics of the meeting were interesting. Harry came in and sat next to Joe. They had been together forever and were obviously comfortable, maybe too comfortable, in each other's company. Joe, who was adamant we needed to be on the front foot, and Wally were obviously going to side with the gaffer to protect their positions. Bondy was in danger of being railroaded.

I love Joe, and have had many good conversations with him, but he rarely challenged Harry. Managers need people around them who will tell them what they don't want to hear, so when he asked me to go through my game plan once again, I had my chance:

'Look, Joe. I'm out on the pitch. I'm feeling this. I'm telling you what the strength of this team is. Even if you don't agree with me, I'm going to change things because I am seeing the game from the centre of the park. I'm able to dictate our shape as the game warrants. I'll just pull those two wingers in. I'll pull the strikers in and get them to sit. And I'll close the shop.'

I could see Joe glancing at the manager, thinking, 'You're going to get fucking told now.' Yet he got a surprise. Harry paused for a second and said: 'Absolutely spot-on. That's how we've got to go there and play. We stifle them, take the game away from them, and beat them here under the lights.' Clearly energised, he then oversaw our best training session of the season.

Bondy was buzzing. The lads recognised the thought that had gone into the game plan. The pattern-of-play session, implementing a 4-5-1 system, was sharp and concentrated. That sense of togetherness transferred on to the pitch at the DW, where we did a job on them and got the goalless draw our diligence deserved.

It was a three-day turnaround, but Harry was on it. I went to see him in his hotel room the night before the game. 'Fuck it,' he announced. 'Now we're going for them.' He played two strikers, recalling Niko Kranjcar in a 4-4-2 that was solid enough to overcome the setback of an early James Perch goal. No one panicked, and Charlie Austin equalised from the penalty spot when Junior Hoilett was brought down by Gary Caldwell just inside the box.

There's a lot of bollocks spoken about the power of the huddle on the pitch. In most cases, they are just part of the show, posturing for the fans. I find them false, to tell the truth. But the one that featured players and staff, close to the touch-line before the start of extra time, was almost a transcendental experience. I'm convinced it put the finishing touch to the most complete team performance of my career.

I remember looking into the lads' eyes and thinking, 'This is over our dead bodies.' I have no recollection of what was said, because words were not that important. It was one of those in-the-trenches moments, when you realise your mates have got your back. I noticed the Wigan players glancing at us. I knew we had them. I knew they were not prepared to go as hard as we were. I felt in complete control.

I'd had the weirdest conversation with Blackie after leaving Harry's room the night before. He told me about his theory that there was an additional energy system, which very few people found because they were so tired, so consumed by cramp, that they lacked the will to push through an invisible psychological and physiological barrier.

I broke through in extra time that night. I was exhausted and in pain when Charlie gave us the lead, six minutes in. I thought I was about to seize up. Remembering what Blackie had said, I kept pushing, pushing. Suddenly, I was filled with apparently limitless energy. It was surreal. It was as if I was in a different solar system. Wigan threw the lot at us, but I had laser-light focus. I ran, I tackled, I dragged people with me. I don't care what anyone says, that was my greatest individual performance.

But here's the thing. I was completely detached from

the jubilation around me in the dressing room afterwards. Emptiness signalled a job only half done. Derby had blitzed Brighton in the other semi-final. Steve McClaren was at Loftus Road as part of the Sky commentary team. Forget the Premier League riches on offer at Wembley, £134m according to more excitable observers – this was a personal crusade, not a business transaction for him.

Harry came back from doing the press with a champagne-soaked suit, but I couldn't wait to get into him, and his coaching staff. We couldn't afford to have a single 95 per cent training session in the 11 days we had to prepare. Every team meeting, each drill, all our thoughts and actions had to be perfect. Otherwise the team with more natural talent, Derby, would win. They had a younger group, a more cohesive system, natural exuberance.

I sat our media team down, and told them we were not giving Derby anything to work with. We would only put up people who would bore the journos to death, like dear old Rob Green and the reliably diplomatic Nedum Onuoha. We couldn't afford to leave something on them in an interview, so Derby could pin it up on their notice board to get them going.

I wanted the comms guys to help by monitoring everything the opposition said, so I could use it as fuel for us. They helped to compile a video, which featured club staff and our families wishing us the best for the final. In return, I promised them a performance.

Memory is a weird and wonderful thing, isn't it? I feel myself getting really emotional as these words fall on to the page. That's pride in drawing a team together, I suppose. That's the joy of being involved in professional football, empowering others by looking them in the eye and telling them what is expected.

I sat down with the lads and continued the theme. We studied Derby with a depth we hadn't found all season. If we had done that quality of work, consistently, we would have gone up automatically. Our preparation was absolutely bob-on. As things turned out, it needed to be.

Harry was inspired. He made a statement by binning Benoit Assou-Ekotto, the Cameroon fullback we had on loan from Tottenham. He had some talent, but was toxic, the biggest egg I've come across in football. He made 31 appearances, but lost the respect of the group in a game against Burnley, when he blamed a suspiciously sudden hamstring injury after losing the ball.

He was a strange one, who took pride in his emotional detachment from football while trying to champion community causes. I'm the last one to complain when players amplify socio-political views through the media, but he acted insufferably, as if everyone was a fool but himself. Cicero, early in this chapter, makes the case against him for me.

Harry's pre-match analysis and team talk on the day filled us with further emotional energy. In that six-week period he had gone from the brink to being reborn as the boss. He was brilliant around the dressing room, having a quiet word here and there. It was personal, intense and above all credible. I studied the lads who had turned on him so recently. They were fucking having him now.

Me, too. I had seen managers, and tough, physical players for that matter, wilt under the sort of pressure Harry had faced. He went up so much in my estimation for having the bollocks to assess the damage, change his outlook, and come out fighting. We were always going to win that playoff final. So many little things, apparently unconnected, came together.

During the coaches' meeting, before the away leg against

Wigan, I caught Joe off guard by asking him what would happen if we went down to 10 men. He didn't even want to contemplate the prospect, because he felt it would introduce an element of negativity. I argued that we had to plan for any eventuality. Plan for chaos.

The scenarios were pretty predictable. Would we shut up shop if we went one-nil up? Would we go for it if we went one-nil down? How would we react if a defender was sent off? How would we reorganise if a midfield player got a red card? What was the contingency plan if Greeny, our goalkeeper, was injured, or hauled someone down?

Questions were almost more important than answers, because they represented a winners' mindset. Fail to prepare, prepare to fail, and all that. Harry took my side when I pushed for us to practise chaotic situations. It wasn't needed in either leg against Wigan, but when Gary O'Neil sacrificed himself for the team in the final, by getting sent off for preventing Johnny Russell from taking a clear goal-scoring chance, the situation was familiar.

We were already being battered and had a minimum of 31 minutes to play with 10 men. At certain stages of the season I would have seen people staring blankly into space, or looking down at their boots. Here I looked around and realised everyone was on it. Players were chirping, communicating: 'Stay connected. Be positive. Talk to the guy next to you.' It was a summary of everything Blackie had worked on with us.

This is going to penalties. Blackie's advice, dig in and win the next five minutes, becomes our mantra. 'We win the next five minutes,' screams Danny Simpson. Other voices, different accents, repeat the message. They build pressure, but we are as one. Simmo notices Nedum wavering. 'Keep connected!' he yells. 'We can see this out.' Chris Martin, the Derby striker, runs past and sniggers, 'No fucking chance.'

There's our marginal gain, our critical 1 per cent, right there.

I see Simmo morph into the inspirational figure who, two years later, would help Leicester City win the Premier League. I see Richard Dunne, the man with whom I have shared so much, good and bad, fill up. I see Bobby Zamora's face harden. I look at Martin and think, 'You have just fucked your teammates over.' Lads who were shattered, mentally and physically, are renewed.

No chance? Really?

Again, another of Blackie's interventions has sudden relevance. He had come into the dressing room at the end of the first half, armed with real-time and historic data. He told us when Derby would be at their most vulnerable; no Championship team had conceded more goals in the last five minutes.

We are in the 90th minute. Junior Hoilett beats Jake Buxton on the right-hand touchline, keeps his balance, and cuts the ball back into the penalty area. Richard Keogh's scuffed clearance merely sets up Zammo to score with a whipped left-foot shot. Fucking hell, it's weird. Zammo goes right, and runs through the corner flag. I wheel away in the opposite direction, both arms in the air.

It is a first for me. I never celebrate on my own, when someone else scores. Yet I'm sprinting towards the left-hand touchline. I'm almost crying. This is phenomenal. I'm still emotionally charged when the final whistle goes, 60 seconds later. It is then, and only then, that I realise something sacred, something special.

These are the days of our lives.

There is so much stuff in football I am not proud of. There are so many things I have forgotten. Images, words, actions, moods stay with me, but I need TV footage to jog my memories of certain games. This is not one of them. The playoff final will be with me until the day I die. That group of players will remain a band of brothers when we are hobbling around on arthritic joints.

We know. We share. We are.

I still get sensory overload when I look back. I have to close my eyes to recapture the mood, envisage the scene. Chris Martin is crying. I console him, because I have been that dickhead. I shake his hand and that of each and every one of his team-mates, before walking up that endless staircase to collect a trophy that means nothing, and everything.

I embrace Tony Fernandes, the owner we had hauled out of the shit. I share a beer with Blackie in the dressing room, and try to take it all in. Hilly, a Herculean figure, engulfs Greeny, the quiet hero. Simmo and Dunney exchange rebel yells. I sit with my old mucker from Manchester City's youth team, Shaun Wright-Phillips. I attempt to explain a vision of Wembley, bathed in golden sunlight, which I had studied from my hotel bedroom window earlier that day.

Amazingly, it doesn't come across as fluffy bullshit.

CHAPTER EIGHTEEN

NO NONSENSE

Actually, it was fluffy bullshit.

We will always have Wembley, our sense of solidarity and wonder, but miracles have a short shelf life. By the second morning of pre-season training I was convinced immediate relegation was inevitable. That famous phrase, 'Those who do not learn from history are doomed to repeat it', had never felt more relevant.

Football is a bit like crossing the road in heavy traffic. If you have a near miss, or, worse, get clipped by a car, you should be very vigilant the next time you need to reach the other side. QPR had been knocked down, recently relegated from the Premier League, but didn't learn their lesson and ran blindly across the carriageway. It was just a question of how bad the collision was going to be.

Lines of communication were open. I had spoken to a lot of people at the club, on a lot of different levels, that summer. I stressed to the owners and to Phil Beard, the chief executive, that we needed to protect and nurture the culture that had taken hold during the promotion run-in. Everyone was blissed-out, eager to agree, but it was a waste of breath.

Madness had descended by the time we reported back. The talk was of money being at a premium and the squad being trimmed. A total of 16 players were moved out during the summer window. That number included accumulated dross from the Mark Hughes era, but also pivotal pros like Gary O'Neil and Danny Simpson.

When, suddenly and inexplicably, the strategy changed and there was money to spend, it went on players who I thought were unfit for purpose. Once again, agents were lining up to staple the directors' trousers to their ankles. You live and die by recruitment, and that means looking beyond players with decent names and extended careers. Bonds slackened, instead of being strengthened.

The first major signing, Rio Ferdinand, summed up the indecision and inconsistency. I thought he was over the hill and didn't have the legs for another Premier League season. If survival was a priority, we had to recruit more pragmatically. Rio was 35. His physical attributes had diminished; he had been in and out of the Manchester United side for a very good reason.

This was nothing personal, since I like Rio as a man. Anyone associated with six Premier League titles and a Champions League triumph has a winner's mentality. But playing for a newly promoted team, at a club that has the additional pressure of being financially fragile, is very different. You get less respect, more distractions, no time on the ball. We just didn't need a player like him, at that stage of his career. He was an unnecessary, unsustainable luxury.

I found myself being dragged into an internal debate I didn't need. I know my candour will be used against me, because it suits my preordained image as a gobby shop steward, but people in positions of authority wanted to know how I felt. In a perfect world such consultation would not lead to confrontation, but this was an imperfect storm.

The uncertainty at the highest level of the club was unsettling, especially when it seemed that Harry Redknapp had given Rio his word he would sign him. When a protracted deal did go through, just before we left for a training camp in Germany, the implications were quickly apparent.

Promotion had been founded on a solid back six, an ability to close out the game. Survival needed similar qualities. Yet Rio arrives, and it is all change, to a 3-5-2 system. I was first choice in that formation, but the first time we tried it in training, against a side playing a bog-standard 4-4-2, it was a shambles. The flaws were obvious.

Rio and Steven Caulker, a lad who had a strangely inflated sense of his ability, made their debuts in a 2-0 defeat in a preseason friendly against RB Leipzig. The conditions, a gale-force wind and a blazing sun blotted out by a first-half monsoon, suited the mood. No one had a clue what was going on.

It was obvious we would go into the season unprepared, with about a 10-point handicap. That's my calculation of the price of a club consumed by confusion. The dilemma was familiar: speak out, and be branded a troublemaker, or keep my counsel. In similar situations in the past I had reacted by lashing out, but this time I resolved to act out of character, and sit and suffer in silence.

Believe me, I tried.

Harry called a team meeting after another chaotic session. He explained that he had been influenced by Holland and Chile at the World Cup – 3-5-2 was the way forward. I was determined not to raise the issue in front of the group because that didn't really serve anyone's purpose, but the manager was insistent: 'If anyone's not happy, let's hear it.'

I'm thinking, 'Please tell me this isn't true', and obviously didn't do enough to disguise my body language. Harry singled me out. He wanted to know what I thought of his master plan. On one level, it was astute management, since it forced the issue into the open. On another, it was dangerously provocative, because I am not known for diplomatic niceties.

Deep breath, Joseph. Here we go again . . .

'No one has played that system successfully, with any longevity. No one, let alone a team going from the Championship to the Premier League. Juventus are probably the only side in Europe to have won things with it, but they are financially dominant in their league, and they have the best players. The system is basically irrelevant, especially here in England with an inferior, newly promoted team.

'Juventus reached the Champions League final because Real Madrid basically fucked themselves by taking their eyes off the ball in the semi, but are usually found out in the latter stages of the competition. Holland used a number of different formations, and did what they had to do to counteract the opposition. Chile are effective in South America, but do you really think they can win a World Cup?

'To play this way you need a really exceptional coach, and players who know the system. You haven't got either. I'm sorry to upset people, but you did ask. You are trying to squeeze a square peg in a round hole. Rio might fit because he can play the sweeper role, but you simply haven't got the personnel to make a go of it.

'Deep down, in your heart of hearts, you don't believe in this. You've gone away in the summer and people have got into your head. What'll happen is, you'll play three at the back and we'll get absolutely twatted. Within five to 10 league games you'll change, go back to 4-4-2, and the previous three months will be completely wasted.'

As you can imagine, this did not go down well. Joe and Bondy were looking daggers. Harry tried to argue his case. It was the sort of subject that should have been discussed calmly, behind closed doors, as part of a more measured process. It hardly helped that Rio made a point of trying to pull me to one side as the lads were climbing back on the bus.

My adrenaline was surging. I'd worked myself up into a bit of a lather. It was neither the time, nor the place, for a reasoned discussion but I did my best in the circumstances:

'Look, Rio. I respect you as a player, for everything you've done in the game, but you're completely wet behind the ears when it comes to this situation. I don't want to fall out with you, but I'm telling you now, I'm absolutely bob-on with what I'm saying. If we go into the Premier League like this, you're going to embarrass yourself and we'll be relegated by February. How will you be remembered then?'

He was adamant it was the best option, and to keep the peace I promised he had heard the last on the subject from me. Steve Black had missed the discussion, but immediately recognised the depth and delicacy of the issue. I needed to cool down, so he agreed to walk back to the hotel with me, instead of taking the coach.

Appropriately, we got lost. A two-minute drive became a 100-minute routemarch. We ended up walking alongside a motorway, navigating our way back to base by Google maps on our phones. It was probably the best thing that could have happened, because it gave us time to work through the options, and plan my response.

I had put myself out on a limb, yet again. I shouldn't have

been surprised that others didn't have the courage of similar convictions, since footballers are conditioned to look after number one, but I was angry. My first thought was to cut my losses, demand a transfer. Blackie was more rational and delivered a simple message: 'You cannot let anyone in this organisation affect your level of performance. We're going to swim in a different direction.'

That's Blackie's magic, seeing things that others miss, and doing things that others refuse to contemplate.

He had got to know me well, in a relatively short space of time. My impulsive reaction is to challenge, to reflect emotion. If a coach or manager decides to take the piss, I will do the same to him. If a team-mate blatantly drops his standards, and no one else seems to care, I will let them toss it off. Inevitably, in either scenario, things come to a head.

Blackie argued it was time to do something different. Take a step back, concentrate on maintaining the highest standards, and allow the politics to become someone else's problem. Do not waste energy by being drawn into internal turmoil. I agreed to start a diary, to purge some of the frustrations. By the time we reached the hotel I had made a commitment to toe the party line, regardless. I would present Harry with solutions.

We did what we should have done all along, and had a mature conversation in private after dinner that evening. He agreed he needed to identify players best suited to the new system, and took the point about the need for specific coaching expertise. I wondered whether he was trying to buy me off when he offered me the captaincy, since I knew Clint Hill, my roommate, hadn't been consulted.

I couldn't agree to accept the job on that basis. Hilly was a friend, with high personal and professional standards. Harry accepted our compromise offer: Hilly would remain as club captain, on the proviso I would fill in if, for any reason, he was not selected. It was a bit of a charade, to be honest. We were shuffling deckchairs without deviating course, towards the iceberg.

At least Blackie had scope to communicate the probable consequences. Since he had not been hired by Harry, his responsibility was to the chief executive. He didn't mince his words, calling it the worst pre-season he had witnessed during 23 years at the highest level of professional sport. As so often in such situations, mistakes were compounded.

Glenn Hoddle was recruited as first-team coach four days before we lost 1-0 at home to Hull on the opening day of 2014/15. He had been out of the game since being sacked as Wolves manager in 2006, and had evidently done little work on his people skills. I took an instant dislike to him because of his aloof manner, and because he was obviously Rio's man.

He was brought in to coach 3-5-2. Mauricio Isla arrived on loan from Juventus, with an £8m option to make the move permanent at the end of the season, because he could play in the system as a right wing-back or a right-sided central defender in a three. Eduardo Vargas, with whom he had formed an understanding in the Chilean national team, was recruited on loan from Napoli.

So much for theory. Vargas needed three weeks to reach match fitness. Isla made his debut in a 4-0 defeat at Tottenham which prompted Harry to pull the sort of tyre-squealing U-turn more usually associated with desperate politicians. No manager likes to be shown up at his former club, and they had to fumigate White Hart Lane after we left.

The holiday romance with 3-5-2 was over. Hoddle's area of expertise had been abandoned. A much-changed team was knocked out of the League Cup by Burton Albion before the switch to a 4-2-3-1 formation paid immediate dividends in our next Premier League match, a 1-0 win over Sunderland. We were basically making things up as we went along.

Another £24m was thrown at unconvincing signings such as Sandro, who was somehow allowed to play without a work permit until the Home Office intervened, three games from the end of another dysfunctional season. Harry detested his image as a wheeler-dealer, and wasn't best pleased when the press boys calculated he'd been involved in 89 separate transactions, including transfers and loans, in his 21 months at the club.

We were bottom after winning only two of our first 12 matches. The dressing room was fractured and the mood was grim. Despite it all, I surprised myself by living up to Blackie's challenge. I could have made things worse by sounding off, but remained relatively restrained. Harry became sombre, detached.

Gallows humour flourished. The fate of Derby's Chris Martin, whose immaturity symbolised their failure in the previous season's playoff final, became a running joke in our dressing room. Whenever we suffered a new setback, or a recurring problem, someone would pipe up with, 'At least we're not like Chris Martin, having another year in the Championship.'

That would happen soon enough. The January window was a shambles. We took a £1.25m hit on Jordon Mutch, who made only nine appearances before being sold to Crystal Palace, and brought in a single player on loan, Mauro Zarate from West Ham. The less said about him, the better. He lasted only four matches.

Harry was good with me, because he was smart enough to trust me, but the timing of his departure, the day after the window closed, was the kiss of death. I've never asked about his motives; it seems a little pointless. Hoddle left with him, citing his loyalty, but that was incidental. Even Jose Mourinho could not have saved a disenchanted, disunited squad from themselves.

Supporters aren't stupid in these situations. Diehards have surprisingly good intelligence networks. They seemed to sense I was doing my best in a truly bad team. I felt for Chris Ramsey, a development coach uprooted from the academy and thrown into the trenches by his mate, our new director of football Les Ferdinand.

Chris was out of his depth as a first-team manager. He was proficient technically, and had a strong character, but lacked authority and political nous. Our relationship was substantial enough to survive regular disagreements on matters of football principle. I fulfilled my promise to keep a lid on things on the dressing room, but he didn't have a chance.

I responded to the inadequacies of my surroundings by choosing to work harder. On Blackie's advice, I did extra training at St Mary's with Jonathan Griffin, a performance coach who specialises in strength and conditioning. Our sessions, on Monday afternoons and all day on Wednesday, footballers' traditional day off, were consistently stimulating.

Relegation, as predestined as turning over a new page on the calendar at the end of the month, was an afterthought. As I assessed my future in the spring and summer of 2015, with my contract coming to an end, I was in transition. It was a little too early to pursue a secondary career in coaching and management, far too late to avoid collateral damage caused by my reputation.

I began to discover that even strong managers, men's

men, were fearful of me. The phone did not ring as often as I assumed it would. It dawned on me, slowly, that it was foolish to expect everyone to see the world through my eyes. I had to reverse the process, and see me from the perspective of others. This was a fundamental test of will.

Football is a corporate world, in which bland people sell their soul. Important decisions are taken on hearsay, the word of mates. Favours are quietly called in. Characters like me, who are determined to remain true to themselves, stand out. I would have followed an easier path had I pretended to be something, or someone, I was not. I would probably have won more England caps and played for bigger clubs.

I'm still judgemental, but I'm learning to take a more considered view. I used to resent anyone who didn't think like me. I used to confuse their determination to smooth their passage, to pay their mortgage, with a lack of love for the game. Now I accept their point of difference. It doesn't necessarily make them bad people.

Keeping a diary has been huge for me. I used to turn inward, because I felt I could not trust anyone. Slights, real or imagined, became greater. Anger simmered. The act of writing those feelings down gives me a sense of freedom. I look back at them and realise they are fleeting emotions. I refocus on a bigger picture.

This is what I'm here for. This is what it is all about. This is what I want to do.

I can reprogramme my thoughts quickly, because I can no longer filter the world according to my mood. My thoughts and actions are down there, on the page, in black and white. I have to respond to them. That might mean apologising to the lads because I have been moaning. It might mean taking heed of a small step forward, or backward.

I used to have no capability to move on. I would self-justify, wilfully confuse malevolence with honesty. I would excuse bad behaviour by convincing myself I needed to be feared in a horrible dog-eat-dog world. Now I refuse to hide. People who back away are fated never to improve.

My fuck-ups are a matter of public record. I've had difficulty fitting in. I've felt obliged to suppress certain elements of my character. It is a leap of faith to suggest I have finally mellowed, but I've learned I am happiest when I am at my most open. This book, and my media work, are elements of my search for meaningful interaction.

I don't bite, but I will have my relapses, especially when I feel I have been backed into a corner. It would be ridiculous for me to think everything is going to be perfect, but if I keep working on things I can control, keep speaking to people in a spirit of mutual respect and tolerance, life will be so much easier for me.

I don't profess to know everything. I am just trying to make sense of what is going on around me. I'm trying to cultivate an ability to think clearly and critically when the distress signals have been launched. How does this particular situation look to other people? Why not encircle the problem, take your bearings, and make a call based upon a 360-degree assessment of the situation?

The fundamental problem is my professional environment. My bluntness is based on the received wisdom that there is no time to waste in football. As a player I have no control over the people around me, other than the delivery of an opinion. I'm changing as a man, off the pitch, but am I changing fast enough to outrun assumptions of who I am?

Jail was a starting point in the process of research and renewal, but it was the Tevez incident that made me appreciate

I had to align alternative worlds, the personal and professional. I matured in Marseille, advanced and then retreated at QPR until I realised I could not afford to be tainted by any club's institutional failings.

My mistake was in assuming that everyone in the game is as analytical as me, when it comes to big career decisions. Whenever a manager phoned me that summer, to test the water, I compiled a dossier on him. I wanted to know about him mentally, physically, emotionally. What was his nature? How did he plan his sessions? What were his tactical touchstones? How did he structure his week?

I know this appears presumptuous, but I almost turned the interview process on its head. Did he have the mental strength to engage with me on those terms? Was he secure in himself? Was the structure above him stable? Money wasn't an issue for me since I was determined it would never again be a primary source of motivation.

I was very impressed when I first spoke to Sean Dyche, soon after the end of the season, but didn't get the same sense of solidity when I went to see Dougie Freedman at Nottingham Forest. I liked him, but he was a bit soft-soapy. I'll admit to having had the unworthy, uncomfortable thought: 'You couldn't handle me. I'd end up taking your job because I'm the stronger personality.'

I spoke to Steve McClaren a couple of times about returning to Newcastle United, but soon got word there was more chance of Mike Ashley renouncing his wealth and reinventing himself in an Indian ashram. That's a shame, but hardly surprising.

Slaven Bilic was impressive. Sardonic, passionate and convincing. He spoke in detail about where he saw me playing for him, and gave me a summary of my strengths. It seemed a good fit. West Ham's co-owners, David Sullivan and David Gold, had tried to sign me for Birmingham City, and I trained with the team for a couple of days. I even successfully completed a medical.

Somewhere it cyberspace, it all fell apart. A vocal minority of West Ham fans reacted as if they were about to be represented by a serial killer. I was in the dark, as most players are in such situations, but there was a change of heart. That's life. Things have subsequently worked out well for them, and for me. There's no bitterness on my part.

I was confident I would be successful wherever I ended up, because I was in a good place mentally, but it was a reality check. It can get lonely up there, on the shelf. There is too much time to think. It was strange being on the outside, looking in. I played golf, went to the gym to tick over, and did things around the house but gradually felt myself withdrawing.

Georgia was first to pick up on my unease. No surprise there, since she knows me so well. I had to level with her. I loved seeing the kids, and appreciated the pleasures of domestic life, but there was something missing. She didn't need to be told what that was. 'You're miserable without football,' she said. 'Do yourself a favour – get out there, find yourself a club and be happy.'

Though comfortable with quick decisions, I knew I could no longer live on my wits. I kept coming back to the obvious conclusion that the next move would help to define my career progression over the next five to 10 years. Burnley was a balanced environment, in which I could learn from the sort of manager I aspire to become.

Sean Dyche saw through the tat and the tinsel. He laughed at the chutzpah of my sales pitch that signing me as a free agent was an absolute no-brainer for a manager who had anything about him. He wasn't bothered by the distraction of a couple of stupid tweets I had posted in May 2014, disparaging Burnley as a town. He was warned off by other managers, but made up his own mind.

The true measure of the man was not in getting Burnley promoted on a minimal budget in 2014, but in his refusal to break the club financially through a mixture of panic and personal vanity when they were in the Premier League in 2015. Other managers would have had no compunction in emptying the cupboards, picking up their compo, and leaving them in the shit.

I liked him for the sense he made of that devalued word, legacy. He will move on in time, naturally, but he understood the importance of his role as a custodian of the club. I'm very respectful of his position, because he has established a clear boundary between player and manager. That hasn't always been the case in my career.

I recognise that, as a leader, he has to be constantly on his guard. He cannot afford to worry about the consequences of his decisions, because he needs to get the job done. I can accept his authority and still have a two-way relationship with him. I studied the nature of his job, and he took time to understand my motivation and mentality.

Football is increasingly cutthroat. Dressing rooms are insecure, because clubs have the disposable income to take a chance on more players. Managers are pressurised by agents who have a vested interest in creating an unsettled environment, which helps them regulate the transfer market. Owners seem happy to allow the inmates to run the asylum.

It helps that Sean still thinks as a player. He identifies with the senior pro who is determined to fight for his place in the pecking order. He recognises the integrity of a player who refuses to yield and responds positively to pressure. He puts up with the sound of my voice because he understands I am a compulsive communicator.

It amazes me that so many football clubs do not carry out due diligence in their human investments. Blackie worked in the NFL with Denver Broncos, 15 years ago. They had two in-house private detectives, assigned to build a character profile of any potential signings. Their recruitment decisions were informed by the objective and subjective, data and personality.

When I joined Burnley, on a one-year contract in late August 2015, the squad underwent psychometric testing. Our so-called Insight Profiles gave us an external assessment of our aptitudes and attitudes. The manager wanted us to share them, but most of the lads took them home, as though they contained deep and dark secrets. I stuck mine on my locker, so that everyone knew what, or who, they were dealing with.

This is me, as a person. It is spot-on.

Joseph Barton

Behavioural Style Overview

Strict. Demanding. Analytical. Introspective. Serious. Direct.

Fast-paced. Intense. Calculating. Pragmatic. Dissatisfied. Impatient.

Problem-solver. Creative. Inquisitive. Factual. Self-starter. Expeditious.

Systematic. Exacting. Critical. Abstract. Resourceful. Logical.

Communications style is direct, straightforward and no-nonsense, perhaps blunt.

Good with abstract, creative thinking and critical problem-solving tasks.

Tends to be easily bored with too much routine and repetitive tasks.

Can seem thin-skinned, often fussy and dissatisfied.

Emphasis is on bottom-line results. May be seen as demanding and tough.

May be critical, sceptical and suspicious. Needs to analyse facts personally.

Often wants to move forward with a decision but needs to weigh facts first.

Good ability to cut through facades and get to the heart of the matter.

May have difficulty delegating work due to a high need to control and monitor.

Makes decisions based on data and logic, not necessarily others' input.

Tends to be goal-oriented but can be fickle and may change mind often.

Not easily impressed. Questions information and wants proof.

Can be defensive when criticised and censured by others.

Job-related Stressors

A lack of challenging work, and opportunities for growth and advancement.

Not having enough time to think, reflect and analyse situations thoroughly.

Too many questions about private thoughts and personal matters.

Not achieving goals at a high level and as quickly as he feels is necessary.

Being confined or having to sit for long periods of time.

Little opportunity for creativity, diversity and spontaneity.

Style Report

Assertiveness – Initiative

Consistently high in initiative, Joseph will be assertive and decisive. Determined and goal-oriented.

He tends to be very determined, enterprising, competitive and proactive. Likes challenges.

Good drive and ambition for accomplishing his goals. Prefers the leadership role.

Sociability – Extroversion

Joseph tends to be naturally serious and selective in his interactions with others.

He tends to be a direct and straightforward communicator with large groups and new people.

Joseph is usually reflective, analytical and logical on the job.

Patience – Calmness

Joseph's tempo or pace is restless, quick and impatient. Emphasis is placed on immediate results.

Change, diversity and variety, as well as being physically active on the job, are important to him.

He prefers a non-routine work environment and will show impatience with repetitive tasks.

Compliance – Conformity

Joseph tends to be somewhat structured, detail-focused and co-operative on the job.

His tendency is to follow policies and procedures and to carefully approach risk-oriented situations.

Decision-making is usually handled with a conservative and thorough approach to ensure accuracy.

Would you have signed me? You decide.

CHAPTER NINETEEN

BUBBLE OF STRENGTH

I turn off my phone at 9.20pm, and settle down to read an article on the aesthetics of football by a Scottish lad named Jamie Hamilton. It is very good. I already sense I will sleep soundly, deeply. I'm never conscious of dreaming, and tomorrow's task is tangible. I intend to finish the season as a champion.

I'm in a typically featureless hotel room in south London, a plastic perception of home. It is comfortable enough, neat but bland. I retrieve my washbag from the bathroom, and pull out a small cream folder. It is worn at the edges, stained and slightly torn down one side.

On it is written: 'Game Preparation and Personal Game Application'. The initials SPDB are inscribed in the corner. Steve Black has the best mindset I have come across in professional sport. If I had met him at 18 I would have captained England. My life would have been so different. That's easy to say when it is hypothetical, but I really believe it.

I understand why Jonny Wilkinson achieved so much in rugby, how he closed off the outside world and explored the darkest recesses of his mind. I appreciate the self-imposed disciplines, the determination to give everything. Blackie was his guide, his soulmate. Now he is my mentor and my friend. People may think I am a hard-nosed, thick-skinned bastard, but we share our vulnerabilities. He tells me we can only get there if we care.

I have a playing career to complete before a new journey, hopefully into coaching and maybe into management. Tomorrow, 7 May 2016, is another step along the way. If I help Burnley win at Charlton Athletic we will win the Championship title. We secured promotion to the Premier League four days previously, by beating QPR 1-0 at Turf Moor.

It wasn't much of a game, to be honest, and I didn't have time to appreciate the irony of the opposition. We were mobbed when the final whistle blew. That's a bizarre experience, a blur of faces and strangers trying to string incoherent sentences together. You are kissed, hugged, unintentionally battered. There's always a scally begging for your shirt or tugging at your shorts.

I somehow crowd-surfed towards the Jimmy McIlroy stand, and my family. Cassius was passed over the barriers. I put him on my shoulders, plunged back into the madness, and headed in the general direction of the tunnel in the corner. My son was bewildered, but I wanted him to share the moment. He will be able to look back at photographs, and understand what his dad did for a living.

It is easy to drift off, and lose myself in other memories. A dressing room awash with champagne and laughter. The Libertines blasting out from Andre Gray's sound system, which incorporates flashing disco lights. A Burnley version of

'Alouette'. A proper lap of honour in the evening sunlight. The subsequent players' party in Manchester, which lasted until 5am. But I've got a job to do.

I visualise everything the night before a game. I enter what Blackie calls my 'bubble of strength'. He uses the analogy of someone wanting to come into my house and traipse across my new cream carpet with muddy boots. This is me refusing him entry. I close the door in his face. I'm in control. I'm empowered.

No one gets to me on match day. Tomorrow will be a little unusual because the Charlton fans will be too preoccupied by their protests against the club's owners to give me the normal welly, but I'll have wind-ups to deal with from their players. They're relegated, disillusioned, but the game is live on TV. They will play for personal pride, if not for the club or the manager.

I pull three postcards out of the folder. The first has an image of Wastwater in the Lake District on the front. I turn it over, and begin to get my game head on. The opening line, written in black ballpoint pen, reads: 'First half. Win it or lose it in the first minute or the last minute.' Underneath, the word 'focus' is underlined. Beneath this lie four complementary messages: 'Keep Talking. Stay Connected. Keep Encouraging. Play at Your Best Rhythm.'

The bottom half of the postcard comes under the heading 'Half-time'. Again the messages are simple, direct: 'Keep Moving. Hydrate. Refuel. Reconnect to Each Other. Start the Second Half Big.' I have read these exhortations constantly over the past two years but they still feel fresh. The pattern is comfortingly familiar.

I respond well to visual, rather than verbal, prompts. The second postcard features a photograph of the ruins of

Dunstanburgh Castle on the Northumberland coast. It has a timeline on the back. The title 'Night Before' frames the first list: 'Rest. Visualisation. Emotional Commitment. Food. Hydrate. Sleep Well.'

My timetable and trigger points for the following morning are listed below: 'Breakfast – visualisation. Commit to Quality Contribution. Rest – hydrate. Lunch – not too much.' The messages merge, seamlessly, into my match preliminaries: 'Warm Up – lots of touches, passing. Multi-directional Movement. Multi-pace.'

The third postcard, which features another Lake District scene, at Ullswater, completes the cycle. It takes me into the dressing room in those precious minutes before the buzzer sounds, and the lino comes in to check whether you have a flick knife smuggled down your socks. There are only two instructions: 'Be Truly Together. Look in the Eye and Commit to Each Other.'

All that remains is a final checklist: 'Big Start. Win Confrontations. Disrupt Their Possession. Play at Your Pace. Get and Keep Momentum. Lightning-fast Transitions from Attacking to Defending (and vice versa).' Since this is the last thing I will read before I turn out the lights, it percolates through my brain.

I am in a reflective mood. I think about the emotional connections I have made through football. They have nothing to do with playing ability. When I look back at my career I will value friendships. Nobby Nolan, Clint Hill, Brad Orr, Shaun Derry, Trevor Sinclair, Jamie Mackie, Heidar Helguson. Good men, great lads. This is about who they are, what they represent as people.

At Burnley there is a new set of lads, for a new phase. Tom Heaton, Andre Gray, Matty Taylor, Matt Gilks, Scotty

Arfield, Ben Mee. Young Keano, Michael, who I speak to all the time. Young Longy, Chris, the former Everton kid I drive in with. Boydy, George, a lad I've grown to like immensely. In a drunken moment, in the days to come, I will describe them as 'the greatest group of human beings I've ever been involved with'.

I couldn't have formed such strong attachments 10 years ago. Maybe I am finally getting out of my own way. Maybe I don't feel as fearful. I am aware of my own mortality as a player. I've got a few years left in me, but I've started to see the end. It is important for me to pass on nuggets of experience. I'm not a player-coach by any stretch of the imagination, but the lads come to me as a senior pro. They look to me for advice.

My last Instagram post before the Charlton match, an adaptation of a 1934 American poem by Dale Wimbrow entitled 'The Guy in the Glass', is part of the informal education programme. I came across it, amended as 'The Man in the Mirror', in a book by Wayne Bennett, the legendary Australian rugby league coach. He sends it to his players, to remind them where ultimate responsibility for performance lies:

When you get what you want in your struggle for self
And the world makes you king for a day.
Then go to your mirror and look at yourself
And see what that man has to say.

For it isn't your father, your mother or wife
Whose judgement of you – you must pass.
The fellow whose verdict counts most in your life
Is the guy staring back from the glass.

He's the man you must please, never mind all the rest,
For he's with you clear up to the end.
And you've passed your most difficult and dangerous test
When the man in the glass is your friend.

You may be like another and chisel a plum,
And think you're a wonderful guy.
But the man in the glass says you're only a bum,
If you can't look him straight in the eye.

You can fool the whole world, down the pathway of years,
And get pats on your back as you pass.
But the final reward will be heartaches and tears
If you've cheated the man in the glass.

I won't cheat him. I promise. The end comes to us all in football. Sometimes it engulfs us, and we go too quickly. Sometimes it toys with us, lures us into staying too long. Infinitely better players than me have had difficult passages out of the game. I look around the dressing room at the Valley, and remind myself I have come to Burnley to enjoy it.

I still have to deal with that inner voice, the insecure kid who tells me I will be shit on Saturday. He will always be there, but now I communicate with him on my own terms. I bombard him with facts about my consistency of performance. It's funny how he quietens when I remind him I'm on the verge of going through an entire season without picking up a red card.

I don't miss a day's training. I still have one of the highest data outputs in the team. Not many 33-year-olds graft in a midfield two. I've seen players five or six years younger than me struggle in that role, which is fucking scary. Other old boys, like Gareth Barry, need to play in a five. That's where the world is at.

The younger lads think it's hilarious when I complain about doing their running for them. Lazy bastards. I tell them age is a state of mind, a number. My prime attributes, awareness, application and competitiveness, are more enduring. So many players are done when they lose even a fraction of their pace; I'm fortunate because I've never had any to lose.

Teddy Sheringham and Dennis Bergkamp never needed extreme pace because they had a brain. That, for me, is the last thing to go if you look after yourself properly. The best players, in any sport, have the intelligence and imagination to see what is going to happen, three moves ahead. Just as Ronnie O'Sullivan is on a different plane in snooker, Roger Federer's anticipation and technique have made him a legend in tennis. I can think my way through matches in a way I couldn't during my mid-twenties.

I believe I have got better as I have got older. Sean Dyche can't get his head round the fact that I play golf on Sunday mornings, as part of my active recovery. I've broken my feet, but my knees, hips and back are fine. My head, my mental approach, is the main thing. If you believe you are fit, you will feel young and strong. Having a young family keeps me active.

The gaffer believes in consistency, continuity. It felt strange not having the foundation of a solid pre-season to build upon, so he gave me a month to work up to full fitness before I started for the first time, in a 2-1 win at Rotherham on 2 October. The match at the Valley will be my 40th appearance of the season, my 37th start. Outside, security guards are frisking pensioners in case they are concealing missiles. Paranoia is in the air. Sniffer dogs are on patrol.

The changing room is narrow, cramped. I settle on the bench and reach inside my washbag for a refresher course. The folder also contains four plain postcards, which contain Blackie's 'messages from the moment'. These are designed to clarify my thinking, and complete the process of immersing myself in the impending task.

The first section involves tactical touchstones when we are out of possession: 'Get Shape. Get in Right Place (make decision). Get in Right Position (body-wise). Direct Opposition's Decisions. Disrupt Their Flow.' It concludes with the following priorities when we are in possession: 'Runs into Box. Getting Shots Off. Pull Trigger Early. Be Aware of Game State.'

They are followed by memory-joggers, mood-setters: 'Play Your Own Game. Play What You See. Get on Ball – change pace. Pass It – drive tempo. Stay Involved – connected. Be Fulcrum. Be Available. Be Passionate. Be Focused. On a Bed of Discipline . . .' The lessons come from other teams, other sports.

I'm reminded of the All Blacks' ability to manage the game, and the disciplines they expect of anyone who wears the sacred shirt: 'Get Officials Onside. No Reaction. Don't Waste Energy. Use It Wisely. Have That Bit in Hand for an Emergency.' A boxing comparison is underlined: 'Jab. Jab. Work the Opening.'

It is personalised shorthand, and works for me: 'If You See It, Do It. Short, Sharp Simple Passing. Work on Availability. Talk – demand it. Lead by Example of Doing It Well. Stay in JB Bubble of Strength and Influence. Solution-based. In Control. Show Football Intelligence. High-energy Execution. Not Physical – that could spill over.'

Pros take pride in the state of their game face. It is meant to be stern, taut and concentrated. Yet the last set of personalised messages seeks to transport me back to the simple pleasures of childhood: 'Enjoy Your Game. Enjoy Your Work. Enjoy Your Skills. Enjoy the Outcomes. Enjoy Influence. A Smile on Your Face . . .'

We have warmed up. Kick-off approaches. It will be a strange experience, since Charlton have erected mesh fences around the pitch, to prevent their fans causing chaos. Their banners proclaim 'We Want Our Club Back'. I understand where they are coming from; a traditional family club has been soured by Belgian owners who know little and care less about its heritage.

I take a final glance at a short list of my responsibilities to my team-mates: 'Talk. Direct. Encourage. Act as Their QC.' Our confidence is high, because we are unbeaten in 22 games, since a 3-0 defeat at Hull on Boxing Day. That loss prompted a team meeting in which everything was up for grabs. I argued it was too simplistic merely to promise to work harder; we had to work smarter.

I've been pretty low-key this season. The first time I showed my teeth in the dressing room was at MK Dons on a cold Tuesday night, 12 January. I had given us a half-time lead, but I ripped into our back four. I'd been on at them throughout the first half. They were casual, slack, and I wasn't having it.

I was walking around the changing room, which is nothing unusual at the interval, because I do so to control my lactate levels. No one appeared in any hurry to visit the toilet, just around the corner. The atmosphere was expectant. My team-mates, sitting at right angles to one another in the main changing area, had evidently been wondering when the explosion would come.

The gaffer's response proved the relevance of those psychometric tests. He used the insight they provided into my methods of communication to frame his team talk. 'He is absolutely spot-on,' he intervened, after I'd had my say. 'Joe is on the pitch. He can smell what I see. He's having a pop at you, but that's not personal. It's a professional opinion. It's blunt, and it is what we need to do, now.'

We won 5-0. It was the start of a run of 10 victories in 12 unbeaten games which took us from fifth to first. The pivotal victory, 1-0 in the return fixture against Hull on 6 February, was secured through a late goal by Sam Vokes. Excerpts from my diary in the build-up to that match, which began with a 1-1 draw at Sheffield Wednesday, give an indication of our mentality:

> The lads were happy with the draw at Hillsborough but that's not us. We can't be like that if we want to win the league. I'm really pissed off. We go into the Thursday meeting and the gaffer's like, 'OK lads, how do you feel?' I tell them I've been sulking, walking around for two days as if we'd been beat. We pumped Sheffield but I can't help but feel we've dropped two points. That's got to be our level . . .
>
> Just be really positive. You've been moaning at the lads because they weren't doing what they needed to do, but go back to pre-season. You came here to learn, to enjoy your football again and get rid of the QPR experience. Let's get back on track. Look at the strengths and weaknesses in the building. What's the level of consistency? How do we plan this?
>
> Interact with the coaching staff. Ian Woan and Tony Loughlan are very good for the gaffer. They're his eyes and ears and they've got a good process in place. I go into their video meetings, and they are on it. Where is this Hull game going to be won or lost? Going back to Boxing Day, they'll play a back four, get behind the ball, screen our

front two. They'll try to win a set piece, or catch us going forward, because their fullbacks, Odubajo and Robertson, will push on ...

Today I am going to get on the front foot. I am going to play exactly how Livermore doesn't want me to play. He's big, done lots of weights, and is very, very strong, physically, on top. But being that big comes with a consequence. He's got to carry that muscle mass around the pitch for 90 minutes. The more muscle you have, the more oxygen you burn. I believe having big muscle, big arms, is one of the reasons Kompany was poor last year.

No one picked up on it. He was too big. If you look at him this year, he looks leaner and he's still picking up injuries. He set off a chain of events by being too big, too immobile. I've got to tell the lads to keep our tempo very high because if we get it up there Livermore is in trouble. Huddlestone, Dawson, Davies. They're in trouble.

We know we are fit enough to do it. We play at our best at that level. It's not great football. It's not pretty on the eye. But keep the tempo up and they'll break. I need Livermore to track me. I need to get him into my game. I need him to chase me, run after me. If he keeps trying to get to me I will tire him out ...

We are potential champions because we know what our skill set is. We train smartly. We know the opposition, and what they hate. Scotty Arfield pulls me up because I am fond of a boxing analogy, but they work for me. I'm not going to trade punches with someone who has a bigger punch than me, but I see so many teams with a weak chin doing just that.

The Championship is a 15-round title fight. With five games to go, I feared we were out on our feet. I used as my inspiration a book called *Relentless* by Tim Grover, who cited Michael Jordan as an example of a leader dragging his team over the line. That entailed straying across boundaries, and challenging authority.

Our training on the Monday and Tuesday, in the build-up to the Saturday game at Birmingham City, was poor. The gaffer was so tetchy I wondered, for the first time, whether the pressure was getting to him. I'd been named in the Football League Team of the Year, and had to resist subtle pressure to attend the awards dinner on the Sunday, 48 hours before a key match against Middlesbrough.

I spoke to Blackie, had a text exchange with the manager, and resolved to be proactive on the morning of the Birmingham game. During the coach journey to St Andrew's, I quietly studied a two-page summary of my thoughts before passing it on to Ben Mee, who sits next to me. I told him to read it, and pass it on. It went around everyone on the bus. When we arrived at the ground I made a point of taping it to the mirror in the bathroom. It was a heartfelt call to arms:

TEAM

- This team's strength is its tried and tested resolve
- We deliver for 95 minutes
- That's our team personality – that's us in action
- When the fight starts we stay in it
- That's a great, great habit to have
- Go out and get competitive – we refuse to yield (unbeaten this year!)
- We get the job done
- We take the initiative and we don't let go

EMBRACE THIS

- Embrace this feeling
- Not everyone gets the opportunity to feel like this
- It's caused by the potential to achieve exceptional things!
- 5 Wins – Champions
- 5 Wins – History
- It starts today – let's go . . .

One of Blackie's theories is that leaders create leaders. The proof of that principle became clear that afternoon, when I had to go off at half-time with a calf injury. We conceded an equaliser, but the team seized control of its destiny. Individuals found their voice, rose above themselves, and were rewarded by Andre's late winner. A crisis of confidence had been averted.

So many things in football are underutilised. Take substitutions. They are rarely positive. It's usually, 'Fucking hell, he's not doing well. Let's hook him and hope the next guy does all right.' Very few coaches take a step back, and analyse the potential advantage of changing a technical or physical match-up.

I'm trying to learn from other sports. I've been invited by Shaun Edwards, who is a coach's coach, to watch the Wales rugby team train. We've had a couple of conversations. His take on his relationship with his players strikes a chord with me. He's passionate, infectious, inspirational. He cares deeply about his craft, and his players.

Why are we conditioned in football to seeking distance between players and coaches? As so often in the game, it comes down to mistrust. Coaches are told their openness will be used against them if they get too close, or care too deeply.

They're brought up to believe emotional intelligence has dangerous limitations.

Rugby may change, because of the money that is creeping into the game, but generally it is less dog eat dog. Coaches realise they cannot make huge strides unless and until players realise they have their best interests at heart. It is completely different in football, where I see a great many coaches manipulate events and relationships so that it becomes solely about them.

Shaun is a strong personality. He was an offensive player in rugby league, creative and nuggety, but not exactly renowned for his tackling. In union, he is regarded as a brilliant defensive coach, whose players willingly put their bodies on the line for him. That's a fascinating storyline, so the media inevitably try to make everything about him. He won't let them, because he knows he is fucked without his players.

He places them in three categories, but insists he can only work with one type. The perfect player doesn't exist. The indolent, disinterested player is a waste of time, and must be driven out of the club as soon as possible. Shaun commits himself solely to the player who is a positive presence, the individual who is not afraid of constructive criticism and is open to anything designed to inspire improvement.

I've studied Bill Parcells in the NFL. There is another strong-minded coach, who understands he is nothing without his players. American football is a very clinical sport, with more than its share of superficial people, but Parcells has been successful because of the human connections he has made. Others shied away from the NFL's drug problem; he made a point of helping players like Lawrence Taylor, who had well-publicised issues with crack cocaine.

Great coaches and tacticians see the big picture, but also

recognise small, simple things. The rest stay in their comfort zones, hoping to get away with it by doing the basics. Their approach to the group is comply or die. I'd love to work with Jose Mourinho, who sees everything. We've exchanged emails and I think I'd get on really well with him. Where better to learn the art of management?

I've worked with a classic bunch of managers: Kevin Keegan, Stuart Pearce, Sam Allardyce, Chris Hughton, Joe Kinnear, Alan Pardew, Neil Warnock, Mark Hughes, Elie Baup, Jose Anigo, Harry Redknapp, Chris Ramsey and Sean Dyche. They've needed to be strong and some, to be blunt, haven't been very good.

Sean is a very good coach but also gives his teams room to self-manage. Right now, for the first five minutes of the interval at the Valley, he is in an anteroom with his coaches. The few punters in the stand who aren't launching stress balls, toilet rolls, paper aeroplanes and plastic bottles over the netting can hear me, in the centre of the dressing room, in full flow.

We are ahead through a well-worked team goal, but should be behind. Tom Heaton is the only player beyond criticism, since he has made several outstanding saves. We are conceding space, lacking pace and intensity. Do we really want to be champions? I go mad, kicking the skip to try to create a reaction. The gaffer comes in, lets me finish, and then loses it.

The bollocking works. We fly at them; confirm the title by scoring twice more in as many minutes, and ease up as the circus cranks up. Five flares, fired into the penalty area we are attacking, are collected, slowly, by a jobsworth with a bucket. Someone throws his shoes on to the pitch in protest. There's an invasion at the final whistle and the so-called Fans' Sofa, which is bizarrely close to the touchline, is torn to shreds.

Mad, but not as mad as us having to parade an inflatable trophy for the celebratory pictures. The Football League, in their infinite wisdom, have taken the real one to the Riverside, where Boro beat Brighton in the shootout for the other automatic promotion place. They obviously don't want to damage their precious brand by giving it to us at a troubled club.

But here's the thing. Winning is not about lifting trophies. It is about making progress every day. It is about the subtle pleasure of being part of a group of people who have a common cause, a will to get better. It is about sharing experiences, pulling others along the pathway. It is about taking the rough with the smooth.

Medals are mementoes, shiny symbols of success. Memories may be less tangible, but they mean just as much. You cannot put a price on the joy we see in the away end at the Valley. You cannot forget the freeze-frame images of fans, waving as we pull out on the team bus, heading northwards through south London's sprawl.

I think back to the uncertainty at the start of the season. Fortunately for Burnley, football is a ridiculously lazy industry, full of poseurs, people who want to posture and pontificate. Sean Dyche is about as far removed from that world, of fake tans and false teeth, as it is possible to be. He did his research, and realised that anyone who got me was going to get a positive me.

Being voted as the club's Player of the Year is a great personal honour, but I'm genuine when I insist that an individual prize misses the point, because we are a collective. I praise my team-mates and tell the audience at the awards dinner: 'I'd go through brick walls for every single one of them.' The following morning's hangover makes me wonder whether I took that too literally.

That clears, soon enough. I attack a new day as a champion, and that's good enough for me.

CHAPTER TWENTY

CALL ME JOE

I joined Burnley because of Sean Dyche. We sat in his kitchen and made mutual promises which were more than fulfilled. He accepted me as the finished article, the older, wiser person I have always wanted to be in a dressing room. I responded to him, as one of the few managers I felt was a friend. Together, we reached the Premier League.

It is very rare to find our level of honesty and human connection in football, an industry infected by fear and restricted by a lack of emotional intelligence. Perhaps that's why Sean understood, intuitively, why I decided to join Rangers instead of accepting Burnley's more lucrative offer of a new two-year contract.

It might not have made financial or football sense to those who misunderstand my motivation, but Sean followed my logic. I have been overpaid at times, and been incredibly unhappy. I've made career choices governed by money, and entered a world of pain. This was a kaizen moment, when I asked myself where best I could improve myself, day by day.

Burnley was the perfect football experience. I was

overwhelmed by positivity and humbled by a lack of suspicion. The fans took to me and I made lifelong friends, from Daisy the tea lady to a group of proper professionals. As strange as this might seem to anyone who has never experienced true team bonding, the saddest part of my departure involved withdrawing from the players' WhatsApp group.

There was a huge temptation to remain as a stabilising influence in what realistically will at best be an initial campaign of consolidation, but I've been there, worn out the worry beads. I would have learned little in another sustained struggle against relegation. Rangers promised something different, something compelling, something elemental. To be honest, they had me at hello.

Ibrox is one of those spiritual football grounds, a stately home which symbolises custom, strength and endurance. The place speaks to you as you walk through its wood-panelled hall, up its marble staircase, and into a gleaming trophy room, where championship pennants proclaim former glories.

The main stand, its red-brick facade decorated by the club crest in a blue-and-gold mosaic, is named after Bill Struth, one of the great managers in football history. A noted disciplinarian over his 34 years in charge, he demanded his players 'be true in their conception of what the Ibrox tradition seeks from them'. I felt the power of those words from beyond the grave.

There are a lot of similarities in the recent trajectory of my career and Rangers' progress from their lowest point, in enforced relegation to the Third Division in 2012. I have had my troubles, but am at the peak of my powers. I feel perfectly primed for the challenge of contributing to the winning culture instilled by Mark Warburton, Davie Weir and Frank McParland.

Anyone who chooses to belittle last season's achievement of winning the Scottish Championship betrays a basic lack of understanding of the professional game. The tired old 'pub league' smears are a reflex action by those who lack insight and basic footballing intelligence. Pressures obviously intensify as standards are elevated, but I appreciate how hard it is to win any title. It requires planning, perseverance, consistency of purpose and above all good people.

Rangers may be a work in progress, but I quickly recognised those constituent qualities once I was given permission to speak to the club. The approach was measured, thoughtful, respectful. The human chemistry felt right. Davie impressed me hugely with his unforced warmth and the depth of his coaching knowledge. As a relative youngster, I was suitably impressed by the example he set as a player, by winning his third league title with Rangers in the week of his 41st birthday in 2011.

Just as I appreciated Davie's passion for the club he epitomises, I related naturally to a manager of Mark's diversity and outlook. Coming from a background in the City of London, he doesn't think in straight lines like most football people, who decried him as an oddity from the moment he began coaching at Watford's academy.

He was a team leader in a different, but equally highly pressurised, environment. He understands the power of ambition, but has a bigger perspective, greater life experience. I will literally be learning on the job with him because I am trying to become a true leader, someone who develops people. My emotional baggage will always be with me, but I know who I am and what I am about.

That helps me communicate, be a better team-mate. I had moments of lucidity at QPR but it wasn't until I got to Burnley that I consistently had the confidence to praise others, to tell them how well they had played and how much they were appreciated by the group. There's no point in worrying about people who want to tell me I'm shit. I have no control over them, no interest in their views.

I had other options. Aston Villa and Fulham saw me as a promotion specialist. I was told Steve Bruce wanted me to delay my decision for a week, until Hull City had established their Premier League place. The most intriguing approach came the day before I travelled to Scotland to complete the formalities of my move to Rangers.

I had just finished a round of golf when I took a call from an agent, who had been contacted by Peter Lawwell, Celtic's chief executive. The message he conveyed was straight and to the point: 'Is there anything we can do together? Can we have a conversation?' To be frank, I respected him for his professionalism. It was a smart move. I sent word back, thanking him for his interest, but confirming my intentions.

Ultimately, I responded to Rangers as an institution that creates icons and demands warriors. I hinted at my decision that evening, by tweeting the lyrics of Bob Dylan's 'Like a Rolling Stone'. Needless to say, the elephant in the room, wearing green and white hoops, began to tap-dance. The usual search of my meanderings on social media inevitably unearthed evidence of childhood affiliations with Celtic. I received a Celtic kit as a present when I was growing up, just as I was given a Blackburn Rovers kit in another phase of my schooldays. I wouldn't insult the supporters of either club by referring to myself as a fan of their team. The reality is I am an Evertonian, born and bred.

I'm not daft, though. I knew my arrival would be portrayed as the equivalent of an invitation to tour the firework factory with a flamethrower. Glasgow bookmakers immediately offered odds on me being sent off in my first Old Firm match. They chose to disregard the fact that I am used to playing with a target on my back, and that I had just gone through an arduous season without picking up a suspension.

Of course, I am mindful of the delicacy of the situation, the unavoidable religious divide between such bitter, perennial rivals. All I ask is to be judged on my actions as a footballer, rather than my philosophical principles as a human being. Playing for Rangers is a phenomenal challenge, but I have never backed down from anything in my life, and do not intend to start doing so now.

My agnostic principles grow firmer with every day. If you want to go through life with a heightened sense of spiritual awareness, fine. It's absolutely no issue for me. You have the basic right to a personalised set of beliefs. The problem in disagreeing with someone about religion is that it is too easy to smear and stigmatise.

A counter-argument is viewed as a deeply personal attack. If I don't agree with the text of your book I am not anti you. I'm not saying you should be banished, driven out of civilised society. I am merely pointing out the nuances of faith. Doctrine impinges on everyday life in so many small but significant ways. Cassius, for instance, was prevented from going to a certain school in Liverpool because he hasn't been baptised, which is ludicrous in this day and age.

Excluding a child because he hasn't had his head dipped in water is the product of the sort of closed minds to which I don't want to subject him. Nan didn't ram her faith down my throat when I was a kid, but I still find it unsettling to visit Liverpool's Roman Catholic cathedral, the so-called Paddy's Wigwam, because it arouses uncomfortable memories of enforced attendance for school services, high days and holy days.

I believe in the power of the alternative view. I may think that Kanye West and Kim Kardashian are the epitome of everything that is wrong with a shallow, materialistic society, but 60 million people quite like what they stand for. It may baffle me, but I am the last person who can afford to be self-righteous.

I'm always being told that my views won't have any validity unless I debate them with a theologian. How could I debate sensibly with someone whose belief system is based on a book? I swore on the Bible when I was in court, but it was a reflex action that had nothing to do with uncorroborated stories which are thousands of years old.

I believe in the longevity of being honest. That might bite me on the arse in the short term, especially when so many are deceitful, but hopefully, over time, people will recognise my virtues. I've been violent, and mixed up in all sorts of stuff, so I understand concerns that I'm engaged in a comprehensive charade, but, as John Lennon sang, let's give peace a chance.

As much as some may not wish to admit it, the Old Firm clubs are vital to one another. I have never really bought into the Brendan Rodgers brand, but his installation as Celtic manager is a good thing for Scottish football. Standards will rise, since the strength of your adversary forces you to examine every option to be at your best. Make no mistake – I intend to win the Premiership.

We are building a young team with long-term potential. Frank McParland proved, in his recruitment work at Liverpool, Brentford and Burnley, that he has an outstanding eye for an emerging player. He has a global network of contacts and a modern outlook aligned to the instincts of an old-school scout. He provides the building blocks; the mortar is applied on the training ground.

My energy is compatible with the challenge because, biologically, I am a lot younger than my 34 years. I am stronger mentally than anyone around, with the possible exception of a Cristiano Ronaldo, whose ability to meet expectations at the highest level is astounding. I can deal with pretty much anything that is thrown at me.

I completed the final assessment for my UEFA A coaching badge in June. Sean Dyche has told me his door is always open, and Frank, who was the initial influence on my moves to Turf Moor and Ibrox, has already spoken of an organic transition within the development structure at Rangers as a natural progression.

Welcome to Joey Barton 2.0. Call me Joe for short. He is the product of a lot of research and reflection.

No one is truly prepared when they go into coaching or management, but if I am not the best at my new vocation – whatever that is – in 20 years, I will have done something seriously wrong. I am already working back from that point, thinking logically, 'What do I need to succeed?' The next phase will have a different tone to my playing career, which until recently has been a warped struggle for survival.

Life is good, rich with opportunity. I know it doesn't always work out as we intend; I'd be gutted if I didn't get the chance of an extended career in football, but I am adaptable enough to change course if that's my fate. I've lost the fear that stalked and shaped me as I was making my way in the world. I'm determined to enjoy this new-found sense of serenity.

I have a viable alternative in media work, but making it as a coach is my priority. I intend to do whatever it takes once I stop playing, and have consciously tried to make the leap of faith as small as possible. Management is a possibility, but coaching is more immediately attractive because it involves dealing with people at an emotional level.

Football is a reflection of modern society. It is impatient, instant. The component parts, its people, are interchangeable. I'm suited to the most critical aspect of coaching – helping individuals to help themselves – because of the perspective life has given me. I could go down the academic route, and qualify as a sports psychologist, but there is no substitute for being out there on the grass.

Initially, I will need someone to guide me, to teach me how far, and how fast, boundaries can be pushed. I've already studied the proactivity and professionalism of Olympic athletes. They work back from their goals, plan with greater clarity and intelligence. That justifies the pursuit of marginal gains; football is so far behind the curve that such a rigorous philosophy is seen as an affectation at even our biggest clubs. We don't even do the basics properly.

Consider something as fundamental as movement. Footballers don't know how to run correctly. They haven't a clue. Apart from an occasional dabble in gait analysis, I've never seen anyone work systematically on the mechanics of running. That's amazing in a sport in which you are, by definition, on your feet all the time. Dexterity is so important.

Look at Lionel Messi, or Eden Hazard in his breakthrough season at Chelsea; their natural fluidity of movement and spacial awareness are fantastic. Zinedine Zidane, the best player of his generation, was balletic, effortless. I'm not saying every player would be a better footballer if he did ballet, but at least we should be assessing the possibility.

Conditioning staff can teach me the technique of lifting weights, but if I can't run efficiently it doesn't really matter how strong I am. I rarely see defenders being given technical drills, to enable them to get their feet in the best position to win the ball. I can stand and moan about that, or do something about it.

As a prospective coach I need to understand how players learn. I would love to sit down with a neurologist, to get an insight into the workings of the brain. How does the skill we refer to as 'football intelligence' operate? How important is the home environment? I look at my kids and know they will have elements of character from Georgia and myself, but what sort of impact will our lifestyle have on them?

My greatest gift was the strength of my mind, forged on the streets, in a rough-and-tumble world. If I had been born with the same footballing ability, but to middle-class parents, I don't think I would have made it. I would have been a more balanced human being, but I wouldn't have been able to survive the turbulence of a Premier League career. Aggression gave me the necessary edge.

My recruitment will be based on the nature of the individual. I'd prefer to work with someone less talented but more open to personal growth, than someone who is very smart but has a closed mind. The latter player has finite usefulness, because either he will soon be bored with you, or you will be bored with him. If someone has a good heart and a good head on his shoulders, there's not much he can't learn.

I am compiling a new file, of discrepancies in my industry. I won't be afraid to delegate. I already know the sort of people I want in the team around me. Peter Kay would have been in it, because of his lifestyle skills. Steve Black will be in it for the uniqueness of his insight and the breadth of his sporting knowledge. It is tragic to think their perfect partnership will never be realised.

It excites me when I consider how many people I can reach as a coach. I'd love to work with a young Joe Barton. I see so many players as I was, messed up and struggling to understand themselves. The happy ones, with a good mindset, are easy to deal with. I will come into my own with unhappy kids, from troubled backgrounds. They are the ones you can get a bit extra from, those with whom I identify most closely.

I can promise them, with complete confidence, that I will make them better. I am a product of a flawed system, a player who was subjected to lazy, results-driven coaching for far too long. I can counsel the kid who is confused, because he is earning 50 times more than his dad without being stretched, or valued, by the club that is paying him a fortune. I was that soldier.

If I stopped playing tomorrow, what could I deliver? Would I have the maturity to soften certain aspects of my personality? Would I have the credibility to command an audience? Would I be able to toe the party line consistently? Self-belief wouldn't be an issue, since I am conditioned to backing myself in any situation.

Thinking rationally, I would have to make huge character adjustments to slot in straight away as a modern manager, who is becoming more of a politically driven, business-oriented CEO. I would need to make only slight character adjustments to learn my trade as a coach. I envisage myself developing into a hybrid figure, a cross between head coach and manager.

Titles are ultimately irrelevant, since it is the quality of your work that counts. Essentially, I've already acted as a surrogate manager at QPR, where I showed the requisite adaptability and an aptitude for leadership in difficult circumstances. I am prepared to do a proper apprenticeship.

I've already mentioned I'd love to work with Jose Mourinho. Someone of his status fits the NFL model, of a head coach being a mentor to younger coaches across his organisation. Football's approach is unstructured, higgledy-piggledy. Players learn certain aspects of management through experience but most fail to make the transition because the process is so haphazard.

Rather than taking time to examine an individual's managerial potential, too many chairmen and owners just say, 'Fuck it. He's got a big reputation; the media will love us. Let's throw him at the problem.' Such lazy thinking disregards the reality that a former player is starting a new career. That, surely, entails starting at the bottom.

Football struggles to find the reset button. Gary Neville fails at Valencia, and suddenly he is shit. Well, hang on a minute. Let's think logically. He went in above his head because people got inside his head. Everyone convinced him he was brilliant, so he took a mad leap of faith. He was told he could fly, so he jumped off the top of the building and was splattered all over the pavement.

Everyone assumed Gary would be successful because he played for Manchester United, a dominant club, and for the most controlling, powerful manager of the past 50 years. Top players have such a narrow spectrum of experience. Gary has more chance than most, since he is open-minded, strong-willed and analytical, but in general terms they can't do anything other than struggle to adapt to coaching or management, initially at least. Their formative years have been too sheltered.

I've played for a weird and wonderful array of people, and for a distinctive range of football clubs in a variety of competitive situations. That background gives me a better chance of excelling in the next phase of my career. I'm fully aware I won't know whether I am capable of flying until I make that leap, but before I do so I am going to be as well prepared as possible.

I have always thought like a coach, as a player. To give an example, I was forced to play out of position, on the right side of midfield, at Newcastle. Danny Simpson was behind me, a great lad who, at that stage of his career, was never going to get outside me. I studied opposition left backs to work out how they wouldn't want me to play against them.

If I tried to run them, players of the quality of Ashley Cole or Patrice Evra would beat me because they were quicker. I lacked a trick to get past them, but if I got a yard and whipped a ball in I had really good delivery. Simmo was a little nervous from time to time but I just gave him very, very simple instructions.

If you pick the ball up and I'm in space, give it to me. If I'm marked, put it in behind me because I'll get one of the forwards to run in the channel. We had a good season because, more often than not, I moved inside and gave the left back a decision to make. Either he picked me up and left the channel exposed by getting overly tight, or he gave me the yard I needed to hit Andy Carroll.

I lost count of the goals I set up for him as a result of yet more simple instructions. If you see me inside and I'm not marked, pull to the far post. Get someone else, Shola Ameobi or Peter Lovenkrands, to run the channel. I will find you. It was all very logical for me. I was very comfortable strategising, thinking ahead.

Nobby Nolan, captain of that Newcastle team, has all the credentials to be a good manager one day. He is an old-school, arms-around-the-shoulder leader and doesn't have a bad bone in his body. Yet he lasted only 15 weeks in charge at Leyton Orient, a mess of a club with yet another dysfunctional foreign owner. He didn't stand a chance because there was no opportunity for him to develop professionally.

I'm concentrating on gradual evolution, a long-term approach that won't involve bells and whistles from week one. I need to find people who share my vision. I'm not necessarily focused on a first-team role. I would find two or three years teaching kids in an academy equally fulfilling. Life doesn't usually offer such solutions, but I'd love eventually to give something back to two clubs in particular: Olympique de Marseille and Newcastle United.

I don't want to jump straight into a bear pit, but I am not the type to play at it. If you transmit even the merest hint that you are not genuine, people will see through you. You cannot be the best if you do not believe in what you are doing with the core of your being. I want to be the best coach or manager in the world but to do that something has to give.

Football demands all or nothing. You can't have a half-hearted go at it. I know I have the force of will to succeed, but am I prepared to sacrifice my family? Will it be worth it if I win five league titles as a manager and the kids are distant from me? The honest answer, as I sit here today, is no, but it is not that straightforward.

I've generally been consumed by my work throughout the time Georgia has known me. She has seen me at my lowest points – going into jail or sitting at home injured, so down that closing the curtains and shutting out the world seemed rational. She has given me stability, in good times and bad, but understands that football gives me purpose.

I have spoken to Blackie, and to friends who balance career and family, to try to make sense of the dilemma. They've told me to recognise my purpose, follow my dream. If that makes me happy, I will be a better person to be around. If I give up on that dream, there is a chance I will eventually grow resentful and become withdrawn.

I want my kids to be positive human beings. Being a good father isn't about being on top of your children all the time. They have to be given the scope to evolve independently, to find their own friends and form their own relationships. Being a good father is being there for them when they need you.

I've thought really deeply about this. There might be the odd night when I am out at a match, and they would prefer to be with me on the sofa, watching a DVD, but I am convinced I can make this work. Football is a brutalising business, but so many people, working all hours on the commuter treadmill, don't even realise their kids are passing them by. I will be there for mine.

I need to address common misconceptions about me. I don't agree with the logic of such unflattering, enduring assumptions, but would prefer to know about them because they give me a base to work from. There will always be those who are determined to think ill of me, whatever I do, but I hope fair-minded people will recognise that I have tried to change.

The knee-jerk reaction is still to dismiss me as violent, outspoken, whatever. That is a view taken from a specific perspective. It has power only if I allow it to affect me. That does happen occasionally, since I am not a machine, but I try to counteract the trolls by wondering just how sad, or lonely, they must be to get a kick out of abusing me.

It is important to have as broad a view as possible on people, ideas, cultures and philosophies. Reach your own conclusions, by all means, but at least make an attempt to see my world through my eyes. Consider what I've experienced, what I've come through. I've never lived in a bubble of entitlement. I know how to climb Everest. I know the good routes to the summit. I've so much knowledge to share.

I have made as many fuck-ups as anyone is going to make, but I've never robbed anyone. I have caused harm and disruption, but I've never set out intentionally to wrong someone. I am not a liar. You could probably argue that such reasoning is me trying to seek some kind of morality in my conduct, but I have principles I hold dear.

Integrity is high on my list of non-negotiables. I live in a world in which strangers pass judgement on me. If they are casting stones they should expect to have their glass houses examined. I may be a bit of a cunt in their eyes, but what about the way they live their life? Does that stand up to deeper scrutiny?

The unadulterated, unconditional love I had for football as a kid is difficult to sustain. That's understandable because the criticism is monotonous. People judge you personally and professionally. They can't wait to put you down, to drag you off to the knacker's yard like a circus animal that has outlived its usefulness.

I have fallen back in love with football with my eyes wide open. I'm aware of the pitfalls, conscious that, by acting the goat on Twitter and trying to fight everyone, I was drawing attention to everything I hated about the game. The easiest thing in the world is to chuck bombs. I enjoy being on the edge, but I am concentrating on being constructive.

I'd like to say I've been scarred by the way the media has dealt with me, because playing the victim sometimes softens the blow. But there has been no way to judge some of my actions, other than harshly. I made a decision to take the law into my own hands, and have lived with the consequences.

For some people anything I do, to acknowledge or act upon past wrongs, will never be enough. I have come to terms with that. Instead of provocatively playing up to the caricature, I'm in the process of making an honest attempt to change things for the better. I go out with the best of intentions, but can offer no guarantees I will never make another bad decision, or another silly mistake.

Human nature being what it is, I'm vulnerable to criticism. By openly discussing my ambitions, I am leaving myself open to accusations that I've got ideas above my station. By talking about social injustice or political philosophy, I am in danger of being labelled a prat with a platform. I'm big enough to take that, as well.

Why shouldn't I have a view on the European referendum (I was in favour of the UK staying in the EU) or the prospect of Donald Trump becoming US president (be afraid, people, very afraid)? What is wrong with seeking to raise awareness of issues that will impact on the lives of millions?

When you think about it, it is completely illogical that in the 21st century, homophobia in football remains a live issue. Other sports and sporting institutions have had the maturity to celebrate our differences, but sexuality in football still causes the collective pulse to skip a beat. I am a huge supporter of Stonewall, the equality charity, and their Rainbow Laces campaign, but the game must be more proactive in prising open closed minds. Independent voices have never been more important in an age in which the Orlando massacre, of 50 people at the Pulse gay nightclub on 11 June 2016, provided horrific proof of the dangers of ignorance and intolerance.

Our mass media is filtered and managed by corporate lobbyists and political lackeys. Supposed newspapers of record are distorted by the commercial priorities and cultural bias of their owners. I sense we are moving towards a financially motivated US-style system, where corporations are allowed to indulge a vested interest by influencing legislation.

I've been to jail, and lots of people still don't want to forgive. What more can I do than try to turn my life around and make a positive contribution? Am I fallible? Of course. Am I proud of what I have the potential to become? You bet. This may sound mad, but I fully believe I can help to change lives through football.

I went through a stage where my life went haywire. I have been saved by the love of good people, Blackie, Georgia, Nan and Tagger. All I want is for my kids to be happy and healthy. If Cassius wants to be a footballer or fly rockets, I'll do everything I can to help him. If Pieta wants to be a tap dancer or a lion tamer, I'll do everything I can to help her, too.

I'm also determined to like myself. I'm the only person I spend 24 hours a day with, 365 days a year. If I dislike myself when I put my head on the pillow each night, I am doomed to a horrible, painful existence. I have to tap into what makes me happy. That's not a new shirt, a shinier Rolex, or a cherry red Ferrari. It is simple things, like tickling my kids so I can hear them laugh.

I'll go and sit on my own. I like reading, thinking. Walking the dog is a good excuse to be alone, and I'm quite content to be in my own space. Football makes me happy these days. I feel so fortunate to have my job. Bonkers, when you consider I spent so many years trying to get away from the supposed pressures by drinking and behaving erratically.

I have no idea whether my sense of optimism and excitement

will last. My study of philosophy, which has evolved from a conventional process of education into a more informal search for insight, has taught me that none of us knows everything about anything. If I could travel back in time and change certain things I would do so in a heartbeat. But I can't.

All I can do is change my world for the better, one day at a time.

ACKNOWLEDGEMENTS

Well, where do you start? I suppose I better start with my parents, because without their love for one another at a point in their lives I simply wouldn't be here. My dad was, is and will always be my hero. To my brothers, Andrew, Michael, Josh, Connor, Noah. And sisters Sharon, Joanne, Molly, Nadine and Kirsty. To Julie and John, Peter, Paul and Tom. Love you all.

To all my nieces and nephews. To Andrew, whom I am fortunate enough to consider my brother and best friend. To my grandparents, especially my grandmother Julia who gave me unlimited love, guidance, belief and support when I needed it the most. Also, a stubbornness and confidence in myself as a person.

To Georgia. My love for her strengthens with each passing day. She came along and showed me a love and a patience one could only dream of before.

To Peter, who helped me better understand my journey in this life. Without him I would never have fulfilled my potential as a human. To Blackie, the Zen master, Yoda to my Luke Skywalker. I share with him a sense of kinship and love of knowledge, along with a great friendship which knows no boundaries. People keep asking me what Blackie does. It's hard to explain. He is unique in every way. One thing Steve always does is make things better.

To all our friends, we love you all, especially the Glastonbury gang. To Raj, Charlie and family, and my class at Roehampton Uni. I hope you have those degrees and are striding on in life, philosophising! To David and Mel who started this book's journey so, so long ago. (We finally did it!)

To the ghost writer, Michael Calvin, who took great time and care to get this book right. He committed himself to me and I hope you find this book as enjoyable to read as we did putting it together. To all the team at Simon & Schuster for their belief and hard work behind the scenes. To Dan Bosomworth and the gang at First10 Digital.

To Harry Tyrrell, my first coach. To Jim Cassell, the academy director who believed in me. To everyone at Knowsley United, who gave me the best football education a young lad could have. To Brad Orr, my childhood friend, teammate and now my agent, who is always there for me.

To all my other teammates, and acquaintances I have spent time with during the course of my life. There are too many of you to mention but your impact, sometimes big and sometimes small, positive and negative, has helped shape me as a person.

Thank you.

Finally to Eddy Jennings and Andrew Taylor and their families, with whom I share a great friendship. I have no doubt that without them this book would never have been written. Thanks for pushing me when I didn't want to do it. You were right! (You know how hard that is for me to do!)

Last and by no means least, to my beautiful children Cassius and Pieta. This book was written with you in mind. I wanted to put down in words the difficulties I had in life. I wanted you both to be able to pick up something and have some context to the man I was, am and will become. A fundamental change occurred in me when you came into this world. A desire to better myself, not for ego, not out of a desire for something material, but for a justification.

I wanted you to be proud of your father. To be proud of who he is. To see all the things he has done. And not attempt to try to justify who I was or what I did. Hopefully, I will get the chance over the course of our lives to prove that, day in and day out. But if I don't, this book can attempt to make some sense of the person I was to date.

Here's to the last 30-odd years. I can't wait for the next chapters to begin.

JB x

A parlour game takes place whenever Joe Barton does or says something significant. Internet search engines are fired up, social media accounts are scrutinised, and his supposed inconsistency and fecklessness are condemned. Headlines generate more heat than light, and everyone's prejudices are confirmed.

In that spirit, and in the interests of full disclosure, I'll save Mr Google and assorted cyber warriors a little work. In a couple of intemperate columns in 2008 and 2011, I suggested he was 'obnoxious' and advised him to 'stop clinging to victimhood and delusions of your own grandeur'. I didn't know him then, as I do now, but we are all entitled to an uninformed opinion.

That's why, when Joe approached me to collaborate on this book, I was intrigued. This was a unique chance to explore assumptions based on 140 characters and a rap sheet read in isolation. When I told him of my doubts about his authenticity, during an initial dinner in Liverpool, he laughed and used them as justification for our proposed partnership.

I had done my homework, speaking to his teammates, coaches and managers. I was struck by the respect Joe commanded within football, and the clarity of the character that emerged from the consultation process. I was advised to 'treat him like a man' and told 'he will give you everything, if you do the same'.

That is what a co-writer needs to hear. Commitment, complete and unwavering, generates credibility. Joe has been open, engaging, thoughtful and thorough. This book isn't an indulgence; he understands its permanence, and has treated it with due care and attention. I cannot make you like him, but I hope it enables you to understand him, and the game that shaped him, a little better.

I knew we were on the right lines in our second meeting, when he tried, unsuccessfully, to wind me up about the existence of God. In terms of philosophy, I still don't know my Aristotle from my Engels, but I like to think I have stimulated his curiosity, examined his intellect and challenged his conscience.

Thanks, first of all, to the Barton family for their patience and assistance. They take their lead from the matriarch, Julia. Joe's deference to his Nan, as he served us tea on the best china in her front room, was as revealing as the manner in which his Dad, Joe Sr, addressed the turbulence of his life and times.

I have been helped immensely by Joe's small circle of close friends, most notably Eddy Jennings, Brad Orr and Andy Taylor, whom I insisted on visiting in Preston prison with Joe.

I wanted to trigger latent emotions by reminding him of the parallel world which could so easily have ensnared him.

He is, and will always be, his own man, but I have come to realise he identifies with individuals whose strength of character is matched by acute emotional intelligence. The insight of two such figures, Steve Black and Sean Dyche, was especially valuable to me. The memory of a third, Peter Kay, moved Joe to tears.

Joe's voice, moods and mannerisms became familiar to Caroline Flatley, who transcribed 350,000 words of direct interviews for this book, a figure which more than doubles when I take into account complementary notes. I can't thank her enough; she is an important sounding board because she is such a keen judge of character. Suffice to say she found Joe fascinating and enlightening.

This book would not have been possible without the wisdom and foresight of Ian Chapman, Ian Marshall and their team at Simon & Schuster. Their professionalism and expertise has been hugely appreciated. It would be remiss of me not to thank Rory Scarfe, my literary agent at Furniss Lawton, and Joe's literary representative, David Riding.

Since writing is such an immersive process, I have to end where it all starts, at home. I couldn't do this without the support of my wife Lynn and the amused detachment of my children, Nick, Aaron, William and Lydia. As I type these words, my granddaughter Marielli is demanding to use this keyboard, so good night, and good luck.

Michael Calvin, June 2016

INDEX

(the initials JB refer to Joey Barton)

41
42
1
2
IY
46
47
5
6
MY
51
52
9
10